CONTENTS

INTRODUCTION TO THE WORKBOOK

This is a workbook with suggested rituals and exercises for working with the main phases of the Moon for the second half of 2018. In these pages you'll find rituals, magic spells, and suggested exercises for each phase. There are astrological overviews, Tarot spreads, and self-development prompts. This is meant to serve as one tool in your toolkit for self-empowerment. This is meant to be paired with your own personal work.

These writings and suggestions come from decades-long work with various spiritual pursuits, practices and studies. My personal concentration over the past six years has been working with the different phases of the Moon, as well as Tarot, and so this workbook focuses on these two practices. Our wonderful contributors focus on Astrology, herbalism, crystals, and more. I have had wonderful results by doing the work, and encourage you try with an open mind. Moontime is a very natural state to live in. It is one our ancestors have lived in. It is of nature. It can be a useful tool at any stage of our own growth—spiritual, magical, or emotional.

My metaphysical focus and expertise is with Tarot, manifestation techniques and magic; not astrology. There are astrological overviews for each month by the wonderful writer and astrologer Diego Basdeo. There are hundreds if not thousands of astrology resources out there you can use as a supplement. Throughout this book I discuss Tarot cards to be used as references and archetypes to utilize. I'm interested in the ideas and suggestions of many spiritual, metaphysical, self-help, healing and psychological theories, to spark inspiration and personal resonance. One discipline or lens is not a be-all, end-all blanket solution for everyone, and I attempt to offer up a mix of many spiritual, practical, and magical suggestions for support and contemplation. My hope is that you take any and all information you consume with a grain of salt. My hope is you mainly rely on what your intuition tells you, what your energy requires of you, and where your natural rhythms and cycles guide you.

In my own personal experience, magic, self-development, and self-inquiry go hand in hand. This book includes all. Magickal exercises and rituals are suggested. There are many journaling prompts to help start the visions and to document the answers coming from inside you.

Self-help work and spiritual practices are complicated, personal, and require commitment and discipline. When we do inner work, our outer world shifts, and vice versa. Like half-whispered spells and empty promises, this workbook will not work if you do not. If there is no trying, no outward energy moved, no shift in mindset, belief, or self-talk, then things stay the same. However, I have found from personal experience that it takes very little time to notice change and to create a different reality.

What we do in the present moment will change the course of our lives in the future. How we direct our energy now will play out in unforeseen ways in days to come. This is why the present is so powerful. I encourage you to listen. To pay attention to messages. To deepen into your own voice, your own messages, your own knowing. To take notes, via paper and pen. To keep track of your own life, and take responsibility for such.

Many of us do not acknowledge all of the power and control we have. We have control over our breath. With practice, we have control over our conscious mind and over directing our thought forms. With practice, through meditation, trance work and ritual work, we have control over our subconscious. We have control over the words we speak, the way we respond to circumstances around us, and how we choose to improve our circumstances. We are able to resist psychic death. We are able to cultivate compassion. We have control over what we can focus on at least some of the time. Within all of us is so much power and autonomy. We do not need any outside tools to access this. Our power is free and belongs to all of us.

All of the tools listed in this workbook are suggested. If you do not wish to purchase any of them, do not. I have had amazing spell results come from scraps of paper, rainwater, and tea lights from the dollar store. I would encourage you to buy only two things, if you choose to diligently follow along in this workbook. These are a journal, and a Tarot deck or Oracle deck if you do not have one. I would encourage you to commit to a key spiritual practice and pursuit during this time. Maybe it is Reiki, Tarot, herbal medicine and healing. Maybe it is breathwork or meditation, palm reading or astrology. Free writing or painting. Stretching, running, singing, or chanting. Delve into a mind-altering, energy shifting practice that will support some of the exercises and suggestions in this book. Cultivate a practice or two that will feel like a sanctuary to melt into.

The end goal of doing spiritual and self-improvement work is to ultimately help others. To help the planet, our earth, our water, our air, our sky. To help the creatures and the other living things that communicate to us solely by their existence. To heal deep pain and damages our ancestors have unknowingly placed upon us, in the hopes that we reduce harm and pain to those around us. To become so financially self-sufficient that we can give freely to those who need it with joy and ease. To eventually create foundations and organizations of love and kindness, betterment and aid. To support and help the environment that has been damaged by greed and ignorance. To become, with our own behaviors, speech, and actions, examples and support to those around us. This is our responsibility as witches, as dreamers, as artists, as healers, as creators, as conscious human beings on this globe.

If something does not resonate with you in this book, do not use it. These rituals and spell work are merely suggestions and guides. Ways to spark thought, inspiration, and evolution. If a different certain spell or ritual is calling to you at a particular time, then be all means, please do that! This is your own very personal practice and only you know what is best: listen to yourself. If something rubs you the wrong way, I encourage you to do your own research! Take what you would like and leave the rest.

You do not have to believe in Wicca, neo-Paganism, self-help, hypnotism, therapy, AA, Judaism, Catholicism, Christianity, Zen-Buddhism, Buddhism, any organized religion, or even anything higher than you to utilize these exercises. (Though all of the suggested exercises take from all of the above-mentioned viewpoints.) There should however, be an openness to energy work, mindfulness practice, and a curiosity to learn more in a specific spiritual/self-development zone that interests your inner voice. You *do* have to believe in yourself and in your incredible power and potential. I invite you to reconsider your life, your beauty, your impact. Believe that there is more out there, more than we can see, more than we've been shown by the dominant paradigm. Know that you are so capable! So special, so loved. So very worthwhile. I invite yourself to step into your legacy and lineage fully.

It would be very encouraged to look into your own specific background and their spiritual practices. Your ancestors' traditions, philosophies and magical practices. Every culture has many; there might be several from your own background you resonate with. Do your own research and your own work in this realm. Again, this takes time. We've all been raised in a capitalist, heteronormative, patriarchal culture. I urge you to examine what your spiritual and magical practice consists of. Why do you buy what you buy, what do you sell, and why? I encourage everyone to connect first and foremost to their background when creating rituals and spells: not take, steal, or profit from another's. Watch your language carefully. Cultural appropriation in white spiritual communities runs rampant. Don't mindlessly grab at images, thoughts, deities. Theft for personal gain and profit is the patriarchy. Think about what kinds of entitlement your privilege affords you, and what impact this has. I encourage you to take the time to develop your own view, voice, and content—not just repost, grab and regurgitate from other sources. (Including this one!)

A note on the language in this book: this is a Queer Feminist project that attempts to center femmes and women. In doing so the pronouns used for the Moon are "she" and "they." Of course we know that gender is fluid— it doesn't exist in a binary. Most certainly the planets nor the Moon do not have a gender, or just one gender. Your Moon can be anything and any gender you imagine it to be; it can change from young boy to mature they to crone she and back around again. Your Moon can have no gender at all or all the genders you can think of at once. Make it anything and everything you want!

A note on the Moon times and dates: all the times/dates are corresponding with Pacific Standard Time. Depending on where you are in the world, you may have to adjust the time/date. All times were taken from "The American Ephemeris for 1950 – 2050 at Midnight" by Niel F. Michelsen and Rique Pottenger. Times were adjusted from Universal Time (UT/GMT) provided in the original print to Pacific Standard Time (PST). If you are reading this and you are not in the Northern Hemisphere, the information in the book that is seasonal will most likely not resonate, however, the majority of this information is timeless.

No matter where you are, no matter who you are reading this, I have love for you, I want the best or better for you. I hope you possess and practice love, forgiveness, and kindness with yourself to create your own most beloved reality for you and your loved ones, for those who have served you, and all we have yet to meet who are on their separate healing paths. May all of us create a more positive, kinder, more loving, more creative world. May you be healthy and safe. Bless you and blessed be!

WHY THE MOON

Because she's a celestial anchor. Because she's both tethered and free. Because she's complicated. Because we can feel her inside of us. When she's inside of one of us, she's inside of us all. Because she's tied to the tides. Because the earliest people obeyed her orbit, timed their months and holidays and celebrations and agriculture to her, and part of that lineage is still in us, cell phone light be damned.

Because she's both the lullaby rocking the baby to sleep and the crashes of waves keeping grown-ups pacing up and down in hallways, all through the night. Because she's heard ambulance sirens, because she's seen every crazy battle from spears to assault rifles, every buffalo herd race over the grasslands. Because we came from the salt water, millions and millions of years ago, and that salt water is still inside of us.

Because she's the divine feminine, every single part and sigh and whisper and scream and giggle, each tiny girl's toes, each teenager's first coat of nail polish, each grandmother's favorite recipe. The different slivers are reflection of our most anguished state, our calmest Mona Lisa smiles. You are lit up with her; she lights the cells within, her fading lumina allows you the space to turn inside and fade. She's complicated and changing, familiar and distant all at once.

Because she wants you to gather, wants you to revel, wants you to celebrate, to harvest and solace one another. The messenger of tears, the bringer of truths. A rock and an optical illusion lightbulb and a muse and a prayer and a song and and a scream and a stifle and a scourge and a spiral of time. La Luna lights up the night, our subconscious, where the deep mind lives. The hands of our internal clocks rotate around her luminescent center.

Because she's back. That bitch, that witch, she's back. Because for some of us she's the best friend and for some the worst enemy. Universal sisterhood sounds so sweet but it is really hard. It might be another chore, a job, an emotional labor—on top of all the rest. She's here to remind us that everything sacred comes back around again. And right now we are ready to dismantle the patriarchy: but we must do so together. With our mindset, our thought forms, our actions and our outreach we are bringing forth a new form of soft power and sisterhood, for all women, queers, weirdos, Transfolk, femmes, non-binary humans—anyone who has felt othered, punished, or abused for being who they simply are.

Tracking time and worshipping by the light of the Moon has been noted across the globe. The Moon was human beings' original calendar. The earliest civilizations relied on the light of the Moon in the desert as a way to mark the passing of time. Without seasons in this climate, the Moon made an easy timekeeper. Hundreds of years later, humans relied on the various phases of the Moon for agricultural purposes; to this day there are agricultural calendars that let farmers and gardeners know when it is time to plant seeds, trim, harvest and till. Biodynamics have shown that the Earth is more fertile during Full Moons.

People who bleed often are synced up to the Moon. Not every woman bleeds and not everyone who bleeds is a woman. An average person's cycle is about 28 days long—obviously around the same cycle as one lunar phase. If you bleed, you can track your cycle to the Moon's. There is much more research and books you can read on this topic. There was a the shift from the reverence for the matriarchy and divine feminine to the misogyny associated with PMS and bleeding. If you are a person who bleeds getting in touch with your cycles and how your body, mind, and spirit act during each phase is a wonderful way to deepen intuition and connect more dots in your self-care map.

The Phases of the Moon

The Moon revolves counter-clockwise around the Earth. One cycle, from New Moon to New Moon takes 29.5 days to complete. While the earliest cultures operated around a Lunar Calendar, the Gregorian Calendar does not. The "Moonth" and the month are not in sync. For much of 2018, the Full Moon is near the end of the month.

There are eight full phases of the moon that Western science recognizes: New Moon, New Crescent/Waxing Crescent, First Quarter, Waxing Gibbous, Full Moon, Waning Gibbous, Last Quarter, Waning/Balsamic. The moon goes around the Earth once and spins on its axis once, all in the same amount of time, and it shows us just one face the whole time. When we look up at the Moon, what we are viewing is a scenario put into place by the Sun, the Earth, and the Moon's orbits and rotations. The earth rotates around the Sun, and the Moon around the Earth. As the Moon rotates, the rays of the Sun hit it at different angles, affecting what we see of the moon. You're seeing the reflected light from the Sun, bouncing off the Moon, which acts like a mirror.

The Moon is not round (or spherical). Instead, it's shaped like an egg. If you go outside and look up at the Moon, one of the small ends is pointing right at you. All of the water on and in the Earth has a relationship with the Moon. Tides on Earth are caused mostly by the Moon (the Sun has a smaller effect). The Moon's gravity pulls on the part of the Earth it is closest to, and with it, the water. High tide aligns with where the Moon is as Earth spins underneath her. Another high tide occurs on the opposite side of the planet because gravity pulls Earth toward the Moon more than it pulls the water. Humans are mostly water. Our insides might just move around, shift, be heightened, much like the water ebbing and flowing, magnetized by the Moon's gravity. Farmers have long understood that working with the Moon's phases, as well as the Astrological sign it is in, will yield more crops. There are optimal times to sow, plant, harvest and weed gardens all based around the phases of the Moon and what its orbit is doing to the water inside of our green veined friends.

As the Moon moves eastward away from the Sun in the sky, we see a bit more of the sunlit side of the Moon each night. A few days after the New Moon, we see a thin crescent in the evening sky. The crescent Moon waxes, and when half of the Moon's disc is illuminated, we call it the First Quarter moon. (The Moon is now one-quarter of the way through the lunar month.) From Earth, we are now looking at the sunlit side of the Moon from off to the side. The Moon continues to wax. Once more than half of the disc is illuminated, it has a shape we call gibbous. The gibbous moon appears to grow fatter each night until we see the full sunlit face of the Moon. We call this phase the Full Moon. It rises almost exactly as the Sun sets and sets just as the Sun rises the next day. The Moon has now completed one half of the lunar month.

During the second half of the lunar month, the Moon grows thinner each night, in its Waning state. Its shape is still gibbous at this point, but grows a little thinner each night. As it reaches the three-quarter point in its month, the Moon once again shows us one side of its disc illuminated and the other side in darkness— the Third Quarter or Last Quarter Waning moon. However, the side that we saw dark at the First Quarter phase is now the lit side. As it completes its path the Moon is a Waning Crescent, then becomes darker, before the New Moon again.

The Moon and Magic

In this book, we will be working with five phases: New, Waxing, Full, Waning, and Dark. Feel free to do more research and play around the subtle energies of more phases than the ones focused on here. The Moon cycle is perfectly suited to this work as it aligns with basic meta-physical and practical principles of magick and manifestation. During the New Moon we set intentions, during the Waxing cycle we take practical steps to move forward, during the Full Moon we celebrate, affirm, aim even higher, during the Waning Moon we release, work through blocks, and get rid of that which is no longer serving us. The Dark Moon is a time for finality, banishing, and deeper magic practices. I guarantee if you begin working a Moon cycle through in this manner you will see change. By addressing the mind/body/spirit shifts will begin to take hold. Witches have long worked with magical timing, taking into account not only the Moon phase, but the day of the week, the sign the Moon is in, and the season we are in to time spells. Some witches are very strict about timing and work their spells down to the minute the Moon is Full or New. This is why this workbook provides the exact Pacific Standard time. My rule of thumb on timing is much more casual. I usually work my spell with a three day rule: meaning that three days before or after a phase is when I do ritual or spell work, with one exception: the Dark Moon phase. (I would never create a Dark Moon Spell during a New Moon.) Feel free to experiment and make up your own rules. Do what feels right and work with your own energy.

If you are an advanced practitioner taking into account all of the above and more may get you more potent results. If you are just starting out, it is quite easy to remember just this basic rule for Moon Magic. While the Moon is from New to Full, the most supported spells are for growing, building, and protecting. While the Moon changes from Full to Dark, the most supported spells are for release, letting go, and banishing. Obviously, there are nuances to each phase which this workbook addresses.

New Moon

In astronomy, New Moon is the first phase of the Moon, rising at sunrise and setting at sunset. It is the moment when the Moon and the Sun have the same elliptical longitude. During this phase the Moon is farthest away from us viewers on Earth. We actually can't even see the moon when it is technically "new". It is a void, invisible, a blank slate. Some witches believe the New Moon to be when the moon appears completely dark. I like to work with New Moon energies on the day when the tiniest sliver of a light smile appears. The glimmering hint of possibilities is shown to us, igniting hope and imparting new beginnings. For many ancient cultures, the month did not start until they could see that small light beam reflected to them.

Any type of positive spell would be optimal at this time. Road opener spells, magnetizing spells, good luck spells are all fantastic to do at this time. Think: invitation and attraction for the New Moon time. Think: Lodestones, hematite, clear quartz and labradorite. Think: Artemis preparing for the hunt.

This Moon phase is wonderful for setting new intentions, for attracting new people into your life, for beginning new projects, for interviewing for jobs, for invoking more clarity and spirituality in situations in your life, and for simply allowing new opportunities to unfold. It is optimal for prosperity spells, for career advancement intentions, for creative endeavors to formulate, and for love and romance spells. Think of yourself in different ways. Allow versions of yourself to expand in your own mind. Inquire and question. I think of the New Moon time as the Ace cards in the Tarot: seeds to be watered. The Fool and the Star cards come to mind as well.

This time of the month is a great time to reconcile situations from last month, forgive yourself and others, and plant the seeds of hope, faith, and optimism. A good time to ground and think about what you would like to protect. It is optimal to wait for the New Moon to begin projects, as the Waxing period of the moon is considered to be favorable for announcing new work. Behind the scenes work, like gathering resources, making meetings, strategizing, and formulating ideas are optimal activities at this time.

If you do nothing else, taking thirty minutes out of your evening to look at the Moon, feel her energy, and write down your deepest desires and intentions during the first three days of the New Moon phase. Put your crystals out on your windowsill or in your backyard to cleanse in the void. When creating a ritual for your New Moon intention, think about what it is that you are ready to get started on or invite into your life. Think about what colors, tastes, sounds, or elemental objects that would look like. Then gather a candle or candles of that color, and set up your altar accordingly with crystals, minerals, photos, and plant life that invokes those desires for you. Maybe your desire invokes fresh tangerines or lemon water. Maybe it summons feelings of lavender and pink rose petals. Or maybe you just cut out a picture of the state you would like. It's your call! Write down your intentions, dreams, or wishes. Then a week later, check in with those during the next phase: Waxing.

First Quarter/Waxing Moon

The First Quarter Moon (often called a "half moon") occurs when the moon is at a 90 degree angle with respect to the Earth and Sun. We are seeing exactly half of the moon illuminated and half in shadow. The First Quarter Moon rises around noon and sets around midnight. A couple days later, the Moon slides into her proper Waxing mode. I think of the Waxing Moon as a period of time between the New Moon and the Full Moon, but I wouldn't think to do any sort of Waxing Moon spell until at least six days after the New Moon period. A great time for a Waxing Moon spell would be six to three days before the Full Moon. In fact, during the Waxing Phase I will frequently do three or six days spells, where I repeat the same spell for that time period to build momentum and strength. (You can work a spell for as long as you'd like, I've even known some people who have worked 30 day spells.)

The Waxing Moon aids the accomplishment of any undertakings. If the time during the New Moon was about planting seeds and gestating in hope and optimism, the Waxing period is about putting the pedal to the metal, so to speak, and not only casting spells but acting on it— bringing the work out into the world. Anything that requires hard work, is an undertaking or needs motivation is our focus during this time. This phase gives vitality, courage, and strength. Think of the Magician and Chariot Cards in the Tarot. All the resources are around you. Summon the correct energy and mindset to use them. At this time concern yourself with the external. Begin building what you wish to see, hear, and touch around you.

This time period is also good for attraction, amplified success, and fertility. Think of the literal light reflecting across the face of the Moon, growing larger and stronger, gaining momentum on the stage that is outer space. That is the energy that is suggested to embody at this time. Waxing Moon time is also good for flexing your intuition and enhancing your perceptions of the world. Think: form. Think: pushing yourself a bit more than you are used to. Prioritize the values and things in your life that are dear. Build structures, better habits, network, launch your new website or new project during this time. Pyrite, carnelian, tiger eye, are examples of crystals that embody this "get it done" energy.

○

The Full Moon

At a Full Moon, the Earth, Moon, and Sun are in approximate alignment, just as the New moon, but the Moon is on the opposite side of the earth, so the entire sunlit part of the Moon is facing us. The shadowed portion is entirely hidden from view. The Moon is closest to us, reflecting approximately seven-second-old light from the Sun. The Full Moon rises at sunset and sets at sunrise. We can see her above our heads all night long, if the sky is clear.

The Full Moon is stuff of legend: humans become werewolves, witches cackle around cauldrons, and people turn into "lunatics". This is the "mother" phase of the maid/mother/crone triple Goddess. Herstorically, this was the time of the month that magic makers would gather as they could see one another and create ritual together under the spotlight of the Moon. (Remember, this was before electricity—the night was usually very dark.) Herstorically, if you got your period during this time of the month it meant you were a witch. (One theory I read was this was because you could have sex at this time and pregnancy chances were rare.) Your lover could look into your sparkling eyes and adore you, smiling under the reflection of moonlight.

Many intuitives believe this time to be the most potent, the most fortuitous time, and the time when our energy and our power are amplified. On that note, absolutely any positive intention setting, manifestation time, or spell setting you choose to do on the Full Moon will be supported. Go big! Dream your heart out! Reach for what you want. Draw down the energy of the Moon and sit with her. This is the time to charge crystals and put rainwater out under the moonlight to use in ritual.

Divination, protection, communication with spirit and other realms are all good aspects to focus on. Downloading information from your guides or ancestors and/or honoring those entities or deities is a good idea under the light of the Full Moon. Channel, write. Calling in abundance, excitement, wisdom, sensuality or other fully fledged components are welcomed. Thank spirit, nature, the universe, your self for all the wonderful things in your life. Appreciation, giving thanks and offerings to your ancestors, guides, and other deities you feel grateful for is a beautiful practice at this time. Things come to a culmination at this time. Pay attention to what is ending. Take note of what messages are around you at this time.

During the Full Moon I tend to take time for myself as I tend to get emotionally and energetically overwhelmed. If I do manifestation work it tends to be more grandiose—reaching for outcomes my subconscious mind may not fully believe can be, or things that are very far outside my perceived sphere of influence. I also work long-range manifestations for my life (healthy and happy retirement, etc.) and spell work/intentions for the Earth, the planet, and her health. When creating a ritual for your Full Moon manifestations, think about what would transpire in your life if absolutely nothing could go wrong; if everything you wanted was in front of you, just waiting for you to choose it?

A couple of days ahead of the Full Moon freestyle in a journal or on paper what this entails exactly: what the elemental properties of these things are—happiness, contentment, safety, excitement, health, hope, etc. What are your top goals, how would you feel in your desired state? Now is the time to write your incantation and gather your ingredients. If it is peace you are after, a white candle, quartz crystals, and perhaps lavender are some of the elements you wish to be working with. Maybe this ritual would include an Epson salt bath, and working with protective deities to enhance calm and soothing elements.

The Full Moon is also a wonderful time to gather with others, if you are energetically inclined. Throw a dinner party or invite loved ones over for a craft night. Create a supportive Moon circle where you can all share your intentions and send it out into the universe, amplified.

These are just some suggestions. The Full Moon is a great time for drawing in energy, making potions, tinctures, or food, spending time with loved ones, or reconnecting to what it is you want to see happen in your life and embodying how you want to feel.

Last Quarter/The Waning Moon

This is the period when the Moon journeys from Full to New. The Last Quarter Moon rises around midnight and sets around noon. You can spot her high in the mid-morning sky. Casting spells for removing problems, eliminating trouble, neutralizing adversaries and reducing harm is most affective when the Moon is on the wane. Protection spells for yourself, your loved ones, home and material possessions are also best cast at this time. It is also a time when our bodies are most susceptible to cleansing, so it is a good time to cleanse yourself through the process of detoxification. Health issues could be worked on now. This is the time to cut loose toxic relationships. Get rid of old stuff: literally and metaphorically. This is one of my favorite moon phases: one of meditation, recalibration, and letting go. During the Waning Moon phase challenge yourself to get rid of as many physical objects that do not bring you happiness as possible. This phase is about getting things in order that are not in order: paperwork, doctor's appointments, closets. Magick loves a void in order to bring in the new opportunities, thought patterns, and positive people and experiences that will help you. But first you yourself need to get moving and make space for the new! This is the time to do so.

Energetically, you might feel tired or low. Recognize the importance of quietude. Spend more time resting or sleeping, more time listening. This is a wonderful time to go inward and connect with your intuition. Ask your intuition questions and listen for the answers. Hunker down on creative tasks that only you get to see the beginning stages of. Self-examination and behind the scenes activities are traditionally favored at this time.

Banishing and banning energies are useful during this time. It is ok to say goodbye and write that letter you will never send. Forgiving yourself and others, as well as making amends internally are opportune exercises at this time. Rituals could include burning items or pieces of paper, meditating with tourmaline, and asking Kali, Saturn, Hecate, or your own preferred dieties for their help. Burying things, and freezing spells work well here.

The Waning Moon also favors forgiveness and release. Going back and examining the past, and blessing mistakes you think you may have made is useful. Trance work into the underworld, and examining the subconscious is best to do under the Waning Moon (as well as the Full Moon). This is a also the most optimal time to cut cords and release energetic pulls to other people, places, or past histories. Of course, anytime is a good time to release and close the door on what no longer serves us.

The Dark Moon

This is the period just before the New Moon (about two or three days before leading up to) when any slivers of the Waning Moon are gone. The Dark Moon rises at sunrise and sets at sunset. I see the Dark Moon as the Waning Moon most amplified: this is the time for finality. Banishing spells, the kind of spell work where you get rid of something that you never want to come back, are best favored here. When you know you need to get rid of a pattern, a person, or an unhelpful behavior the energy of the Dark Moon will help you to do so. You may call upon your ancestors or particular deities, crystal or plant energies to help you with this task and to help protect you during this shift.

This is also a very optimal time for deep magic. Shape shifting magic, divination exercises, going into other dimensions and portals, accessing the void, scrying, creative meditations are all ways to honor the dark Moon. Hecate, the Queen of the Witches, is an archetype that corresponds with this time. The Moon Card in the Major Arcana can help you as well: getting weird and wild and swimming into surreal landscapes of your mind and imagination help to shift your subconscious.

Last but certainly not least, the Dark Moon is a time to practice concentrated rest. Take a long bath, lay down and close your eyes. Focus on being quiet and sleeping more. Our culture does not often reward allow us to prioritize rest. Yet now is the time we need it more than ever. Can you give yourself one or two days of committed rest and relaxation during the Dark Moon time?

Eclipses

Eclipses generally take place between two and four times a year. There are two types: Solar and Lunar, each appearing within approximately two weeks of one another. The maximum amount of eclipses in one calendar year is four Solar, and three Lunar (Nasa.gov.). Eclipses happen when one heavenly body—in this case, the Moon and the Earth—obstructs another. When the Earth moves between the Sun and the Moon, Earth's shadow appears on the Moon, creating a Lunar Eclipse. There are total and partial eclipses. A Lunar Eclipse only occurs at a Full Moon. Some people believe that a Lunar Eclipse has to do with inner motivations and emotions. Our perspective can get shifted, our subconscious disrupted. With that comes change. Others believe a Full Moon Lunar Eclipse is like a Full Moon times a zillion: emotions are heightened, as is the opportunity to attempt potent spell work and create more grandiose waves. Be sensitive to information and patterns that come up before and just after a Lunar Eclipse, particularly if this is a theme from the last Eclipse from six months ago. This could be a chance to break patterns or release unwanted energies. Lunar Eclipses can herald an ending to a situation that was started six months prior at the Solar Eclipse in the corresponding sign.

A Solar Eclipse occurs when the Moon moves between the Sun and the Earth. The Moon blocks the sunlight from reaching Earth and casts a shadow on the Earth. Like Lunar Eclipses, there are total and partial Solar Eclipses. A Solar Eclipse only occurs at a New Moon. Solar Eclipses can feel like amplified New Moons: ready for fresh starts and break aways. A true beginning of a different journey. People might be making choices around you that will affect you, or vice versa.

Any Eclipse, like any time, can be used as an opportunity to make magic, set intentions, and address lingering unhelpful patterns. Like anything, your experience of an Eclipse may fluctuate wildly depending on where you are in your life and what needs to come out. The key is to notice and listen to your energy and intuition. Go slow and watch the reactions of other people, but do not engage immediately if you can help it—others might be stirred up by the shift in energy.From anywhere from two weeks before an Eclipse, to the period to the next Eclipse is referred to as "Eclipse season." There are two or three Eclipses during every Eclipse season. At these times you may feel unstable or raw. Be extra kind and compassionate to yourself and those around you. If you feel called to make a vast change around the Eclipses, note it—and perhaps wait a week or two to follow through.

Void of Course Moon

When the Moon is said to be "void of course", that refers to a time, lasting anywhere from minutes to a few days, where the Moon is not in any sign. Astrologers (I got my info from the Mountain Astrologer) advise to not start anything new at this time, so see this as a sort of resting and hanging out period, as the Moon is not charged in any specific way.

Blue Moon

The original definition is that a Blue Moon is the third Full Moon in an astronomical season with four Full Moons. A normal year has four astronomical seasons with three months and normally three full Moons each. So a "Blue Moon" would be the addition of one. Recently, this definition has stretched to include a Full Moon that happens twice in one month. This is quite rare: taking place four to five times a century. The month could feel heightened and especially shining. This year is a year where we have two Blue Moon Months, in January and March.

Super Moons

A Super Moon is a Full Moon or a New Moon with the closest approach the Moon makes to the Earth on its elliptical orbit. This makes it appear very large. A Super Full Moon looks about 10% bigger than an average Full Moon. This happens frequently; usually three or four times a year. Tides will be affected, and perhaps your emotions. Go outside in bathe in her luminescence.

Astrology and the Moon

In Western Astrology, the Moon rules Cancer and the Fourth House, the House of home, and ancestry. It is feminine energy and it represents our deepest personal needs, our basic habits and reactions, and our unconscious. The Moon spends roughly 2 1/2 days in each sign. What do we feel we need for a sense of security? Look to the Moon in your natal chart for answers. Sometimes the Moon is our shadow side, the hidden parts of our personality; our emotions, the unconscious, our intuition, our spontaneity, and how we make ourselves feel comfortable and safe. The Moon can represent the parts of us only our nearest and dearest experience. It can represent what we need in our intimate partnerships to feel valued and loved.

Some astrologers believe it can represent our relationship with our mother or how we mother. Some astrologers believe that when the Moon is in your sign, or falls near your birthday, then it is a "power moon." Likewise, we can use elements and energies of the sign the Moon is to help us with our spell casting and manifestation. There are thousands of books and websites on this topic for you to read!

Ways to Work with the Moon

First, get to know her and how you feel during the different phases of her cycle. Go outside every night and look at the Moon. Notice her. Notice how you feel. Talk to her, listen to her. To know what cycle she is in, make your right hand into a semi-circle. If the Moon fits in the crook of your palm, on the right side of your right hand, the Moon is New/Crescent. Do you feel energized and excited when the Moon is Full? Or completely exhausted or wrung out? You can plan any rituals or self-care activities around that. Let your energy tell you whether to take a bath, or cast a group spell then go out partying. If you are someone who gets their period, then your energy might also ebb and flow based upon that. Notice if your period coincides with a particular phase of the Moon. Most people who bleed get their periods around either the New Moon or the Full Moon. Obviously this will effect your energy levels as well.

Look up what phase the Moon was in the day you were born, if you know that info. Does this correspond to how you usually feel during a specific phase? I knew instinctively that I was born during the Waning Moon because I feel so grounded at that time. It felt like home to me. When I looked it up, it was confirmed. Think about your Moon sign. If you don't know it, you'll be able to look it up pretty easily if you know your birth date and time information. Some people suggest your Moon sign could explain where your strengths lie in casting spells.

There are so many different avenues in which to do this work. One way could be simply as a journal, a way to remember what was going on for you each month. Naming and writing are very powerful tools, especially when done by hand. The Moon acts as natural time keeper. As you observe each cycle pass, you can think about where you were at the last one. What were you doing? What was going on? What has changed, and what remains the same?

You can use some of the exercises as prompts for topics to think about in your own life. There are many questions asked between these pages to get you thinking about dreams, goals, ambitions, emotions, intentions, points of view, blocks, fears, etc. Through the year the topics of relationships, self-love and self-esteem, work and career, money and abundance, community, service, and making changes are all addressed and introduced. The idea is that when a little or a lot of reflection and action are taken in each sector then positive change occurs.

It could be a good idea to hone in on your most important desires for each month, season, or even this half year. Pick between one and three main goals and desires, then work a Moon cycle for one (or two) of them at a time. You can go back and forth between a couple if one is more practical, and one is more based on internal or magical change.

Looking at the year as a whole expanse is a helpful guide as well. For this particular edition, I've based each month loosely around the seasons of the year and the Wheel of the Year. I've also taken into account phases of manifestation, all built from a base of self-love.

Each cycle gives us the opportunity to examine what we want manifested, what external work we have to do in the world, reflections and downloads on greater expansion, and what we must let go of, release, and sacrifice in order to do so. When we address these emotionally, energetically, mentally and physically, true shift will begin to take place. Once carried out consistently, results will be seen.

Cycles of the Moon, Our Life's Cycles

At a workshop I once gave, I told the participants earlier that day I jotted down a note about utilizing the phases of the Moon. *Cycles of mindless repetition, or spirals out into freedom?* I asked myself. We come across the same patterns and themes in our lives many times. They come around continuously. Themes of love, control, betrayal, ambition, ancestry, thought patterns, reactions, relationships. So easily the mind can be trapped on autopilot. The cycles of Moon remind us that we can process constructively to make positive change and lighten heavy patterns and burdens. Otherwise, we just automatically repeat the same habits, mindsets and perspectives. Then we wonder why our life feels the same. We wonder why we aren't getting results.

Every hardship and challenge can ultimately be received as a gift for us to take our power back and still move forward with love. For us to acknowledge the bullshit, yet not let our core goals and visions get blocked or swayed. For us to feel our feelings, and rise up even stronger. For us to remain heartfelt and conscious as the machine threatens to break us down. To stay connected to our highest ideals and deepest intuition even as those around us tell us the opposite—this is our evolving journey through this world.

Are you in another repetitious, mindless cycle, or are you creating your spiral into freedom?

Encounters with our inner and outer demons remind us of how far we've come. Bending into our fallibility with kindness and compassion, acknowledging achievements no matter how miniscule. Charting our progress through introspection and reflection. Letting our inner Moons, our inner wisdom shine through and reflect our highest self. Moontime is not linear. It isn't a start and finish line to pass through, rushed. It is a spiral. A circle. Touch base with what cycle, what phase you are in. Notice if it syncs up with nature, if your inner is aligned with your outer and what the Moon can tell you each night, as you walk around underneath her noticing her light cloaked shadows and glow alike.

Moontime can transcend even the literal cycles and phases of the Moon. You might be in a New Moon phase for a year: starting new projects and making new relationships. Your Moon work could revolve around dreaming, inquiry and introducing a beginner's mind to your work. Likewise, a Waning Moon phase could be spent organizing, strengthening boundaries, protection, and your intuition.

As you get deeper into this work, allow your intuition to guide you. Can you trust yourself more? Can you allow yourself to open up to messages? Can you make more space for mystery and exhale fully out, into your whole self, into a vibrant and aware life?

You can begin your Moonwork at any time of the cycle. You will see more rapid and potent results by working through the whole cycle, or at the very least a balance. This can be carried out in magical, practical, and energetic ways. For example, honoring the New and Full phases of one moonth brings seeding and blooming into focus. Releasing and/or banishing negative thought forms during the Waning Moon, then replacing them with positive or supportive actions during the Waxing Moon is another example of this balance.

This all depends on what you wish to work with, what energies you feel most aligned with, and what Moon phases feel most comfortable for you. The more you work consistently through all the phases and cycles on one topic, theme, goal or dream, the more potent the results. Journaling how you felt, and what you did during each phase is very helpful. Note your actions, and what spells and rituals you decided to embark on. Also keep track of any uncanny or incredible results you've seen as a result of your diligence in mind/body/spirit. There will be many, if you do the work, I promise! Obviously, as with everything, use your intuition as a guidepost to your intentions, goals, and magickal workings.

The Lunar Cycle and The Wheel of the Year

If you look at the Lunar Cycle from the illustration on the next page, you can see how it is a mirror for the seasons of the year. Take notice of the time of year it is, and what you are trying to work through. The New Moons around Imbolc (February) to Ostara (March), or through to April, the time of quickening Earth, may be more potent. You might feel more in tune to start things, to plant items to grow. Likewise, the Waxing to Full Moon period of the year (Beltane, or May, to Lammas, or August), may feel much more naturally charged towards embodiment, harvesting, and sharing.

We can take this a step further and compare this even to a day: the New Moon with sunrise, a Full Moon would correlate with noon, the Waning Moon with sunset to night, the Dark of the Moon landing somewhere between 3:30 AM and 6 AM (depending on sunrise time). What time of day do you feel most energized? Does this correlate to a specific Moon phase?

We can experiment with manifestation and flow utilizing both the cycle of the seasons as well as the lunar cycles. At the cross quarter cycles we may feel more balanced, even while there are tests. Transitions and choices might feel more heavy and weighted. During the disseminating Moon, the 3-4 day period after the Full Moon, we may find ourself integrating our downloads and lessons, and sharing what we know. At the Waning Moon we may wish to slow down and fortify our energy. If we match up our activities to the energies of the Earth as well as our personal energies, our efforts may flow better and have more impact. This is a process that can change as you change.

In our lives personally, the month of our Solar returns could feel like a New Moon time. If birthdays usually feel like a fresh start to you, then it might make sense to start wrapping up "your year" in the 2-3 months before your birthday.

Any creative human (which is most likely every human) can also see how clearly this cycle also mirrors any creative project or cycle. We get the inspiration, the idea. It is New Moon time. We try different ways, we work on things we love during the crescent to the First Quarter. Once we find something we are excited by, a direction to flow in, we keep going and building. We find the discipline to finish tasks, and find the courage to show ourselves to the world. We are in Waxing Moon.

The Full Moon marks the culmination of the project. It is in a finished state, it is ready to show us and others around us its particular message. (For those of you who have made many creations, or who got a degree or certification, we can also reflect on the exhaustion and drained energy that also might be present at this culmination.)

During the disseminating Moon, we process our work, we glean further lessons. During the Waning time we organize, archive, recenter, adjust to new blank spaces, any lulls that occur. During the Dark Moon we may receive more messages, or spend time in one more period of mourning, or of a letting go as we detach from who we were when we made the original creation. We may feel like a different person or feel unmoored, not knowing what comes next. We rest, and conjure our inspiration again at the next New Moon.

These cycles are a mirror for birth and death, destruction and resurrection. It is a perfect mechanism in which to lean into life. It mirrors the spirals of time we all experience: wishes, dreams, beginnings, learning, trying, buildings, fruition, illumination, sharing, becoming, shedding, decay, and transformation.

If you are naturally feeling more drawn to a Moon phase, go into it deeply.
Spend time with it, listen to yourself and the messages that come from within,
that come from the Moon as you sit underneath her.
Sit with these messages, learn from them.
There are no "good" or "bad" Moon phases.
Every single moment of them can tell us something important, if we listen.

EARTH
North

IMBOLC
YULE · DARK · NEW MOON · OSTARA
WANING · CRESCENT
SAMHAIN · FIRST QUARTER
West
WATER
LAST QUARTER · BELTANE
MABON · *East*
AIR
WANING GIBBOUS · WAXING
LAMMAS · MIDSUMMER
FULL MOON

South
FIRE

*This Wheel of the Year & Lunar Cycle illustration goes
clockwise, however the orbit of the Moon is counter-clockwise.*

Here you can jot down some basic wishes you have for the second half of 2018.

Dreams I have for self-love:

Dreams I have for myself and health:

Dreams I have for myself with career:

Dreams I have for myself, my relationships, and community:

Dreams I have for myself and my talents and learning new skill sets:

Dreams I have for myself and my abundance:

If you have an Oracle or Tarot deck, you might want to take the time to pull cards for each month that this workbook covers.

July:

August:

September:

October:

November:

December:

JULY 2018
JULY 6TH : LAST QUARTER MOON
JULY 9-11TH: DARK MOON
JULY 12TH: NEW MOON SOLAR ECLIPSE
JULY 19TH : FIRST QUARTER MOON
JULY 27TH: FULL MOON LUNAR ECLIPSE

July, the seventh month of the year, asks for a pause. This month begins eclipse season. July contains both a solar and lunar eclipse at our New and Full Moon. The previous eclipse season of 2018 kicked itself off in the start of the year, in January and in February. Now we are halfway through this year, and many of us are due for a reboot in various aspects of our lives. This month asks you to take what you need and leave the rest.

This month, blue jay is at home, nestled in their oak tree branches, high in the sky. The dahlias stretch up like fireworks growing from the earth, brilliantly waving to greet the Sun. How will you continue to come home to yourself? How will you be at home in yourself?

Make sure to be dedicated to the changing sky above, just as you notice the changing tides inside of yourself. Eclipse season generally brings some shake-ups. Do not accept fear-based thinking around any cosmic event. You can choose to be obsessed. Umbraphiles, coronaphiles, eclipsoholics, ecliptomaniacs and eclipse-chasers—these are the names for those who live to photograph eclipses. Obsessions can overtake the experience of watching a different movie unfold in the sky of your awareness. Similarly, fear-based thinking can block your own abilities to witness the subtle shifts happening inside. Fear-based thinking stops us from stepping into our own power. Eclipses are about shadows emerging, and different ways of seeing. And so, we reflect. We value our awareness. The awareness grows into a different blueprint—a safer way to hold ourselves.

Many of this month's workbook prompts concern themselves with the work of love. When we are very young, our eyes are made of stars when we think of love. We believe in love as fairy tale, love as cotton candy ether that happens to us—not as a miracle that happens from us. The topics of this month serve to support our inquiries into the miracles of self-love.

When we are young, we would like to believe that the miracle of love involves no effort. We are taught that we simply chance upon it like a rare shooting star. We are taught that when it gets difficult, it isn't love anymore. As we get older, we understand that one of the many miracles of love is the work of caring for it. We must continue to dig into it, tending and tilling. Even when the ground gets familiar, or becomes hard to fertilize. Even if at times we've misplaced our shovels entirely. The work of self-love is the theme of this month. There are guides to remind you to show up for yourself and to come home to yourself, missives on forgiveness, and the fruitfulness of rest. Let self-love form the basis of your magical practice this July. Whether it resides in simple pleasures or something more grandiose, be sure to take the time to fill your cup in some way every day. This work of love isn't meant to be a punishment. The best kind of work continues to remind us why we do it. The Moon above reminds us that no matter what phase we are in, we are part of a circular whole. What is the pleasurable work, the fulfilling work, the transformative work? This month, how will the work of love translate into magic?

July 2018 Astrology Insights
By Diego Basdeo

July 12th: New Moon Solar Eclipse in Cancer, Opposing Pluto

July 25th: Mercury Retrograde in Leo

July 27th: Full Moon Lunar Eclipse in Aquarius, Conjunct Mars, Squaring Uranus

Release Me: July Astro Overview

There will be a purpose. When something is taken away, something else is planted in its place.

Healing is nonlinear, illogical, and many times repetitive. It is against our instincts to sit quietly while bombs drop around us. It is counterintuitive to surrender to what feels like a war. It is hard not to beat ourselves up for being too intense or vulnerable or needy. It's hard to acknowledge that things you thought you were over are not done with you yet.

On the 12th, a solar eclipse will be happening in the sign of Cancer directly across from Pluto. Solar eclipses have everything to do with the ego and having it in Cancer makes it about how our ego interacts with our emotions and what shifts or changes need to happen. Emotions are signs that develop from our experiences and our processes. They tell us, based on synaptic and intuitive memory, when something is awesome or terrible. Pluto is the massive, generational movements, the cosmic tides, and is concerned with one thing that is important for us to take an unflinching look at this month: Power. Let me tell you about one of your many powers. Knowing, listening to, and loving your emotional body is power. Our emotional body is our connection with the universe. You can think emotional health is control, mastery, or restraint and that's all fine. True power starts with connecting with your feelings, and not just your reaction to them.

Pluto can often be a catalyst which brings about strengthening or destructive storms from the cosmic sea into your personal harbor. They are the type of storms that you can see gathering on the horizon. I think the trouble brewing may be something left unsaid, perhaps a less than savory part of you that is making its way to the surface. We all have shadows: undesirable feelings, thoughts, and even intentions. Our shadow side is connected to some of our most instinctive reactions, primordial animal-brain feelings and impulses like lust and grief. You know, the kind of things that are really tough and sometimes impossible to talk your way out of? The scandalous and sometimes shameful, heart churning, gut gurgling feelings that only patience, time, and process can transform? Pluto fucks with that.

One reliable interpretation of this tells me family power dynamics will be shook. Perhaps the voice of a family member in your head needs to get the boot. Maybe it's actually your voice and you need to make a change. But this is a fucking eclipse. Expect to be transformed. Expect distress, birth, and relief. All things change, they pass, so please press on.

When I think of Cancer, I think of the ocean, I think of the tides. When you are caught in a tide, the worst thing you can do is try to fight against it. This is our natural inclination, to survive, but this isn't how the ocean works. Old survival skills do not apply below the horizon of the sea. When we surrender to the tide she may pull us in deeper, but we can save our energy once the rolling tide passes, and swim to the surface. Of course, this is a metaphor for emotions. Of course, this is a metaphor for healing.

How can we gladly do that which we must do?

This question guides us in the next eclipse in the series that calls us to take action after the storm. The second eclipse of July will be a lunar eclipse in Aquarius where Mars is spurring our Moon into action and deep transformation. This Moon fiercely guards our experience as valid and true. To center ourselves and to hear our own voice in a crowd of our histories, we detach from possessions both material and interpersonal, we detach from circumstance, identity labels, and patterns. We do it fiercely, because we have so much love to give, and much of what love is yearns to be given it without attachment. Mars is right behind the Moon, giving us Kelly Rowland "Motivation" all night long. How is compassionate detachment an action? The Mars/Moon duo is talking to chaotic Uranus—it may make it easy for you to see when you need to let go (or be let go of!) through an unexpected turn of events! Uranus shows up to disrupt our "nice secure systems" we've built to keep things running smoothly. Uranus knows what it is to be free. Uranus knows that getting free is a responsibility. This is its paradox and its work is WILD.

There is a lot of passion behind this eclipse and it can turn into haste if we are not careful. Uranus, sometimes called the "queer planet," challenges normative roles. Traditionally we can see a disruption to mother/daughter parent/child relationships both literally and figuratively when Uranus aspects the Moon. In a broader reading I think the relationship between us as adults and our childhood or child-selves can create some transformative moments. Remember loving detachment.

As if all of that wasn't enough, Mercury is retrograde. Please be patient with communication, with yourselves, and others. With Uranus, sometimes the worst, most offensive way of saying something leaves your lips before you get a chance to use your stellar tact skills. Sometimes someone else will do that. Jessica Lanyadoo has a really great policy on processing with people: "My rule to processing with people that you don't trust is simple: DON'T." Definitely don't do it during a retrograde. Focus on you and your transformation this month instead.

Take care, lunar babes.

Showing Up For Yourself

The Last Quarter Moon occurs this month on a Friday. You may feel the urge to spend some time this weekend, or the following week, in a quiet space alone with yourself. Re-centering your fire, your aspirations, your momentum after our vibrant Strawberry June Full Moon. Reconfiguring what you'd like to summon up to stay, and what you'd like to see go. You may be able to get clear on what is to be pulled out or fastidiously trimmed back, which dying weeds need a caring hand's cut.

The Last Quarter Moon phase is when the Moon is halfway in her voyage from Full to New. The light across the face of the Moon lights up half her face space; the reflected sunshine dissolves a little bit out into more darkness each evening. She rises while most of us are asleep, save for the owls and the bats and the datura blooms, and sets at 1:30 pm, about halfway through the day. The Quarter Moon times can offer a sense of balance—we've been able to settle into the new ripples brought up by last week's Full Moon. We've allowed any shocks, truths, or new decisions about who we are becoming, and what we must do, flow into answers and actions. If emotions came up, coursing like quicksilver through your nervous system at last month's Strawberry June Full Moon, by now, they've subsided some. You've been able to gain more clarity around what they are an arrow pointing towards—big picture style—in larger themes of your life. You may have been feeling the pull to show up for your Self more.

Showing up for ourselves is one of the most profound gifts we can give ourselves. It can also be a very challenging task. In a world that has taught us to rely mostly on the external for validation, to rely on outside authorities and systems for permission and resources, to base our value on other people's virtually uncontrollable perceptions of us, making the choice to be our own best advocate can feel deeply dicey, almost absurdly risky! Making the moves towards prioritizing self-advocacy can bring up a lot of uncomfortable emotions—especially if we were never taught to do it, or if we have only begun enacting it as a valid option recently.

Who are we, if we aren't waiting on everybody else? Who are we, if we decide to put ourselves into the picture? What does that say to all the others and other parts of ourselves trying to hold us back? How do we loose the unwanted weeds of shame and self-doubt?

Nobody owes us anything. We owe everything to ourselves.

At the root of magic, of life, of ritual, is this showing up. This practice. This practice of living, which is a practice of living for one's Self. For living by one's needs, desires, alignment, health, value systems, ideals, and for the greater good. For remaining in one's resilience, bending and waving in the wind. Like The Magician, who makes a pledge to his own power and prowess; like The Hermit, who turns inward to mine her struggle into solace; like The Star who shines for themself, for everything, or no one and nothing; we must remain on our very own path. Time after time, moment after moment, breath after breath. This is what all the cards, as vastly different as they are, have in common. They are all *there*. They have all turned up, in their chaos and their callings, in their vibrancy and their violence, to be precisely where they need to be. No blame and no judgement (well, except maybe in the Judgement card, wocka wocka). They've turned up where they are, simply how they are, learning on their paths and in their ways. Teaching us their lessons as we practice, and practice again.

At this time, identify a couple of key places where you'd like to show up for yourself more.

Some examples of showing up for yourself could be:

Speaking up, letting someone else know what you need. Showing up for yourself could mean asking for help more: telling someone you need more guidance or support. It could mean simply telling someone you do not have the bandwidth at the moment, and figuring out what you can help them with, or when the best time would be for both of you. If you are a caregiver or a caretaker, showing up for yourself could mean allowing yourself to enjoy a little bit more Self time—5 minutes, 25 minutes, or even an hour a day—so that you can show up for your family or friends with that much more presence.

Showing up for yourself could be doing things you have a resistance, anxiety, or fear around: taxes, cleaning, rejecting someone or declining an opportunity. Showing up could mean admitting to yourself that certain behaviors and certain crutches aren't working anymore.

Showing up could mean you want something different. Something wider, more expansive, more exciting. You could end with the noticing. Noticing can be the showing up, too. Or, you could keep showing up and keep inquiring, keep naming, keep working on defining what it is you do want.

Showing up could simply mean you show up. You are tired, distracted, and bedraggled, but you made a promise and so you go and you honor that promise. To your studio. Job. Therapy. Your friend date. Your meditation mat. Etc.

Showing up could mean slowing down.
Showing up could mean you need more time.
Showing up could mean being aware of the activities in your life to focus on now, to bring more balance and support to your energetic body, your physical body, your mental body, and your spiritual body.

Showing up could mean redefining what feels right and true for you. Specifically if you are sick, ill, have a chronic illness or mental health condition that needs managing, or have a beloved in that situation. It could mean that caring for your health and physical body is what you need to show up for now. That has immeasurable value all on its own.

Showing up for one's Self is going to look incredibly different for each person. If you have a traumatic brain injury, or serious and limiting health conditions or illness, and are unable to work, showing up for yourself might be creating new methods of redefining success that exist outside of dominant ableist culture.

If you are in a level mental state, and financially and/or energetically abundant, then showing up for yourself might actually be showing up for other people who need your help, your resources, and your privilege. Showing up for yourself might mean using some of your resources, whether it be time, energy, or money, to go to people, places, or elements that need your efforts.

If you are a creative person who has trouble showing up for your creative practice, there are some different ways to start showing up—specifically if your issues are around mindset, or fear, or not knowing where to start or how to begin. First things first: You begin where you begin. You begin with the practice of showing up. If you stare at a screen for an hour, that is how you begin. If your heart is racing and your stomach feels sick, that's where you are. Schedule a time. Move forward one step at a time. One breath in and one breath out. I've written this book on a plane with a cold, and in the desert all alone with anxiety. I've written on days when I've had mild headaches, when my muscles are stiff and sore, after I've cried for hours over death and politics and protests and hope. I've written this book while being in the best mood imaginable, literally feeling as though I was dancing with Spirit and her messages were cascading out of my fingertips and onto the screen. Looking back, I can't remember which paragraph I wrote when I was grinning a wide smile, or which word was typed while tears fell against my cheeks. If you are a creative, find a way to make your practice, your process, an anchor. That goes for a spiritual or magical practice as well.

Whenever we are starting something new it is uncomfortable. You may meet a resistance, or an acute opposition that can also be defined as an edge. An edge can be where you find growth. Eventually, with practice and compassion you come out the other side with a new way of view-ing yourself and a new way of valuing yourself. There bursts forth a new understanding of who you are, outside of all the noise trying to define you. Practicing introduces new understandings of what you need. Through this process, there are a few things to remember:

Patience. You must cultivate patience. We are focused on the longer results of deepened self-love and self-awareness. We need to suspend expectations when we practice showing up.

Practice. This is a practice. Some days the practice will be discouraging. Other times will be revelatory. Keep practicing.

Process. This is a process. Cultivate your own specific loyalty of the unknown. Accept that you will not have all the answers all the time. The process is also a practice.

If this showing up is rubbing against the grain of your family patterns, friend groups, or society, this can feel splintered. Especially if there has been some deep subconscious programming that you will not be safe to take up more space. If your subconscious has deep-rooted beliefs around value and worth, if your subconscious does not believe you worthy or valuable, this is another aspect to take into consideration and address with kindness, or with the help of a therapist or support group.

Above all else, you get to define what this showing up entails.
You get to believe you are infinitely worth it, infinitely valuable.

In the very first Many Moons for the very first Last Quarter Moon three years ago, I brought up a wonderful exercise that one of my teachers, Ariel Gatoga of the Druidic Craft of the Wise, shares. It is called the "Waning Moon Flips." In this practice, one lists all the limiting core beliefs they can think of at the time. All the fears, anxiety, or anger that holds one back. The thought forms and energy that keep us looped in unhelpful spirals. We then reframe it by rewriting those down in a positive or helpful way. For example:

"I am a bad person because I am in debt. I will always be broke and hopeless" could be replaced with "I am a great person who never had any familial financial support and who never learned about money. Every time I learn more about saving, every time I make a $3 payment to my credit card, I am remembering that I am able to get out of debt. I know that I have more agency to make better decisions, because I love myself and I am hopeful for an abundant future. I begin this abundant future today."

When we are doing little things we don't want to do, like doing the dishes, having a hard conversation, or going to therapy, reframing helps. Reframing is an important practice. "I GET to go to therapy." "I GET to do my dishes." "I GET to be alive." Etc., etc., etc.

"Every time I show up for my creative practice, I am showing myself that I care about my process and the gifts I wish to give to humanity. I know that every brushstroke is an amplification of my love of the Earth and of color. It is safe to express my voice."

Continuing to show up for ourselves enacts a great homecoming. We are allowed to come back to ourselves. We are allowed to feel at home in our desires and our needs. We are allowed to feel safe in caring for ourselves and for others.

During this week, during this Waning Moon period before the New Moon, ask yourself: What do I need today? What do I need from myself? Where will I give this to myself? How will I show up?

This would be a very good week to:

Do one or many things you've been putting off doing, that in the long term, will give you great benefit. (I.e., start a savings account, quit smoking, research and find a therapist, send out a couple of grant applications, etc.)
Do your own version of the Waning Moon Flips. Do one or two reframing exercises around smaller patterns in your life. If you feel ready, try it for larger issues.
Show up for yourself in ways that have been a challenge previously. Maybe it is meditating every day, or drinking enough water, or saying no thank you or keeping boundaries around when you leave work. Ask for help or for an accountability buddy who needs help, too.
Show up for someone, or a group of people, you've been meaning to show up for. Ask them: How can I help? Or take the lead yourself.

Journaling questions, or questions to pull cards to:
How do I need to show up for myself more?— allow myself rest when I need it,
What will that look like?
Where do I have opposition or stubbornness to this? Why?
What am I ready to reframe?
What damaging expectations do I have of myself that are ready to be swept away?
What positivity would fill my life if I dropped my resistance to caring for myself—or the collective—more?

Tarot cards to reflect on:
Two of Cups, Six of Cups, Nine of Wands, Nine of Swords, The Magician, The High Priestess, The Lovers, The Star

JULY 12TH: NEW MOON in CANCER 7:48 PM PST, SOLAR ECLIPSE 8:01 PM PST, 5:22 AM PST MOONRISE, 7:55 PST MOONSET

All Our Water Holds

Sound Piece VII

Tape the sound of the moon fading at dawn.
Give it to your mother to listen to
when she's in sorrow.

—Yoko Ono

The Moon is New on Thursday, July 12th. She shows up in the sky at the same time as sunrise, but we can't actually see her, as a New Moon is technically invisible—hiding between the Earth and the Sun. Her potential is embedded in this glittery black, blank slate. Her power, in part, lies in the mystery of her magic.

This Moon is a Partial New Moon Solar Eclipse in Cancer. Next month, on the 11th, we'll have a New Moon Eclipse in Leo. Themes in your life from the lunar eclipse in Leo this past January might already be surfacing in scenarios and shifts in your life. Think back six months, all the way back to January of this year—practically another lifetime. What has changed? What still needs attention or a different form of awareness?

Eclipses come in a series: either two or three eclipses take place in a time period of about one month. A solar eclipse will always be in the same sign that the Sun is in, while a lunar eclipse will almost always be in the opposite sign of the Sun. A family of signs will keep occurring in pairs, at the New and Full Moon, approximately every six months, for aound 18 to 24 months. This series of Cancer/Capricorn eclipses starts this year, builds during 2019, and continues on into 2020. Thematically, we could be addressing concerns around how we mother and care for ourselves, and one another. We may be revising our definitions of power—it may be more nurturing, more collective-focused, more fluid, more horizontal. We could be exploring, personally and collectively, how our intuition and our emotional superpowers can posi-tively affect our career, our ambitions, our relationships. Stalwart structures our egos may have depended on for safety may begin dissolving or evolving into more sustainable and flexible arms to hold us as we work. We may find that the more we connect to our intuition, the more we learn to accept the riches our own mysteries and magic offer up. The more we lean into our clearest instincts, the more safety we end up securing. The more we listen to our inner voice, the more our lives open up. Once we are more open, there is more dolphin laughter to enjoy. There are more rainbows after the rain.

A New Moon Partial Solar Eclipse is when the Sun and Moon conjunct one another and align with the Earth. The shadow of the Moon covers—eclipses—the Sun. The Moon is a meta-phor for our subconscious, our intuition, our instincts, inner desires and safety, and our sometimes intangible cycles and waves. The Moon is the emotional power of our life force, the ways we mother ourselves and have been mothered. The Moon rules our emotional body— and so connects us to all other life, also alive in the lunar light. She is our acceptance and aware-ness that everything comes in cycles, externally and internally. She reminds us that paying attention to our intuition, our emotions, our physical state in the present is an altering of our future state. The Sun is a metaphor for our consciousness, our self-realization externally, and our growth (Liz Greene and Howard Sasportas, *The Luminaries*, York Beach: Weiser, 1992, p. 81). The Sun is also about rebirth, our search for meaning and happiness, and the continued development of our personality, our energy and life force. The Sun highlights intentions and external attention. When the Sun is shining brightly, it allows us to experience a life divinely lived. We need engagement and involvement with both Lunar and Solar qualities for our evolution. Integration and balance of our inner states and our external behaviors is what compels an opening seed to crack and unfurl. Reflection and action are needed in equal measures if we wish to grow and transform. The components of our soul's mission are fertilized when we prioritize interior realizations with exterior pleasures.

The Moon is crossing in front of the Sun at a New Moon Eclipse. Our subconscious is maybe coming to the forefront. There is an opportunity to examine where our ego is helping us, and where it is constricting us. We can ask ourselves at this time: What has been failing to appear in our lives? Internally, how will we summon the permission to prioritize our needs? Can we accept certain needs as non-negotiable? Can we reframe our needs so as not to be burden, but as a way to experience a more authentic, compassionate life?

At this New Moon Partial Solar Eclipse, both the Sun and the Moon are in the astrological sign of Cancer. Cancer correlates with emotional mastery and psychic ability, with caring and creativity. The sign of Cancer correlates to the mother archetype, the home, and our homecomings: psychic, metaphorical, or literal. The archetype of Cancer is exalted when they are able to identify their emotions and work with them constructively. When their psychic abilities and sensitivities are able to be manifested in the spirit of service and healing, the archetype of the Cancer is empowered. Themes of this eclipse may be feelings and how we feel them, nurturing and how we allow ourselves to be nurtured. We may be rethinking our care, and the care of the collective.

Can we allow this eclipse to open us up to transforming our feelings into healings? Can we find ways to work more deftly with our emotions, not be flooded by them? Can we allow our emotions to give us more information about what to let go of and what to hold holy? Can we allow our intuition to discern what new riverbeds are safe to flow into?

Cosmically, and elementally, we enjoy a dose of double water, as both the Moon and Sun are in Cancer, a water sign. Magically, the element of water corresponds with the direction of West. It has to do with emotions, intuition, psychic abilities, spirituality, nurturing, and is introspective. Water is also a symbol of fertility and renewal, whether it be be in a womb state or by tears—cleansing drops of release. Water is fluid, receptive, and changing. When we work with water, we are invoking the unknown, our intuition, our mysteries, the lotus, the eel, the dove, the serpent, the succulent, the tides, the ocean, pearls, our blood, our sweat, the Moon.

Water has been used in ritual since ancient times. Many early ritual sites have been found in estuaries; where the river meets the sea is where Indigenous/Pagan peoples would make magic. It is healing and cleansing: a way to access our intuition and wash unwanted energy away. Some ancient practitioners believed that the spirit of the Moon goddess was strongest in caves and caverns near the ocean, and so would gather there. We pour out libations to honor the dead and to connect with Spirit. We dunk in bodies of water to celebrate baptisms, we immerse ourselves in mikvah baths for many different reasons, we luxuriate in a salt bath before a spell to relax and reconnect, we release our tears into bowls of water to be held and reflected. Holy Water. Florida Water. Moon Water. Our Body's Water.

From a Jungian standpoint, water is feeling. Water correlates to the subconscious and unconscious. Our subconscious (or pre-conscious, as Freud called it), and unconscious make up between 80-90 percent of our brain. This is where much of our power resides, so deep and so vast. Our subconscious is our own personal ocean of mystery and intuition. How will you access your subconscious at this New Moon Eclipse? What does it wish to communicate? How is it turning up by way of themes, symbols, or reoccurring dreams?

In the Tarot, the suit that correlates with water is the suit of Cups. The realms that Cups correlate with are emotions, intuition, instincts, spirituality, intimacy and relationships, emotional patterns and behaviors, service, reflection, joy, contentment, happiness, and love. Many of these themes rely on our ability to blossom. Our care, compassion, our ability to be in flow and to let things flow with us and around us. As we gain versatility in the ways that we process our emotions and connect with our intuition, we enact a homecoming to ourselves. Our magic increases. Our appreciation of the many mysteries in our lives opens portals.

Part of what makes our magic so intriguing is precisely because it is unknown. It will always have aspects of intangibility, of indescribable sensations and breathtaking mystery. Part of what makes our magic so powerful is that, like water, it is so fluid, so shape-shifting, and it shows up in so many states and in so many ways. It is changeable, and in that change lies the hope, the faith, and the possibilities that move us forward and connect us all.

When water is in its fluid state, it is so versatile that it moves ships along, caresses seahorses in its navy depths, and travels down through the soil to offer sustenance to emerald green roots that weave their way through the fabric of this Earth. When it gets too cold, it freezes: it becomes almost impenetrable. It gets too hot, it scalds. When our emotions, our subconscious, or intuition are ignored or imbalanced, our life can become dangerous. The sweet sprinkles become a thunderstorm; a warm spring becomes a boiling cavern.

Some people try to act like everything is rigid, static, unchanging. That the rules are the rules and this way is the only way. No waves allowed. Water teaches us that we are fluid. In fact, we are mirrors of the ocean, of the rivers, of the rain. We hold this very dynamic fluidity inside of our own bodies. Our identities, our feelings, our intuition. This Moon can teach us to embrace our own fluidity. In embracing our own fluidity, we are open to more change. We can see others as changing as well. This Moon can prompt us to embrace changing forces in our lives, to turn into any natural cycles we have previously been resisting.

Some people try to act like water is free, but it is in fact priceless. Water is life. Water covers 71% percent of the Earth's surface, and our bodies contain around that much water as well. We came out of the water, billions of years ago, little life forms, looking to evolve into another incarnation. Keeping our water with us as we grew to stand and evolve on land. Protecting water, being mindful of how we use water and what we do to it is protecting our own life. Protecting that water is to honor all kinds of sacred stories. Protecting water is to honor all kinds of sacred life.

Some people try to act like femme, feminine, and emotional labor is free, but it is in fact priceless. This work makes the world go round. This work literally saves lives. The work of patient caregiving, caretaking, of explaining. The work of processing and presence. The work of fierce, hard, and soft determination. The work of hair brushing, bottom wiping, hand holding, sweeping, and dinner cooking. The work of surviving being screamed at, ridiculed, cat-called and gaslit. The work of support and sweetness, softness and story telling. The work of teaching, empathizing, channeling, and sharing. The work of the truth. The work of organizing, making phone calls, offering up resources, checking in about dietary restrictions, asking preferred pronouns, and finding everyone rides. The work of tending to the hearth, bringing forth the ritual, conjuring the circle. The work of shielding others from the pain we carry in a disturbing world, as well as the work of rebuilding it. The work of comforting, providing solace, the work of carrying on. This is all work that must be acknowledged more, valued more. Can you take the time to acknowledge all the work you have done and continue to do? Can you promise to celebrate this work, as well as celebrate this work that other women, femmes, feminine folks, and queers do? Will you promise to protect your intuition, your work, your water? Will you promise to see it for what it is: a magical superpower, a gift to the community, a shining chalice of success?

This is the collective web of water that we are all in, together and individually. May we hold ourselves more lovingly so that we can hold one another—securely yet fluidly. Allowing for collaboration, missteps, apologies, conversation, engagement, listening, laughter, understandings and misunderstandings and acceptance and evolution, ebbs and flows, deep wells of sustenance, and knowing and patience and space. Because one person's needs are different than our own: our Black Trans sisters have much different needs from our white cis sisters; our Korean-American sex worker sisters have much different needs from our bisexual undocumented coven members; our Queer disabled Latinx sisters have much different needs from our Filipina Intersex community; as do our Gay Russian witch sisters. What we all have in common is that we all need one another. We can acknowledge our differences, hold space for one another while simultaneously holding space for ourselves.

When we are full of sorrow, let us be reminded that we can still hold ourselves. Let us be reminded that we can still hold one another both while our eyes are dripping tears and when our arms are strongly outstretched. Let us be reminded that our suffering is not ours to carry alone. We can find new ways to help ourselves and ask for help. We must look for an abundant array of healing modalities and methods that include connecting, sharing, reaching out, ice cream, dancing, laughing, and taking care not to overburden ourselves.

When we are overjoyed, let us rejoice. Let us use the stardust of our energy to inspire others. When our chalices are overflowing, Ace of Cups style, let us not feel guilty. Let us enjoy and take more time to relax into the inspiration and feelings of flow. Let those of us with abundant resources—time, energy, ideas, money—help those who need them. Let those who need help be brave enough to ask.

Consider The High Priestess card, the card of the Moon. When she is in tune, she is an embodiment of the divine. The witch. The herbalist, the scholar, the channeler, the inspiration. The cosmic mother, the gatekeeper of the underworld, the safe keeper of the subconscious. When she is misunderstood, when her knowledge is degraded, she is withholding, withdrawn, has no sense of herself, may even harm other women. Considering all the violence enacted on women, on femmes, on witches, on empaths, on mothers, on daughters, all the shame and violence and blame, can you now understand her shadow?

Consider the Queen of Cups, the Tarot card of double water. The Queen of mothers, the psychic songstress. She holds the standards of her heart, and the hearts of those around her so high that she runs the risk of dissolving altogether. When she is balanced, her psychic abilities help her make decisions, access Spirit, and care for all. When she is imbalanced, when her water levels are too dry, she's the mean mommy. The abuser and enforcer. The codependent, emotionally manipulative, overly concerned parent.

Knowing all that she was up against, the many times her water was polluted carelessly, her invisible labor unappreciated, how many times she was taken for granted, for generations upon generations, can you soften into more empathy for her pain? And for your own?

Because your mother birthed YOU. And YOU are rebirthing yourself. Consider your mother, your intuition, your most holding patterns, your most holding self. The holding that is positive and the holding that hurts. Try to give yourself more compassion, more space, to heal as you must.

At this New Moon Eclipse, let's practice enacting even more space, more holding for our healing, individually and collectively. Our power, our work, our worth. Know that the water goddesses and water gods of the world are living through you, as you exist via your grandmother's grandmother's womb. Sedna, Venus, Oshun, Neptune, Poseidon. Know that the water bearers, the well diggers, the deep sea divers, the dowsers, the mermaids in their oyster shells, are supporting you. We can hold ourselves with more sweetness, even if at first it tastes like too many tears. The tears are the salt washing our sorrow away. We are allowed to redefine healing and holding for ourselves and for the oceans of people who swim alongside us. We are allowed to let the ocean of creativity, of wonder, of miracles that we hold inside ourselves out.

We can do this with our healing processes and work. We can do this with our vulnerabilities and our fierceness. We know that healing is not linear. It comes in as you float on lapping waves, get refreshed at the base of a waterfall, or when you are down at the bottom of a deep sea floor. It comes as you reconnect with your own mysteries. It comes as we allow co-creation with the elements, the universe, our communities, and our own water.

The following suggested ritual centers around accessing intuition and asking the cards questions about our healing, eclipsing harmful sub-conscious patterns, and our intuition. If you do not feel drawn to this ritual, you can create your own. If all you feel called to do around this New Moon is listen, is notice, is touch base with your own water, or think about how to protect our precious planet's water more, that would be excellent. It is suggested to use the element of water in some way during this eclipse. If you are not feeling called to enact a ritual at this time, there are many small activities you may wish to do instead. Up your water intake. Commit to drinking a tonic or herbal infusion daily. Allow yourself to feel more fluid.

Connect with water. Cry into it. Know the water can take away your pain. Water can hold tears and salt and still flow. Spend time with your shower or bath. Clean it, scrub it, change the shower curtain, add eucalyptus sprigs under the shower head, or put a bowl of salt nearby to add to a body scrub or a salt soak. When you shower, thank the water, thank the pipes, thank the tub for helping you cleanse and get clean.

Charging water spell. Charge a bowl of water under the eclipse with a water-safe crystal, then with love and intention. Pour it into a water bottle or pitcher after it has been charged. Decorate with tape/stickers, words of love, words of intention. Every day, for at least 3 days, drink the charged water. Imagine all of the water in your body filling up with your intentions and desires. Imagine them going into your cells, your subconscious, and allowing new breakthroughs and new magic to begin in tandem with new outlooks and behaviors you are cultivating.

Consider mothering. Think of a couple of mothers you know. Reach out to them and ask them if they need anything. If you are a mother, think about what you need more of at this time, and ask for it from those around you, from yourself, from the universe. Think of someone with no mother, or who is not a mother. Reach out to them and ask them if they need anything. Write your own mother a letter. Depending on your relationship with your mother, and what needs to be in the letter for your healing, you may or may not send this letter. If your mother is no longer in physical form, you can still contact her and communicate with her. Depending on your relationship with her, you may need to forgive her, set a boundary with her, or recognize her as an angel in your life, watching over you and continuing to protect. You may need to look for and identify other people, other than your mother, who hold you and help heal you.

Remember, the Moon is New; it is a blank slate to be used however you'd like in the spirit of fresh starts and seedlings. Happy New Moon!

Suggested Affirmation: "I allow my intuition to guide my healing. My healing is fluid, and allows for others to be healed in the ocean of our collective."

Circles of Water, Reflections of Intuition: A scrying ritual and Tarot pull

You will need:

a bowl, large enough to scry in (look into comfortably)
Tarot cards
a journal
other crystals, tea lights, or herbs you feel called to use
(magickal ingredients associated with Cancer, the Moon, and intuition are: selenite, moonstone, Herkimer diamond, Lemurian quartz, mugwort, motherwort, angelica root, among others)

You may wish to begin this ritual with breath work, or a guided meditation or Yoga Nidra, or anything else that helps get you in a relaxed and open state. Get grounded, cast your circle, call in the elements and your deities, if that is your practice.

Dim the lights so you can just see what you are doing. You may wish to turn out all the lights, and light tea lights or candles.

Put out a bowl of filtered water that has a pinch of salt and a squeeze of lemon in it.
Set the bowl of water on a table or on the floor. You may wish to place any of your magickal ingredients around it.

Once you feel centered, peer into your bowl of water.

Ask yourself:
What is my intuition telling me at this time?
What are my emotions telling me at this time?
What about my power scares me?
What next steps does Spirit want me to focus on taking?
How will this help my healing, and healing of my matriarchal line?
Where am I ready to flow?

Make note of any clear messages that are coming in by writing them in your journal.

Spend a bit more time with the water, seeing if any other messages or insights come up.

New Moon in Cancer Circle Spread

Pull the cards and place around the water bowl one by one in a circle. (Be careful not to get water on them!)

1. What is healing for me at this time, at this New Moon Eclipse?
2. What harmful patterns in my subconscious am I ready to let go of now?
3. Where can more support be found?
4. What, in my heart, do I know I am ready to manifest?
5. Where must I put my energy at this cycle?
6. What portals are opening for me at this New Moon Eclipse?
7. How will I welcome and affirm these portals?
8. What will shift and change as I continue to show up for others and hold others in this greater collective?

Make notes on what your circle spread tells you.
Depending on your state of mind, you may wish to:

Cry into the water.
Charge the water with positive intentions and use it in the bath or drink it after it has been charged with the New Moon. If you are asking the water to hold your pain or suffering, after the ritual is finished, lovingly pour it into the earth, or into a body of moving water.

Promise yourself that you will pay attention to your healing, your intuition, and any messages that come through to you, via your subconscious, external synchronicities, or through your larger community in the coming days. Promise yourself will practice holding other's water.

Promise you will act on some ways to reduce how much water you use, or consider protecting water in some way, or helping those who do not have easy access to water obtain clean water.

Notes on Ritual / Spell:

Notes on Tarot Spread:

1. What is healing for me at this time, at this New Moon Eclipse?
Card I pulled:

2. What harmful patterns in my subconscious am I ready to let go of now?
Card I pulled:

3. Where can more support be found?
Card I pulled:

4. What, in my heart, do I know I am ready to manifest?
Card I pulled:

5. Where must I put my energy at this cycle?
Card I pulled:

6. What portals are opening for me at this New Moon Eclipse?
Card I pulled:

7. How will I welcome and affirm these invations?
Card I pulled:

8. What will shift and change as I continue to show up for others and hold others in this greater collective?
Card I pulled:

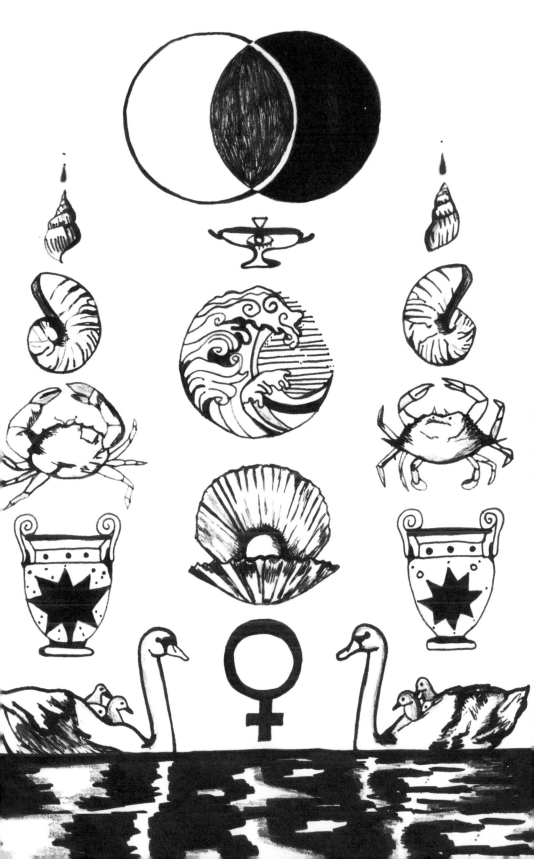

JULY 19TH: FIRST QUARTER MOON in LIBRA 12:52 PM PST, 2:52 PM PST MOONRISE, 12:17 AM PST MOONSET

Soul Retrievals: Ending Self-Abandonment

Content Warning: This piece touches on trauma and abuse. You may wish to skip over this piece if these are intense subjects for you.

Today, the Moon revolves into its First Quarter Moon phase. It is one week after the New Moon, and one day and one week before the Full Moon Lunar Eclipse. Shifts we are wishing to have taken place are taking place. If they seem imperceptible, it might be time to notice and focus on them until they grow wings. If they aren't feeling quite the way you had hoped, remember that life sometimes unfolds at its own speed. Recall that this is one bead in a longer string the length of a lifetime.

Practice suspending judgment. Maybe you don't have all the information you need yet. Maybe not enough sand has passed through the hourglass yet. Maybe the dust has to settle—hard when we lack patience, but necessary. Maybe more unwinding, unraveling is needed. It is your call to focus on what will give you long-term sustenance. While we are retraining our brains, our thought patterns, our behaviors, it can feel we are wading through sludge. Keep going.

From a magical perspective, the Waxing Moon is an excellent time for building and growth spells. Drawing and attracting are the name of this Moon's game. This First Quarter phase comes in on a Thursday, ruled by Jupiter. Libra—the sign the Moon happens to be in—is ruled by Venus. These next few days is an opportune time for love or self-love spells, beauty, attracting, and abundance spells. Try one for 3 days in a row. See what sweetness comes your way, as you offer up your wishes to be charged by moonbeams.

The topic for this Waxing Moon is around Soul retrievals, calling your energy back, and in doing so, ending self-abandonment. If we are women, if we are people of color, if we identify as Queer, Trans, disabled, different in any way, we can be taught at a very young age to abandon ourselves. To play small. Ignore our talents and the ease of our joy. Not get in the way. Change our behavior to fit in. If we have been abused, misunderstood, if we have threatened others by our very difference and our many talents, if our souls have been bright and singing and jarring since an early age, these might have been squashed down. Tampered with, ridiculed and gaslit by others who are intimidated by our light.

This may have resulted in self-abandonment as a safety measure.

Some of us abandon ourselves to nurture and nourish one another, some to keep the peace, some because it was imprinted onto us that we were dangerous, our talent was powerful and that power was one that we were not to be given access to, that power was one we weren't allowed to experience. If you remember feeling or being stifled from an early age, no matter what the source, it is time for you to call your power back.

It is time for you to call your energy back.
It is time to show up for yourself in all your rainbow colored glory. All your confetti sprinkled joy. It is never too late to do this. It is never too late to give yourself more pieces of you. It is never too late to get back to your soul and your self.

In this short piece, I will discuss four basic soul retrieval categories, and techniques to address them. These are on a spectrum, so you may identify with one, some or multiple practices.

✓ it is difficult + essential work that I must do - in order to love myself + move forward

The first practice of ending self-abandonment is to calling in your past self in order to forgive them. Welcoming and accepting yourself, in all your forms, makes peace. It grants yourself permission to love all the parts of yourself. In this, we are able to integrate. We are able to be present. We are able to move on.

A simple practice to help yourself with this is to practice forgiving your past self. There can be shame, blame, or guilt for how we behaved. We may wish to bury our past selves or not address them at all. We have to understand that our behavior, as ashamed as we may be about some of it, was innocent. In many cases, we were doing what we were doing because we didn't know any better. In many cases, these past selves were a survival mechanism. We did what we needed to do to survive. We did what we needed to live! Practicing gratitude for our past selves for helping us get to this point is important.

A simple yet potent practice for this is to look at old pictures of yourself. Really look at yourself and allow yourself to see the wonderful person you were, doing your best. Speak to these pictures. Thank yourself for allowing yourself to stay alive and for growing and changing. If it is hard to do, start with a baby picture. Babies are literally the most innocent stage of our evolution. Look at yourself as a baby and you can't help but love yourself. Give thanks to yourself as a child, as a teenager, as a young adult, and as an adult. You made it. At times it was brutal. There were times you didn't behave as your best self. A lot of time, you didn't know any better. You were drawing the map! You were attempting to create a diagram of a path in the dark with a velvet blindfold on. In the mistakes you found your answer. In the unknown you summoned your knowing.

Thank yourself for surviving. Allow yourself to be proud of yourself for living. Have you thanked your past selves lately? Have you honored them for not giving up, for regrouping, recommitting, over and over again?

The second touchpoint on this spectrum is calling in more of yourself. Taking up more space in your life. Yes, you are allowed. To exist. To cry. You are allowed to have people hear your adorably freaky laugh that sounds like a seal. You are allowed to pitch your idea. You are allowed to relax, to take a salt bath with some rosemary sprigs thrown in for good measure. You are allowed to order the extra side of whatever it is that you want. You are allowed to say no thank you and let that be that. You are allowed to ask for what you want and what you need.

Hematite is an amazing stone for this. Working with hematite reminds us that our greatest protection against the psychic vampires—that come from outside and inside us— is by filling ourselves up with ourselves, cell by cell, whisker by whisker. When we fill ourselves up with so much of ourselves, there simply isn't room for anyone else to try to steal our shine or zap our energy. We are protected.

A very effective practice begins with calling back your energy back every day verbally and psychically. You can do this at any time during your morning routine and even add it to your evening routine before bed. Simply state:

I call my energy back to me. All my energy that is scattered other places, I call back to me. All energy in my body this is not of me, I return to the earth to be transformed into something greater. I lovingly release all energy that no longer serves me. All the energy inside of my body, all the intentions I set forth is of me, for me.

If you feel called, practice this at least once a day, in your own way, with your own words.

Call back the person that hid in the closet. Call back the person who hummed alone in the forest, making up myths out of moss. Call back the person who had to shut down to find a way out. Call back the person who reveled in performance, who felt fiercest in a leotard. Call back the person who desperately needed love but never was allowed to ask for it. Call back the person who hid their light, their inspirations and their ideas out of a very actual fear. Call back the person who could hear messages from birds, who found answers in clouds. Call back the person roaming in the wildness of their forest, sweatily seeking an answer that was inside this whole time.

This practice helps us accept and helps us make peace.

We can enforce this practice of calling ourselves back with a devotion to staying in our energy. One way of doing this is to frequently give ourselves what we wish and what we desire, in tangible ways. It might be very simple. Not holding in your pee or waiting to go to the bathroom, not holding your breath, not facilitating constriction in your body, or clenching your stomach. Eating what you wish, scheduling activities you like before consulting others, voicing your opinion on where you'd like to go, what groceries you'd like, or if you have any allergies/limitations. Crying when you need to cry. Doing nothing when you need to do nothing. Invest energetically, with time and intention, activities that interest you—especially activities you have always wanted to try but somehow got told you couldn't or were not allowed to try. In work and in relationships, volunteering to do the activities you want to, instead of waiting to take on the work of what others do not want to do. Setting boundaries with certain harmful relationships in your life. Honoring the you in you.

If this seems like a lot of work, it is. This takes practice and this takes time. A very simple, focusing practice is making a list of things to do when you wake up, before you start your day. Decide to put 2 minutes, 20 minutes, or 2 hours, whatever your schedule permits, into one thing you want to do for yourself, whatever it is.

The third practice is one of working with the different elements to bolster your energy. It is a common practice in witchcraft to work directly with an element we need more of in our own energy system. When we feel uninspired, we light a match and get our body moving to upbeat music. Putting our bare feet into the earth and feeling her alive energy, we feel more grounded. Watching the hawk circle slowly in the sky brings us the essence of our own ideas and imagination, our own ability to vision. Any witch knows that when crafting a spell, we not only bring in the elements energetically as we cast our circle, we also have a representation of the elements we honor on our altar. These elements are a balance of our intentions as they reflect the essences of nature and bring the anima of all life forms into our spell work.

Are there any elements that you feel like you need more of in your life? At this Waxing Moon time, do you need more fire and water? More earth and air? More space, more stillness? Do a check-in at this time. Promise yourself you will give yourself more of what you need, elementally.

I was excited to learn that is also a Buddhist practice. In *The True Source of Healing* by Tenzin Wangyal Rinpoche, the author outlines a soul retrieval practice as part of his Bön dzogchen tradition. This practice is based upon connecting with one or more of the five elements: water, earth, air, fire, and space. The beautiful part of this practice is that it requires nothing but our attention. Wangyal Rinpoche suggests we get out into nature, even if this means we are looking out the window or through the room in our apartment. Nature could be a park, our bathtub, or a vase of flowers. If we cannot get out into nature, we meditate on the element. We stare at the sky. We connect and relate, interdependent as we are.

While at this time of the year it is easier to submerge oneself into the ocean or a river, to rest one's body on the earth, or to find a space to build a summer bonfire, we can work with the elements at all times of the year. Wangyal Rinpoche suggests simply meditating with the thought of the element inside of you. When we go outside and feel a breeze, we can meditate on how flexible we are, examine if we need to work on our communication. We can put our feet or our body on the floor of our room, and feel the stability of the Earth. We can thank her for giving us structure and we can meditate on where we must find the trust and strength of our inner resources. We can take a shower, a bath, or a foot bath with herbs and salt, and imagine being held with love, imagine our intuition bubbling forth freely. Looking at the sky is being the sky. Allowing yourself stillness and space with an element is invoking that element into your body and psychic space.

The last soul retrieval I will discuss is the one generally associated with the subject. This is a soul retrieval practice that involves Shamanic journeying, EMDR therapy, hypnosis, biofeedback therapy or somatic therapy. Shamans and some therapists believe that when something traumatic happens in one's life, a part of the soul flies away. When I say "soul", I mean: your spirit, that part of you that cannot be destroyed, your higher self, the *you* part of you, the part of you that cannot be replicated, your true identity, which involves your own gifts and unique talents that come from inside of you.

When parts of our soul are missing, we are disconnected from ourselves on a fundamental level. Symptoms of this can include numbing, dissociating, addiction, freezing, blacking out, forgetfullness, anger, depression, codependency, and difficulties staying in the present moment (*Soul Retrieval: Mending the Fragmented Self*, Sandra Ingerman). There can sometimes be a very clear "before" and "after" period with deep forms of trauma. A person can, with or without prompting, recall the age or even the incident in which part of them flew away or broke off. This sort of soul retrieval is best enacted with professional help. Working with and journeying with an experienced practitioner who is deeply knowledgable can facilitate this sort of soul retrieval. Twelve step programs, recovery communities, women's groups, and other similar support groups can help along with concentrated therapy. It is only recommended that doing work around soul recovery lost due to trauma and abuse should be undertaken with a highly experienced counselor or specialist. If what you read about healing trauma resonated, do not do this work alone. Enlist therapy and community for support.

The benefits of doing this work are immense. In my personal experience, soul retrieval work, done with a trained, experienced practitioner, combined with ongoing therapy and a self-love practice, result in clarity, bravery, an enhanced intuition, a deep self-love and reverence, and a loss of listlessness, depression, and feeling powerless. In my own life, there has been a commitment to staying in the present moment as much as possible, and what can be more magical than that? The present moment is the moment of all potential, and being clear, engaged, and in love with it is where potent transformation can take shape.

Please remember that this takes time.
Please remember that this kind of work is intense.
Please remember that this will often look like one step forward, two steps back.

As we begin to address our deep pain and our suffering, more may burst forth. This comes up to come out. Over time—time that is not linear, time that is somatic, time that is of breath, of the middle of the roots of the trees that had seeds that were planted long before you knew how to crawl— this will shift and change. Give yourself all the love, all the compassion, and all the space you need to simply be, simply breathe, as you refrain from judgment in your own process.

Your healing is ultimately for the healing of all. If you are not used to taking up space, stating your needs, fostering your gifts, nurturing your unique talents, as you begin to do this work, it may feel like sabotage. You may feel guilty for taking up so much space.

Darling, take up space. All of it. Darling, share your natural gifts and talents just as the eucalyptus freely wafts her fresh scent in the breeze, just as the black-tailed jackrabbit feasts on sagebrush, and just as the manatee floats unencumbered in the sea. You don't limit other people's space, so why would you hinder your own glittering expansiveness?

You deserve to be in fully present in your body, loving and accepting all the parts of yourself. You deserve to hear your own true soul sing.

During this Waxing Moon time, allow yourself to give yourself a little more of yourself. It benefits the collective. Our year cards are the High Priestess, and Justice, (or Strength, if you use a Marseille-style deck). The High Priestess is very much a card of healing trauma by connecting to one's own intuition at an unwavering level. To opening the portal to our own underworld, our vast subconscious in order to gain our own wisdom. Justice is all about Karma. All about doing what is true and right for you, independent of your programming, when the fear has been cast off like so many heavy, rusty chains. Justice also points to where in your life you must cut cords to belief systems that do not serve. These two cards together—the High Priestess and Justice— tell a story of letting go of patterns that are harmful. They tell a tale of reconnecting to your personal power. There is a sweet strength that surfaces when an individual can be wild and free and laugh long and openmouthed. When they can sing and cry and process and feel safe: exactly how their body, mind, and spirit need to. These become more articulated after all the parts of yourself begin to get called back inside.

You deserve to be whole.

Books on this topic: *The Body Keeps the Score* by Bessel Van Der Kolk, Md, *The True Source of Healing* by Tenzin Wangyal Rinpoche, & *Soul Retrieval: Mending the Fragmented Self*, by Sandra Ingerman.

Helpful herbs / plant essences: Yarrow, nettle, rosemary, borage, bamboo, Cypress, Galangal, High John the Conqueror, Hyssop, blackberry
Helpful crystals: Aragonite, desert rose, apache tears, Tiger eye, rose quartz, hematite, tourmaline, Botswana Agate

Journaling questions:
Where have I been abandoning myself?
Do I need to call my energy back?
How will I do this?
Where do I deserve to take up more space?
How will I speak up for myself more, become more of
my own advocate?
What are some elements I want to work with more at this time?
How will I use them to build and grow?

**Thank you to Joanna Buchmeyer for mentioning this topic, and for encouraging me to address this for the collective.

What my intentions are for this Waxing Moon time, going into the July Full Moon:

JULY 27TH: FULL MOON in AQUARIUS 1:21 PM PST, LUNAR ECLIPSE 1:22 PM PST, 8:04 PM PST MOONRISE, 5:48 AM PST MOONSET

Rest for the Revolution: July Full Moon Lunar Eclipse
by Layla Saad

Welcome to this Full Moon Lunar Eclipse. The Moon is in full bloom. But Mother Moon's light is absent from our view in the night sky, because our planet Earth has moved directly between the Sun and the Moon. We know she is there, carrying her messages of abundance, personal power, and healing, but we cannot directly access her blessings because we—planet Earth and all of its inhabitants—are blocking them from view. We have plunged ourselves into darkness, and we are frantically groping around, trying to find our way back to the light.

That is how it feels for many of us right now—in our personal lives and our communities.

We are square in eclipse season. In two weeks' time, there will be a partial solar eclipse with the New Moon, and two weeks ago we experienced our first eclipse of this season. This is a time that can feel both dramatic and chaotic. It is a time where layers are being pulled back, truths are being revealed, shadows are being exposed, and uncomfortable paradigms are being brought to the surface to be examined and processed. It is therefore also a time where we may be feeling very vulnerable, raw, drained (physically, mentally, and spiritually), battle-weary, lost, confused, and defeated. We desperately desire to make our way back to the light—individually and collectively—but with energies eclipsed, we may be finding it a challenge to access that energy within us.

If you are feeling like the victim rather than the victor of your life right now, know that this is okay. If you feel in despair about the state of the world, yet you find you have run out of energy to keep fighting for justice, know that you are not alone. If you find yourself questioning anything and everything (your work, your creativity, your relationships, your beliefs, your activism), know that you are not losing yourself. If anything, you are trying to find yourself. To find your wholeness. And to find wholeness for a world that is so very broken.

This Full Moon Lunar Eclipse (and in fact this entire eclipse corridor) offers us an opportunity to step away from the light, and allow ourselves to find rest and nourishment in the darkness. This time invites us to lay down our mental and emotional weapons. To take a break from the chaos. To press pause. To soften and release. To remember that we do not have to figure it all out right now. To remember that we are always, always, already whole, perfect, and free—but we have to allow ourselves to feel it.

Mother Moon speaks to us now:

"Dear Beloved,

Though you may not see me fully right now in your night sky, I am still here, in full bloom. In fact, I am always in full bloom. I am always big, round, whole, and complete. 360 degrees of lunar magic—24 hours a day, 7 days a week, 365 days a year. But from your view on planet Earth, I appear to cycle through different stages. To you, sometimes I am completely absent, other times I am a crescent, other times a semi-circle, and other times still, a glowing orb. But my truth is that I am always whole—whether or not the Sun's light is fully shining on me.

This is what I want you to remember, as you sit in the darkness (literally and figuratively).

In the same way that I am already whole, whether or not the Sun's light is reflecting off of me, you too are already whole. Your wholeness does not come from being seen and honored by others. It comes from seeing and honoring yourself.

In what ways are you not seeing and honoring the wholeness that is you? The beauty that is you? The miracle that is you? In what ways are you negating and shaming yourself because you are in a period of darkness? In what ways are you denying yourself rest and replenishment because you believe you have to work hard to deserve it? In what ways are you participating in your own victimization, by placing yourself in situations and relationships that are oppressive to your humanity? In what ways are you holding healing and replenishment at arm's distance because you believe you need to be performing all the time?

Can you imagine, Beloved, how it would be if the Sun's light shone fully on me every single day? Can you imagine how exhausting that would be? To never have times of slowness, quietness, and darkness? To always be shining, always be accomplishing, always be giving myself to everyone else, while asking nothing in return? Yes, you can imagine—because you do that to yourself, too.

There is great wisdom in the dark, Beloved. In the mystery. In the outwardly inactive. Allow yourself to rest now. Give yourself permission to Be. To just Be. For yourself, and for the collective. For as long as you need. The work will still be there when you are ready to return. And you will be better resourced to do it—with newfound energy, compassion, creativity, humor, generosity, power, empathy, patience, pleasure, awe, and innovation.

Take as little or as long as you need. But not a moment sooner. Remember, whether or not the world can see the fruits of your labor, you are always whole. You do not have to prove it with your Doing. It is already true with your Being. If every person on your planet understood and practiced the depth of this truth, a collective healing would sweep the Earth.

Maybe it starts with just one person. Maybe it starts with you."

Suggested Affirmation:
"I now give myself the gift of rest.
My rest is radical.
My rest is resistance.
My rest is revolutionary."

A Tarot Spread for the Full Moon Lunar Eclipse

Audre Lorde once said:

"Caring for myself is not self-indulgence, it is self-preservation, and that is an act of political warfare."

Self-care, particularly rest, is a revolutionary act. Especially so while living under white supremacist, heteronormative, capitalist patriarchy. And even more so if you belong to a marginalized or oppressed group (e.g. woman, person of color, LGBTQIA, disabled, poor, not a member of the dominant religion, etc.). Many of us live under systems that do not reward or value our rest, and in fact actively work against it—by keeping us working overtime (by being "on" all of the time) to try and prove we deserve it.

Your rest—not just physical sleep, but actually consciously taking your time, energy and attention away from the people/situations/dynamics that are exhausting you—is an act of radical resistance. By drawing your energies back towards yourself and giving yourself the grace of rest, you give yourself permission to have your cup refilled. Once refilled, you will be able to go back out into the world and give of yourself in a way that honors and serves you, thus honoring and serving the world.

This three-card Tarot or oracle card spread, arranged in the position of a Full Moon Lunar Eclipse, can help you discover what you need rest from, what is stopping you from giving yourself this rest, and what healing you can receive if you give yourself this rest.

I invite you to make some space for yourself during the eclipse to pull three cards and ask yourself the following questions:

Card 1: SUN – What people/situations/activities do I need to take a rest from right now?

Card 2: EARTH – What is getting in the way or stopping me from giving myself this rest?

Card 3: MOON – What wisdom or healing will I receive if I give myself this rest?

For the next two weeks, during this eclipse period, I invite you to give yourself the gift of rest from whatever you need a break from right now. Allow this period of rest to do its work on you. Receive the wisdom and healing you need for yourself, so that, when you are ready to emerge, you may share this healing and wisdom with the world.

Rest is radical.
Rest is resistance.
Rest is revolutionary.

Notes on Tarot Pull:

Card 1:

Card 2:

Card 3:

Notes on this month:

Intentions for the next:

AUGUST 2018
AUGUST 1: LAMMAS
AUGUST 4th: LAST QUARTER MOON
AUGUST 8-10TH: DARK MOON
AUGUST 11th: NEW MOON SOLAR ECLIPSE
AUGUST 18TH: FIRST QUARTER
AUGUST 26TH: FULL MOON

August is a month that reminds us to celebrate. The Sun is high in the sky—nothing to do but bask in the heat. A time to take stock of our light, our life force, and how we continue to burn and shine alike. The Sun—our life force and expansion—takes center stage in the month of August. Many practitioners of the Neopagan or modern Craft will tell you the Sun is masculine. Yet many religions have goddesses associated with this magnificent star. Bast was an Egyptian cat goddess associated with the Sun. Japanese people from the Shinto religion named their Sun goddess Amaterasu Omikami ("the great divinity illuminating heaven"). Sol, or Sunna, was a Norse Sun goddess, riding her horse-drawn chariot far across the sky (Monica Sjoo and Barbara Mor, *The Great Cosmic Mother*). The list goes on and on. Why wouldn't we associate the source of the Sun with birth, giving life, with femininity, with endless collaborative abundance, with glowing brightly and sharing visionary creativity?

Where is it time for you to make room for more fullness and depth in your life? What can you do this month to invite the warm rays of the Sun inside?

August 1st is Lammas: a cross-quarter Pagan holiday that celebrates the harvest. This is the day that marks the halfway point between Summer and Autumn. We celebrate all of our abundance by giving more away. We celebrate our abundance by allowing ourselves to enjoy it. This is the time to bask in the brilliance of Summer and all of her pleasures. As the Moon passes above in the sky each night, connect to her beauty, examine her stoicism. As the Moon passes by our heads each night in the sky, allow her light to fill you up, head to toe, outstretched arms to wide open hands to the tips of your fingertips, caressing the moonglow.

August may be a very intense month for some of us: we have a New Moon Solar Eclipse. Some of us may still be feeling and dealing with the eclipses of last month. We can go deep. We can examine our shadows. We can think about what fortifies us physically, emotionally, and mentally. In this workbook, we go deep into some meaty topics of life: ways to practice witchcraft, dealing with shame, expanding our consciousness, blood, and death. This month, we can release. This month, we can stand even more in ourselves without shame. This month, we can honor our bodies, our practices, and the infinite paradoxes of death and life.

August 2018 Astrology Insights
by Diego Basdeo

August 11th: Solar Eclipse New Moon in Leo, Conjunct Mercury retrograde, Opposing Neptune

August 14th : Mars Retrograde enters Capricorn

August 19th : Mercury Direct

August 26th : Full Moon in Pisces / Square Uranus in Taurus / Earth Trine with Saturn in Capricorn: Uranus in Taurus and the Sun in Virgo/ Mercury square Jupiter

August 28th: Mars Direct

Leo Season

This month, it's all about that new new. Unexplored territory, new boundaries, wild feelings, and new ways to jump to totally new conclusions! Fun! But let's start with the basics. The New Moon on the 12th is standing real close to Mercury, which is all about talking about those feelings. Let it out, let it flow, and let it be a little more private than you want it to be. Move through your feelings—don't run towards the first "answer" or "reason." The Moon/ Mercury combo is making a deadass square to Jupiter which tends to blow things out of proportion.

A Leo New Moon is less about showboating and more about creating something to perform. It is a beginning of an individual's quest for its source. Leos are known for creative force but remain mysteriously underrepresented in famous artists, poets, and musicians. I believe a Leos' greatest creations are themselves. Leo is the vulnerability that, through maturity, brings our awareness to profound unconscious thought—if we are to work out our feelings with words, put them in a song, a poem, a chapbook, whatever. Give your feelings creation. Give this world some light on the source of who we are.

There's a chance to take a minute and allow these wild thoughts to take you to previously unexplored parts of your emotional wilderness—this is a time for writing. There are revelations about money, resources, and property that started back in May that are being touched on again. What are the multiple currencies you deal in? Are you the accountant, keeping track of every emotional transaction? Are you getting paid for your labor? Are you paying too much for rent in that relationship when you're looking for a home? How much are you getting paid for your performance of solidarity? Then there's real money. This is going to change. How are we using the tools of capital for the greater good? When is money not the answer?

It's really important to not freak out if things feel financially unstable right now. Security is not an achievement. It's a measure between where you are and the danger a lot of people have to experience on a regular basis. Don't get me wrong. Security is really important! But I think we are being reminded of how many of the privileges entailed in safety are built on the subjugation, incarceration, and slave labor of other people. It is absolutely in our favor to take the feelings of scarcity or fear and channel them towards solidarity with people who experience these constantly. It is a strength to allow it to remind us that everyone deserves security and well-being.

While your intentions are generally good, you might overestimate what you are capable of, and promise more than you can deliver. Be careful not to develop a reputation for being unreliable, simply because you desire to make others happy with what you say or promise.

Towards the end of the month on the 26th, the Full Moon in Pisces glows very close to watery Neptune. Illusions run strong, but keep in mind that when we are present with both pain and pleasure, we can learn to use them to develop our personal power. Being present is the BIG surrender: surrender to change, surrender to circumstance. Acceptance is not passivity but being present makes us available to understand the true task at hand.

It's been said that the Pisces is made to suffer or to save, that each of these choices are the emblems of fish we see which represent Pisces today. Pisces as a sign understands that chaos, chaotic nature, is always very close and that in each human generation there is an iteration of that chaos. However, just outside that chaos is art, music, pleasure. The closer to the strange wild, the more creative we may be. A Pisces Full Moon may illuminate when we tend to get involved with people who linger a little too close to that art of chaos. We are closing this month understanding that boundaries are built for love, can fall for love, and be rebuilt for love. To save or to suffer is a calling on our hearts. Ensure that our well-being is so on point that if someone we love needs a life raft, we won't sink bringing them aboard.

Deprogramming for Witches

Our Moon enters its Waning phase in this first week of the month. Our lunar eclipse was one week ago. Feelings might be parading around your mind, no end in sight. Breakthroughs disguised as breakdowns may have challenged your will and your focus. During this Last Quarter Moon time, take some moments to regroup. Remember who you are and what you want. In seven days, we will have a New Moon Eclipse, our third and final of eclipse season. How are you taking care of yourself? What must you take care of more in order to move forward? What are you ready to compost? Name it. Forgive it. Love it. Light it on fire. Let it go.

As release and internal work is favored at this Moon phase, this week's topic is around deprogramming. Do flowers speak to you? Can you feel other people's feelings? Do you just somehow know certain things you can't explain? Do people frequently describe you as "sensitive"? Are you completely strange? Really weird? Extravagantly queer? Does The High Priestess card come up for you in Tarot readings, like, almost every time? Are you reading this workbook? Surprise! You are probably a witch. You are definitely an empath, an intuitive, a creative, a magic maker. (Spoiler alert: many, many more people are these things than not. I stand behind the idea that every person is creative, every person is intuitive, every person is magical—or at the very least, has these abilities inside of them.)

So here you are, this holographic rainbow of stardust experiencing a holographic array of existence, outside the bounds of normalcy—whatever that is. You dream and you doodle and you draw down the Moon. You help and you hear things and you heal and you send out lovingkindness whenever you can. However, greater society may not see these traits and actions as worthwhile. This is precisely because people who are their own thinkers, people who are not easily controllable and who are empowered, are panic-inducing to the overculture. We've seen this happen time and time again with the demonization of social justice movements and leaders. We've seen this for thousands of years with witch-hunts. Magical people are powerful, and this is why they are feared. This fear leads to control, and in many cases, violence.

Witch hunts were political, enacted for control over women's bodies and labor, as well as Indigenous folks' autonomy and knowledge (Silvia Federici, *Caliban and the Witch*). In Europe, the power in place was the church and the state; in America, it was the colonizers. (And, yes, is also now the church and the state.) These powers wanted even more power, attempting to control physical bodies and labor power. Witches were healers, community counselors, oracles, folk medicine women, sex workers, herbalists, doulas, and knowledge holders. They knew all about healing illness with plants, birth control, abortion, and saving lives. They passed this knowledge around to the community and to one another. So much of their magic was forged in this connection. This magic was created in collaboration with the elements, with spirits, with source, and with one another, outside of money or capitalist systems. This was terrifying to the state.

And so the war against witches, which was also the war against women, weirdos, gender non-conforming folks, and other non-compliant folks, began. Witches were sluts were power holders were deviants, in extreme rebellion against capitalism, and the notions of hierarchy and control that came along with it. And so this is how witches became inherently political. This is how witches, and all the other attributes of a witch—creative, sexy, knowledgeable, wild, intuitive, mysterious, psychic, intimidating, to name only a few—became demonized. To this day, we see the remnants everywhere. The ashes of the hundreds of witches burned in this country, the millions of Indigenous people killed and displaced from their own land, the millions of slaves stolen, tortured, and murdered still smolder. We still live with the violence of extreme capitalism and its discontents. We are still attempting to heal from it, still resisting it.

In many cases, mass murders were carried out not just for control, but to eradicate these price-less forms of knowledge off of the face of the Earth. Know part of what we deal with as witches, as empaths, as conscious beings, part of our path is to reconnect with these practices and rituals. Being connected to the seasons, the Earth, and one another is to remember. Research-ing and enacting our ancestors' knowledge and memories. Know that this remembering and reclaiming is where much of our magic lies. Know that part of the remembering may be in re-remembering the witch hunts, the burnings. Know that this might be a painful thing for your psyche to experience. Give yourself permission to begin healing this experience. Know that you are allowed to define your practices for yourself. Know that there is no wrong way to be a witch, so long as you remain connected and compassionate, so long as you remain committed to dismantling capitalist and patriarchal philosophies.

Narratives around witches and magic not being real or being evil are an attempt to erase our birthright. Stereotypes around sensitivity being bad are designed to destroy us. We must resist these paradigms. It is no easy feat, even if we pick apart the shadow stereotypes of the witch: lonely, ugly, cruel, shunned, evil. We may be afraid to say the word because of these connotations. These stereotypes are toxic masculinity at its worst. They lead to dehumanization and violence. Kathleen Hanna famously proclaimed: "Resist Psychic Death." As witches, that is what we have done and that is what we must continue to do. We see treasure where many see trash. We seek out pathways of survival when there are none easily available. Resist psychic death. Resist spiritual death. We start our healing with ourselves. We start with our breath. We follow through with our thoughts, our language, our actions.

At this time, I encourage you to continue, or to begin, deprogramming yourself from the stories that tried to break you down by using your superpowers as a shaming device. Being empathetic, soft, kind, caring, psychic, or intuitive is wonderful. Feeling things deeply, having relationships with animals, plants, the elements, guides, fairies, spirit, the spirit realm, or certain ancestors is a gift. If you are clairsentient, clairvoyant, or clairaudient, it is for a reason. If you are a channel, medium, however it looks, there is nothing wrong with you. You are just as Source intended you to be. Connect with it, be it. If it is time for you to come out of the broom closet, fly your witch flag high.

So you are a witch! Thank the Goddess! The word "witch" comes from Middle English "wicche," and means "sorceress." Other derivatives of the word are "to foretell, warn" (Proto-Germanic), as well as "to dowse, divine", and "to know" (Wikipedia.org). If you know where your ancestors came from, look up the source of the word "witch" from that geographical region. While these are positives, over time, "witch" became a derogative term, which we are now reclaiming.

A witch can be many things. The witch is untamed, wild, full of rage, ready to cry in public, generous with her gifts, able to communicate with nature and spirit, able to heal bodies by sticking acupuncture needles into them, and shows up as a psychedelic lighthouse during a drab foggy night. A witch is so tender, so gentle, so sweet, eyes overbrimming with tears at the first sign of injustice or cruelty. A witch is overflowing with talent and inspiration and she uses this ingenuity in unexpected ways. A witch locks herself in a room with a pen and comes out 12 hours later with an indescribable masterpiece. A witch gets an idea after her lap is stained with elderberries and creates a fortifying elixir. A witch fucks however she wants and whoever she wants, whenever. A witch is uncontrollable and exciting. A witch is measured and slow, carefully figuring out her strategy. She's found foraging in the forest, carefully caressing crystals in caves, climbing trees for a better view of the egrets, and holding her breath for long periods of time under the waves that crash on the horizon, so sun-kissed and salty. A protest is usually full of at least seven hundred witches. Witches are in classrooms teaching the children, in grocery stores stacking your produce just so, on movie sets directing actors, in abortion clinics holding clammy hands, dawdling in parking lots on their phones too long swiping left, seducing the crowd on strip club stages, parallel parking just right inside the lines in too tight driveways, walking your dog, taking your temperature, and shuffling the oracle deck across from your burning questions. Witches are brujas are wizards are priestesses are seers are rootworkers are sorcerers. Witches are Muslim, Jewish, Buddhist, and questioning. Witches are everywhere and they are diverse. Your witch identity can look exactly how it needs to look for you and you alone.

If we are to consciously deprogram ourselves from the negative, patriarchal, transphobic, capitalist, racist connotations associated with the witch and feminine identity, we must also take care to deprogram our magical practices in a similar way. Decommodify our witchcraft. Decolonize our witchcraft.* Question our magical practices from top to bottom. Question our need to buy things, to consume things, and why. Question whom we are stealing from, and why. Question what sort of language and framing we are using in our communities and how that might need updates. For example: "white" being good and "black" being bad. Using "love and light" as an excuse not to look at racism, classism, ableism, transphobia, and misogyny, among others, that burden so many in our collective.

Think of the witch adage: Harm none. Obviously, in the system we are in, this task is an impossible one. But creating *less* harm is sometimes as easy as a pause. As simple as an inquiry. The real truth is that language is important. How we treat one another is important. What we do with our privilege is important.

Capitalism has this way of brainwashing us into thinking that if we like something or someone, we have to own it/them. Capitalism has this way of confusing the accessories of the thing with the thing itself. In this case, the thing is magic. Magic is priceless and it cannot be bought and sold, only shared and experienced.

Let's not confuse the commodification of spirituality with spirituality itself. Capitalism can sully the sacred quite quickly. The lessons of the witch, and the ways of the witch, get confused with what a corporation can sell easily. Let's be wary of who is getting the microphone now, and what this current trend of spirituality is reflecting. A great portion of it seems to be echoing the patriarchy. I'm suggesting we question who is getting attention and why, especially if they are white, straight, and cisgender. Let's deprogram our spirituality from the dominant patriarchal narrative as much as we can. Let's make sure we know where we are getting our information from and be sure we ourselves are experienced practitioners before teaching others.

Your spiritual practice does not need any external tools in order to be valid; it does not need to follow along capitalism's trajectory of rampant consumption and endless productivity. You do not need certifications or the approval of a mainstream in order to be a magical creature. We can examine multiple ways a spiritual practice and a magical life can look. This is deeply personal. This can be private and slow. It is intimacy, vulnerability, consistency, and engagement that defines a relationship with the sacred.

We can use gentle inquiry and pause to think about what we are learning. Think about all you consume. Do you know if the books or articles you are reading are written by people who are anti-racist, feminist, and against oppression? If you are a writer, are you properly citing and referencing the origins of your ideas and concepts? Do you give credit where credit is due? Are you buying services or products from people who cannot speak to where they are receiving their information, or who present information that is not their own as if it is?

Consider what you are buying and why. I am not advocating to totally stop buying and selling products completely. I am advocating for a consciousness and awareness around the items we consume and why. (Magically and otherwise!) If time and time again you are getting messages to purchase a certain crystal, or a certain tool for your magical practices, then of course, go for it! If you feel called to make your own wand, steep your own infusions, do it! Knowing why you feel pulled to ownership is important. This can also lead to wanting to protect things from being pillaged and extracted to extinction. Knowing where the items are coming from is important. This can lead to even more information for your magical practices. Questioning certain impulses around ownership—whether it be physical objects, or intellectual or conceptual works—is important as well. You can ask yourself: do I NEED this thing, or do I WANT it? Do I NEED to call myself a certain type of practitioner for my ego, or is the language I use appropriative, and ultimately disrespectful to the culture and the practice it comes from?

It is important to be mindful and conscious in the world of witching as much as it is anywhere else. Because if you are a witch, then you are very aware of intention and of consciousness around your thoughts. You are aware that as a witch you are in a relationship WITH nature, water, air, fire, animals, plants, yourself, your intuition, your guides, other humans, angels, ancestors, archetypes, and deities. You are aware that if this intention or relationship is imbalanced or misused, problems will arise. A witch must know the difference between cultural exchange and cultural appropriation. A witch must be able to define what they do and why they do it.

This could also be a great opportunity to identify certain practices you'd like to experiment with, take classes in, read books about, and deepen your knowledge around. A deeply enriching practice is to connect to your ancestry, and dive into what the specific practices were from your country of origin. If you are unsure of this, and still wish to be respectful, it is simple. Every single group of people across the globe have used candles, and some form of cleansing with sage, dried herbs, or dried grass for magical purposes. Most practices include burning, burying, ritual baths. Most practices include prayer, meditation, trance. Most practices include saying thank you, leaving offerings, and having a connection to animals, spirits, and other astral helpers. Find what works for you, and what feels good. Find a way to have a balanced practice full of connection and exchange.

We are reclaiming what is ours. We are taking back what has been stolen from us. We can remember and we can tell new stories. We can create new practices that reflect our realities. Remember that there are always opportunities to listen and to learn. Remember that we are witches! Remember that we are strong, resilient, brilliant, and are most beautiful when we come together with love.

For more deeply detailed work on the links between witchcraft, healers, capitalism, and feminism, read *Caliban and the Witch* by Silvia Federici, *Dreaming the Dark* by Starhawk, and *Witches, Midwives, and Nurses: A History of Women Healers* by Barbara Ehrenreich and Deirdre English.

Journaling or questions for inquiry:
How do I define my magical practice? Where does my magical practice come from?

What would I like to learn more about?
What magical or spiritual practices do I feel called to practice that are related to my ancestry?
How can I deprogram and decolonize my witchcraft more?
Where can I deprogram my own ideas around my gifts?
What are my magical superpowers and how must I cultivate them?

Following is a basic banishing spell for confusion or self-doubt. Banishing spells and release work are favored during a Waning Moon.

A Banishing Spell to Banish Confusion and Doubt

Before you enact this spell, you must get very clear on what you are banishing. Examples could be: behavior that is time wasting, addiction to social media, dependence on being scattered. Pick one thing. (You can always do this spell for different things at every Waning Moon!)

You will need: A pen, a small black candle that will not burn for more than a few hours, a small pin to carve the candle with, a small bowl or cup, 5 very small pieces of paper, a small piece of black tourmaline, a small piece of quartz crystal.

Get centered and cast your circle. Write down the thing you are banishing on the 5 pieces of paper. Charge the candle with the thing you wish to banish. Feel it leaving your body. Carve the name of the thing into the candle.

Light the candle.

Say: I banish _____ with the power of fire. Cross the name out on the paper until you cannot see it, and burn it.
Say: I banish _____ with the power of water. Cross the name out on the paper until you cannot see it, and put it in your bowl of water. Say: I banish_____ with the power of air. Cross the name out on the paper until you cannot see it. Tear it into tiny, tiny pieces, then breathe on it.
Say: I banish _____ with the power of earth. Cross the name out on the paper until you cannot see it, then crumple it up into a ball.
Say: I banish _____ with the power of my center. Cross the name out on the paper until you cannot see it, then poke it full of holes with your pin.

Burn the candle all the way to the end. You may wish to envision all of the confusion, doubt, or anxiety leaving your body in the flame.

Take all the paper that has been burned, and bury it somewhere far away. As you step out of the spell, visualize yourself stepping back into yourself, with more clarity. Promise yourself you will no longer do activities that lead to confusion, strife, drama. Carry a small piece of tourmaline with you for several days for protection. If you feel confused, take out your clear quartz. Connect with it for clarity. Imagine your mind being wiped clear of the clutter and replaced with a calming color or grounding object. Direct your eergy towards what is true for you when you are your calmest.

*I need to thank some contemporary witches and spiritual leaders that I very much look up to for having conversations about this subject, and for teaching me through their writing, dialogues, and example. Some of these people are: Layla Saad, Diego Basdeo, Janeen Singer of Holy Sponge!, Pomegranate Doyle, Erin Aquarian, Brandie Taylor of Magic Hour Astrology, Asali of Asali Earthwork, Rebekah Erev, and Dori Midnight. There are many, many more!

Notes on this Waning Moon time:

AUGUST 8TH - 10TH: DARK MOON

Processing Shame Under A Dark Moon

"Shame is the lie someone told you about yourself." — Anaïs Nin

From August 8th to 10th, the Moon is Dark. A Dark Moon phase is generally categorized as the three days just before a New Moon. The Dark Moon is one of the most potent and magical times of the Moon's journey. The light of the Moon is gone from the sky. The Dark Moon rises and sets with the Sun—it is missing from the symphony of the stars. We must find this light inside of ourselves. This time is optimal for rest, quiet, reflection, release, decluttering, and detoxing. Getting rid of what is no longer serving us is one of the first steps to setting the stage up for future successes. From a magickal perspective, the Dark Moon is perfect for banishing spells, divination work such as Tarot, communing with your spirit guides or helpful ancestors, pendulum work, scrying, and past life regression. Think of the ashes that the Phoenix will rise out of beginning to stir. This is a time for facing aspects of ourselves that the Waning Moon phase may have brought up, and having the strength and compassion to face them head on. As always, experience each phase for yourself, in different ways, over different time periods. See what feels right and works best for you.

This Dark Moon's segment will focus on a very common binding spell that witches, weirdos, empaths, queers, people of color, disabled people, fat people, sick people, people with learning disabilities, intersex folks, trans folks, people with mental illness, neurodivergence, and women—to name just a few—experience. This is a spell, a movement that has led to the squashing of our power, our sweetness, our strength, our laughter, and our success. It is the mistress of patriarchy, white supremacy, and capitalism. What I am speaking of can be as violent as a dagger yet has no blade. It is the sword and the skewer of shame.

Our last prompt was around deprogramming our witchcraft. Shame can come up heavily here. Millions of witches were systemically wiped out over the millennia. Witches have been demonized, dismissed, and we have been simultaneously feared and revered. With fear will always come the urge to control and destroy. You may have shame around your identity as a magical practitioner in our modern world. Your shame may be separate from your witch identity. Your shame could be related to a history of abuse or bullying. If we think of shame as negative thought forms, as a hex, as an unhelpful entity, or a spell, we can parse it apart and think of ways to diminish it.

Shame is one of the deepest, darkest, most powerful binding spells that exists. This is because shame is a pervading feeling or belief that no matter our behavior, no matter our intention, no matter how much work we do, we are worthless. We are useless, undeserving of love, disposable, and damned. Our compassion, our success, our kindness in the world is meaningless when shame rears its vicious head. Shame is particularly dangerous because it is literally derived from nothing. It can be manufactured from anything at all: a chipped manicure, a mispronunciation, walking around with a zipper down. Just from your innocent, brilliant experience of being alive, shame can pounce, can demolish, can rip through to the bone. And, if left alone and unleashed, shame will never stop biting, never stop gnawing at your self-esteem. It is toxic.

Shame gives many other voices that are not ours power over us. Whether or not these voices are actually present does not matter. Shame sneaks into our psyche, lodges its way into our brain, and polices our behavior. Shame is the master controller, as it convinces us that we will always be unworthy. Shame threatens us with being shunned, ejected, ousted from the group.

Shame silences us, and leads us to believe that whatever abuse happened was our fault. Shame renders us powerless no matter how high up we climb. Shame promises us that if we do not do the work of banishing it, it will never leave us. If we always allow it to lurk in the shadows, it might kill our souls and dash our dreams. It is tricky to hex shame, as it is a shape-shifter—it is found virtually everywhere: in the media, advertising, in our family of origin's beliefs and patterns, our workplaces, the spiritual community, as well as the world at large. The consorts of shame are humiliation, silence, and self-hatred. The accomplices of shame are racism, fat-phobia, classism, transphobia, capitalism, and sexism. The chains and ropes keeping shame upright are guilt, blame, embarrassment, and paralyzation. The enforcers of shame are perfectionism and competition.

Manifestations of shame in others are that of the non-constructive critic, the blamer, the defensive defender, the controller, the aggressive or passive-aggressive bully, the psychic vampire. While it can be hard to pinpoint some of these archetypes while we are dealing with them in the moment, the endless painful impossibly large sinkhole inside our stomach during or after a run-in—where nothing or no one will ever be good enough, worthwhile enough, healthy enough, happy enough, clean enough—is usually a giveaway that we've been shamed. No level of enough is ever ENOUGH. This internalized sharp-edged hunger can leak out into all interactions with others: being overly critical of our loved ones, friends, strangers on the screen, or random people at the mall. This behavior feels the need to contact perfect strangers on social media and insult them, use gossip and ridicule of others primarily as a connection device, and pick apart unknown members of one's community. It is a hex that hexes in both apparent or intangible ways. This hex grows and feeds on itself.

Perfectionism may be by far the largest societally accepted byproduct and behavior of shame. It is a shield as well as a distraction device. If we must be perfect, that will most certain-ly take up all the energy for living life! Perfectionism is a cover-up for shame. A crutch for feelings of vulnerability. It is enforcing a cycle of shame-based and shaming blame and behavior. Perfectionism can feel like a never ending sinkhole, sucking out all the energy of a process. Perfectionism is also incredibly exhausting, as nothing or no one could ever be perfect enough.

This behavior is never satiated. If it is never satisfied, it will always have places to hide the shame and hatred. It will always look at people who are happy and content, empowered and excited, particularly people who "shouldn't" be happy because they don't abide by societal standards of beauty, behavior or success. These behaviors are distractions that keep the blamers from looking at their own deep-rooted seats of shame, sadness, and existential unhappiness. These behaviors also keep us completely separate and alone, when at our base it is our vulnerability that needs to be expressed. It is our heart that needs to be acknowledged and seen, our human-ity that needs to be witnessed, in order to give us support and comfort, safety and self-worth.

Perfectionism also can be a stand-in for a deep, deep fear around the messiest, least control-lable, yet inevitable outcome we all face: death. Death is beyond the limits of most humans' perception. It is the void of all voids. Hard to explain, yet easy to experience. Hard to relax into, yet the greatest teacher. To be in the void is to be in a zone of insecurity. It also promises openings and revelations. The Dark Moon is a time of both. During these next few days, you may wish to ruminate on the void and your awareness and experience of it. What lessons around emptiness does this Dark Moon have to teach you?

There are ways out of shame, and ways to work with the curse of shame. Vulnerability and connection are antidotes to shame. Laughter, humor, fun, silliness, and joy smooth over the pain of shame. Living your dreams is a powerful antidote to shame. Living the best life you can is a balm to the pain and blame. Connections to creativity and creative expression alleviate shame. So does surrounding yourself with a positive support network. Remember that we are all going to die, and use that as a complicated positive motivator, not a negative.

Here's the thing. In most of life, there's no right and wrong. In art, in creativity, and living life, there isn't. You know there isn't, and I know there isn't. The bees climbing into the inside of the trumpet flower on a bright green field in mid-August know it. The quails skittering across the brush know it, the cache of golden birches on your favorite hike know it, but many people in this world don't know there is no right and there is no wrong. And they use these ideas as boxes to cage other people in—whether over their mere existence, or in smaller ways.

I frequently get hate emails from people who need to tell me how disappointed they are in my work or who I am as a person, and messages from strangers criticizing me, my words, my behaviors, and my output. A recurring complaint I receive is about the typos in Many Moons. Because of my own history of learning disabilities, ADHD, and abuse, I can react quickly to insulting or critical messages with shame if I am not grounded. I have learned that in one stranger's eyes, I am wonderful and amazing, a transformative witch and brilliant creative. In another person's eyes, I am a heaping pile of kangaroo poop: useless, messy, and rude. Which one am I: a useless heap of kangaroo poop, or a wonderful witch? I can't be both, can I? Well, actually, yes I can—or the projections of me can. As these qualities are in the mind of the pro-jector, so they exist in a certain aspect of me, if I choose to accept them. This is why I've found it incredibly useful, when dealing with shame, to detach from the feelings of shame that arise in me and from the person insulting me or sending me a critical message.

When we detach, we can be free to reconnect to our personal flare-ups and reactions. We can focus on going in and recognizing what is happening internally, and name the feelings coming up, as well as the origination of the pain. We are also cutting energetic cords immedi-ately with the cause of the discomfort, which is important to do as soon as possible. The person who insulted you or said hurtful things to you did not cause fire to well up in your throat and a clenching in your gut. We don't want our attention to focus on them, we want to clear the emotions inside of us. It is important to redirect awareness back to the somatic sensations of the shame. Allow it to come up. The coming up is a way of getting it out. This might include journaling, walking, crying, or talking to a trusted friend or a therapist.

Another aspect of this shame work is to get clear, Ace of Swords style. Is it true that there are typos in my work? Yes. Is it true that it could be annoying to people who are in publishing or literary fields, and that these typos could devalue the work, or determine my work "invalid"? Sure. Does it mean that the books are utter garbage, that they should be wiped off the face of the earth after having all of my critics throw javelins at it over and over, while cursing it out in every language they've every learned? No. Should it stop me from ever typing another word again, should it cause me to throw my computer from the highest mountain after stomping on it repeatedly with my highest heels?Absolutely not!

Distance your behavior from your intrinsic value. Yes, maybe you made a mistake. Maybe it was truly horrible, and maybe it was just simply slightly uncool. But that doesn't make YOU any less awesome, or any less valuable. If you need to take accountability, take accountability. Apologize, figure out how not to repeat the mistake, absolutely. Then move on with the wisdom you've gained.

Once you've detached from the welling up of the shame and embarrassment from originat-ing scenario of that shame, you can put the focus back on the roots. This is where the some very fruitful shadow work comes in. (This may be where, depending on where you are in your process, you may wish to get help in the form of a therapist or a support group.)

When the shame comes up, do your very best not to contract, run away from it, or to judge yourself. Try to have compassion for it. Sometimes, this inquiry could surprise you. Personally, I have found that shame in my life tends to pop up when I am about to get wider, more expansive, when I'm ready to take up space. Because part of my herstory is that of abuse, my subconscious and my ego have told me that to stay small is to stay safe. My subconscious' default is to be tiny, to be silent— that way, bullies will not notice me. That way, others will not see my power and try to co-opt it, or be triggered by it. While I frequently get insults and unasked-for critiques that do not affect me in the least, I have found that it is when I am about to uplevel in some fashion is when they actually sting and stick around. My subconscious is looking for proof that I'm meant to stay small, that I'm unworthy or underserving of my hard work, and it comes out in shamed-based spirals.

Challenging emotions always come up so they can be released. Not stuffed down and shoved into the dusty trunk under the bed. Not to use as a flagellation tool to prove to yourself how undeserving of awesomeness you are. Challenging emotions come up because we are human. Many of us were abused, mistreated, or not taught to process our pain effectively. That's all, nothing more. Obviously, for those of us who suffered abuse and trauma, the feelings can certainly be deeply disturbing and excruciatingly painful. That doesn't make you broken, and you can work on healing them. Be gentle with yourself through the process.

Shame, however, can be a teacher. It can very specifically, very painfully locate Our Deepest, Darkest Fears. These also are almost always either related to our very early childhood and upbringings, or to jarring episodes that happened in our life. These deepest, darkest fears are sometimes also linked to our deepest, darkest desires: what we would like, above all else, if we could have anything we want. A life with more time. A life with less stress. A life of less caring about what others think of us. A life of dignity, of bravery, of service. A life of adoration, of love, of acceptance. A life of joy, creativity, fun, laughter. A life that sometimes is what Our Deepest, Darkest Fears and our Shame are stopping us precisely from experiencing.

Whether we want to manifest great heaping barrels of abundance or happiness, evolve our consciousness more, lighten our load, enjoy a little less physical pain, or simply lower our stress, working with our shadow will always be useful. It is always useful to check in with our ego. To see how far away it wishes to fly away from the Towers we've built. Looking at our shadow is to look at our Self.

The ego—the Sun, our consciousness, our awareness—will always have a shadow. In fact, the brighter the Sun shines, the more opportunities there are for the shadows to come out. Our shadows, our states of vulnerability, are natural, healthy, and normal. Part of having a shadow is acknowledging it and getting to know it. Use it as a teacher and a guide. Play around with it, see what it needs. It might need nature and staring contests with cats. It might need to be sung to coyly, "You Don't Own Me," while dancing around a dirty kitchen with spinach on your cheek and mismatched socks.

Gentle and powerful witch, fierce and indescribable spell caster, sexy and genius wizard, you are not alone anymore. You have the stars and the trees, the waves and the wind. You have the caverns and the friendly internet and friends who love you and see you. You have your guides and flickering tea lights and the twinkling tornadoes of energy that well up in your body, waiting to be used. Yes, you are imperfect. So is your favorite song, or the pebble you took home with you from the beach. Yes, you are wounded. There are gifts in our wounds. These gifts teach us what we are capable of, what we have survived, and how we have thrived. How we have chosen to not pass our pain on. How much we are committed to loving and accepting ourselves, in all our imperfect wholeness.

You can deal with your shame. You can give yourself understanding and patience. You are part of a growing web of wonderful weird witches who are doing the same. You are perfectly whole. There is nothing wrong with you. There was nothing EVER wrong with you.

At this Dark Moon time, as we are so prepared to ripen, to harvest, to work on blooming even more brightly than before, you may wish to have a check-in around shame. Where do themes of shame pop up in your life? Where do you use shame as a weapon, to create distance from yourself and others, or even from having an intimate relationship with yourself? What are some recurring limiting thought patterns that hold you back? How are they based on your self-worth? How are they linked to shame?

After we are dead, after we are dust, after only memories, photos, and our legacy remain, no one will be able to detect the shame we held onto like static cling. After all that remains of us is in stories, in our creative artifacts, in the archives of our behavior, the amount of shame we carried in our body will not matter. It will not tip the scale against you. Insulting emails, gossip, and other petty cruelties will not matter. What will matter is that you moved past your shame and fear into bravery and love. What will matter is what you did with your one true life in your own amazing body.

Below are a couple of ways to work with shame. If you feel called to go deeper and really work through limiting patterns, therapy, especially somatic-based or trauma-based therapy, is useful in dealing with deep-rooted issues. And last, but certainly not least, a consistent forgiveness practice is encouraged. Forgiving yourself and others who inflicted pain on you is a wonderful way of cutting energetic cords to the past.

Tarot cards to meditate on: The Five of Pentacles, Three of Swords, Five of Swords, Nine of Swords, Ten of Swords, Queen of Swords, Knight of Pentacles, Seven of Wands, Nine of Wands, Ten of Wands, The Tower, The Devil, The Moon

A Tarot Pull for Shame/Guilt/Embarrassment (or other painful emotions)

You will need: A journal, a Tarot or Oracle deck, water or tea

Find yourself in a calm, comfortable place. You may wish to light a candle or put on calm, soothing music. You may wish to do breath work, or spend time in meditation before this Tarot Pull. Shuffle the cards until everything feels ready. Drinking tea or lots of water is always a good idea.

Row 1:
1. Why is my shame surfacing right now?
2. What is the root of this shame?
3. What does my shame need from me at this time?

Row 2:
4. What does my shame want me to release?
5. What is my shame holding me back from expressing or doing?

Row 3:
6. What lies on the other side of forgiving myself, of laying down this heavy burden and working through my shame, or other painful emotions?

You may wish to pull one or two clarifying cards for cards that do not make sense to you. However, before you do that, you may wish to journal or write through your understandings of the cards pulled.

A Smashing Spell for Banishing Shame

You will need: An egg, or a tomato, or another round object that splatters open after being thrown

Do this spell in the night, as late as you can stand it.* Before you leave your home, set up your bedroom so you are all ready to go to bed. Maybe you wish to take a salt bath right after the spell—have any loving or soothing set-ups done before this spell.

Go to an isolated yet safe place. (You may wish to do this with a friend, for safety's sake.)

Call all your energy back into your body. Dismiss any energy that is no longer yours out of your auric field.

Ground, and cast your circle of protection. If you work with protective deities or angels, you may wish to call them in at this time to enforce your power.

Hold the object in your hand. Charge the object with your shame, with the emotions that have been haunting you or holding you back. Really focus on moving any energy from within you into the object. You will know when you are done.

Scream, or speak as loudly as you can, something along the lines of: "I do not deserve to be shamed! Shame, be gone! Shame, I banish you! Shame, you leave my energy field! Shame, I no longer have use for you! Leave my energy, now!"

Throw the object far outside your energy field. Smash the shame-charged object with all of the might you can muster so that it dissolves.

Thank the earth and the air for transforming your pain. Ground. Close your circle and go home. Conduct any loving activities you need, and be sure to get a long night's sleep.

In the next few days, leave the earth and the air an offering, or build an offering to them on your altar. You may wish to work with the stones hematite or tourmaline to deflect negative energies.

For the next month, watch your thoughts and your behaviors very carefully. Be compassionate with shame-based thoughts and behaviors, and immediately distract yourself by mindfulness techniques, or doing an action you must focus on. If there are people in your life who continuously shame you, distance yourself from them. If you have noticed that you tend to shame yourself and others, work on lessening that behavior.

A few books that address shame are *Daring Greatly* and *I Thought It Was Just Me (but it isn't)* by Brené Brown, *The Mind-Body Code* by Dr. Mario Martinez, or *The Soul of Shame* by Curt Thompson.

AUGUST 11TH: NEW MOON in LEO, 2:48 AM PST NEW MOON SOLAR ECLIPSE 4:58 AM PST 6:24 AM PST MOONRISE 8:17 PM PST MOONSET

New Moon Expansion

"Three things cannot be long hidden: the sun, the moon, and the truth." — Buddha

Happy Saturday! Happy 11th day of August! Happy New Moon Solar Eclipse! This is our third solar eclipse of 2018, and our final eclipse of the current eclipse season. For some of you reading this, you may have undergone some shake-ups, shake-downs, some ego deaths all around. These changes may have been internal—emotional patterns coming up to be released, stronger desires being built in the corridors of your strong heart. More decisions made in the spirit of letting your true soul shine. These changes may have been external—people leaving, situations coming to an end. Remember to let the dust settle. Remember that it takes time to make shifts. You may need some time to catch up to your new self and your intentions. Have you been giving yourself enough time to process? Have you been allowing the newness to just be, whether raw or roughly howling, tenderly sparkling or almost unbelievable in its goodness?

A solar eclipse is when the Moon is between the Sun and the Earth. The Moon blocks the light of the Sun from getting to Earth. Eclipses are total (like the one North America experienced last August) or partial; this eclipse is partial, which is more common. It will only be visible from northern North America, Greenland, Northern Europe, and Northern Asia.

This solar eclipse happening today, on this Saturn-ruled Saturday, is in Leo, a fire sign. The themes that we will be talking about will be solar power, consciousness, energy, and the embodiment of joy, pleasure, and fun. It is Summer, we shine bright, the goldenrod has come into her full bloom, and the chrysanthemums waving in the breeze nudge us to take a longer lunch break. It is long glittering days and warm humid nights, sitting on porch steps talking about the meaning of life, crickets providing the soundtrack. August reminds us that there is nothing more magical than simply living life. Enjoyment, and pleasure are easily attained in August. The light is so very present in our every day.

Leo, the lion, takes its stage on the night sky. The fifth sign of the zodiac, the archetype of Leo is generally associated with royalty, deep self-love, creativity, performance, and a flair for drama. Leo is a sign of successful self-realization, which is obtained through childlike joy, bolstered by bravery, and imparted with playful radiance. A cause of stress or sadness for us during Leo season might be not feeling appreciated enough or that our gifts and talents are being ignored. Having to be in situations where we aren't allowed to shine, to be adored, or to have fun is also cause for tension. Question if you are allowing yourself to soak up all the light and warmth you require. Take responsibility for expressing your gifts and talents outwardly. If you aren't beaming your rays of radiance out into the world regularly, make a promise with yourself to do so more frequently at this New Moon.

While most modern-day practitioners associate Leo with the lion, ancient Babylonians named this constellation Ursula, the Lioness (Barbara Walker, *The Women's Dictionary of Symbols and Signs*. New York: HarperCollins, 1998, p. 291). It is the lioness, not the lion, that does all the hunting for their pride. Lionesses hunt in groups. A pride of lions consists of many related females, was well as their offspring, along with a few unrelated males. Female lions live together for life. There is no rank hierarchy; they depend on one another to survive. Even though they are certainly busy raising children, hunting for food, and protecting and nourishing their young, female lions still find time to play, while male lions give up play along with their youth. During this New Moon weekend, do you need to get together with some of your most hilarious and alive friends and make magic?

Leo is ruled by the Sun. The Sun, the center of our universe, is about halfway through its life, at an impressive 4.5 billion years old. The Sun is one of 200 plus billion stars in our spiral galaxy, and while it isn't even the largest, 1 million Earths could fit into one Sun. The Sun is over 92 million miles away from us, yet we can feel its rays on our skin, the concrete, on our phones left out too long in the grass. Compare that to the Moon, which is so, so much closer: only 238,900 miles away from us, an easy ride on a rocket ship. Compare that to the width of the Earth: 24,8120 million miles, all the way around, from pole to pole. When we consider that scale, when we consider us in the petri dish of the universe, it sort of makes the not so important thoughts clogging up our brains not so, well, important, doesn't it?

Let this New Moon show you where to align your mind.

The Sun's energy powers our weather, our water cycle, and, alongside our other elements, makes life on terra firma possible. The Sun's inward and outward pressure, created by fusion reactions, is balanced, which results in a steady stream of energy coming our way. Solar power is powerful indeed. More power from the Sun hits the Earth in a single hour than we use in an entire year.

The Sun can act as a metaphor for our own energy, our own seats of consciousness. The Sun can be bright and generous, yet if left unconscious or unaware, its presence can burn us. The Sun creates shadows—places for us to check our perceptions and truths, or places to be scared by what we do not understand. The Sun warms us, gives us enough brightness to pass on to others, has enough energy to support many—or can be blinding if stared at it too long. It is all how we use and choose to work with our energy that determines much of the outcome of our fate.

The Sun card in the Tarot is one of evolved consciousness, engagement with life, and balanced alignment between embodiment and one's own higher power. It is a card of new beginnings and rebirth. This card is on the last line of the Major Arcana: the line of the superconscious. The superconscious has been called many things all over the planet throughout history. It has been called source, universal mind, the collective consciousness, messages from spirit, our higher self, universal consciousness, our most aligned alignment. It is seeing or feeling both form and the energy behind that form: the energy that links us all.

Because The Sun is in this last line placement, this card is a rebirthing of our most evolved state—a visceral reconnection with the light through the embodiment of our authenticity. A falling in love with our own divinity. A return to our core ideals and the innocent confidence our higher self has around its gifts, its goals, and its path. In the first row of the Major Arcana, we have a different illustration of this energy: The Magician. After The Magician, we have The High Priestess, who is close sisters with The Moon card. In this last row, these archetypes make an elevated pairing in the reverse. First we have the experience of The Moon: intuitive and psychic states, cyclical messages, and a surrender that lies in deep trust of the waxes and wanes, the ebbs and flows. An acceptance that time is non-linear, a step into the spiral, and the balance that comes from mining the depths of our wildness. After this inner knowledge can come the outer action and integration of The Sun. The Sun is a seeker, but not for validation's sake. The Sun is so in love with life, so in love with the whole, that the simple yet profound qualities The Sun seeks are more joy, more source, more connection. This master generator of energy is activated by wonder and exuberance. These cards together form the inhale and the exhale of an entirely new state of being: our subconscious and consciousness are unified. Our goals are in alignment with our soul's purpose. We've got the trust; we've stepped into our confidence. There's nothing left to do but create our own unique blend of magic, nothing left standing in our way of expressing our own captivating forms of creativity.

The young figure on a horse—the image on The Sun card in the traditional Rider-Waite-Colman-Smith deck—is riding away from a wall; presumably a wall that they have just jumped over. Other, older versions of this card have two figures dancing with one another. Some interpretations have one figure as the "eternal self" and one as "the mortal body" (Rachel Pollack, *Seventy-Eight Degrees of Wisdom*). Again, we see a reference to the brightness of OUR individual superconsciousness, and the ways our very being-ness infuses that of that collective superconsciousness with this brightness, and vice versa. The shadow side of The Sun was touched on previously. The Sun represents the blinding truth. This can be horrid, or it can be a liberation. Reclaiming doesn't always feel like a helium balloon. If you are bursting through tired stories at this time, give yourself credit for doing so, even if it feels like a drudgerous cement-filled elephant tied around your ankles. Change is frequently challenging. The Sun card encourages you to keep going. Maybe you need a pair of sunglasses to shield your vision.

This superconscious relates to the use of our own consciousness. Consciousness begets consciousness. What we focus on grows. When we find peace and calm, we desire more of it. When we experience inspiration and elevation, we keep seeking it. Until we become it. Then we radiate it outwards: we mirror the Sun. We become ourselves.

Accessing the superconscious can give us great gifts. There is an endless supply of potential and inspiration in the universe. Once we begin working with this energy, we can see how wondrous the endless possibilities that tapping into source grants us. Like a Sun, it feeds on itself. People can access this energy in a number of different ways. Meditation, running, breath work, making art, walking, being in nature, being creative, taking part in interesting conversations, taking baths. It looks different for everyone. An easy way to identify when you've accessed your most potent conscious state is when you feel really alive. Present. Connected. Flowing. Trusting.

Connecting with our inspiration, our mindfulness, and our consciousness is key to changing our realities. Our consciousness is only about 5%-10% of our brain power, but accessing it and using it to train our subconscious can drastically alter our narratives and completely flip the script we are automatically running on. Our subconscious is the soil that grows the seeds. Our consciousness is the Sun that guides the seeds into the kind of growth we want. Working with retraining negative thought patterns that hinder us from expressing ourselves fully is key to living our best lives.

Do not let your inner critique scream at you all the reasons not to try:
It is too late. As long as you are alive, it is never too late.
I'll never get there. There is no there, there.*
There is only here. And here is the present, and we all know the present is a gift.

Utilizing our consciousness comes in a number of different ways. First, we mindfully observe our thought forms and our behaviors. We clearly define what it is we would like more of, and we correspond our consciousness to this reality. We tell our thoughts—our consciousness—to stay in patterns of this correspondence. When fear, anxiety, or thoughts that are not in tune with our desired consciousness bubble up—and they will, to the tune of hundreds, if not thousands of times a day—we shift away from them and refocus on what we do want: on what thoughts we would like to think, on what ways we would like to feel. It isn't so much spending time trying to fix what we don't want, as it is filling ourselves up, as much as possible, energetically and consciously, with our true self and our most desired thoughts and feelings. We change our belief systems about who we are, and what we are capable of being in this way.

After all, belief systems are just thoughts we think over and over.

To be clear: this is not an ask to ignore pain, suffering, or challenging experiences that come up for ourselves and others. It is an invitation to feel them deeply, look to the truth of the situation, and take full accountability and responsibility to ourselves and others. Then we can move through them. We can detach and observe our patterns and our thought forms. We can see the source of them, and respond accordingly. We are no longer trapped in the cycle of reacting, and causing more pain to ourselves and others. This is how we transform. This is how we evolve.

The Strength card, the card that corresponds to Leo, speaks to this transformation. This card reassures that we have what it takes to look into the belly of the beast and come out stronger for having passed our hand through the flame. This is a card of compassion, of finding source, pleasure, and completion through raw and authentic looking and experience. The figure in the card is listening as much as she's making peace with the lion. She's happy to breathe in the same air, knowing she can learn from the wildness she is engaging with.

There's a famous saying: "Don't believe everything you think." We can see this statement is certainly helpful when we consider thoughts we have about ourselves that are not helpful to us, or that are downright abusive. Our world is certainly a world that enforces thinking that is harmful to our self-esteem and our self-love. Once we acknowledge that we are more than our thoughts, so much so that we can observe, redirect, and direct them again, over and over, we get free. We can be the child on the horse jumping over the walls of self-doubt racing forward in the light. We can be the lion roar and the silky smile that soothes the scary beast. Knowing that so much of our existence takes place in our mind, with our consciousness, and that we can shift and change our thoughts with practice and focus is freeing. We can protect our energy, in part, by using it in exciting, truthful, invigorating ways.

There's another aspect here to bring up at this Solar Eclipse. And this is the part about taking risks. Being brave. Living a more exciting life. Stepping into more thrill. This solar eclipse wants to remind us that there is no reward without risk. Every entrepreneur, every person who walked up to another cute person and introduced themselves, every artist and maker, every person who offered an idea to the group, every weirdo and witch, every lioness and horse rider alike can attest to the fact that there is no reward without risk. Where are you ready to take risks in the coming days, weeks, months?

This eclipse wants us to remember that it is time to step into the light, time to be vulnerable, time to be brave as never before. This eclipse asks us to take the shadows and the hardship and really look at them, learn from them, and burn them up. Say I'm sorry and I love you and I wish I had done better and this is how I will do better but my shame has only been an anvil around my neck so far and its one I'm shedding because I didn't actually even put it there and those ghosts are gone and I'm here with my heart out instead, I'm here running up this hill, dirt stained knees, windblown cheeks, with precious gemstones of my dreams in my hands and fortune cookie messages from the future in my pockets and I'm ready to take hold of my life for myself and for everyone I know and love and for the greater good of the planet, the Moon, the stars, and the Sun herself. Because this is it. This moment is all we have. Our awareness is our key and our embodied joy is our keyhole.

Remember, sweet treasure, to cultivate your pleasure. Because at the end of this lifetime, we are what we love, and how we love. We are what we do. And what we do is based on what we think and what we believe. And what we believe is based upon our consciousness and what we tell ourselves we are capable of achieving and becoming. During this New Moon time, hold enough space for your soul to sing powerfully. Your aligned consciousness is the basis of your future. Cultivate an enriched soil to plant the golden seeds of your beloved belonging. Allow these seeds to be magnetized up into existence by the shining rays of your one and only imagination.

Some activities as ritual ideas for this New Moon time period:

Starting today, ask yourself this simple question: Does this make me feel good? Does this person make me feel good? Does this activity make me feel good? Be mindful of things that make you feel good in the moment—like watching Netflix for three hours a night—but over time, make you feel bad. Maybe there's a compromise; maybe one hour of Netflix with more sleep or meditation ends up being the balance. Be also mindful of things that make you feel uncomfortable or scared in the moment—like working out or working out a debt payment plan—that will, over time, make you feel really good. Try to take away a few of the things that make you feel bad and add a few of the things that make you feel good.

If you have a child, or know a child who is open, create a ritual together. Ask them what they want more of in their life. Share with them your hopes. Draw pictures of what they are. Light a candle, sing a chant you've made up together, clap your hands together. Create collaborative magic. Create your own safe space for joy, for growing, for creating, for innocent engagement. You can do this ritual with another trusted childlike adult as well who is open to making collaborative magic. There are no limits!

Be in the Sun. Sit or stretch out or lay about. Invite a friend with you so you can slather one another with sunscreen. Invite sunshine inside you to light up the corners. Allow yourself to smile with the sunshine on your face. Thank the Sun for its light and warmth. Live. Flow. Examine the grass and the dirt, the clouds and the sheet of wondrous blue that is the sky, with equal delight.

*This is a Gertrude Stein quote. Gertrude Stein, *Everybody's Autobiography* (Random House 1937, p 289)

Journaling questions:
Where is my consciousness ready for an uplevel or upgrade?
✴ What narratives am I being called to bury in the past?
✴ What new narratives am I currently planting?
✴ What words am I using to describe myself and my life?
Where is my joy and pleasure pulling me?
Who am I, right now?
How will I carry out this truth with joy and fun?
What do I need, internally or externally, to carry this out?

Suggested Affirmation: "I am joy. My consciousness is the celebration of all that I am."

New Moon Ritual: Releasing the Past, Invoking the Future

Note: You may wish to do this spell on Friday, the day before the eclipse. Friday is ruled by Venus, planet of love, and the Moon will be in Leo after 5:17 pm PST. You may wish to do this spell on Sunday, the day after the eclipse. Sunday corresponds to the Sun, which rules Leo. (However, the Moon will be in Virgo, starting at 4:58 pm PST—so you may wish to do your ritual in the morning.)

You will need: Lemon water, paper, pen, kitchen salt, something to burn paper in (such as a cauldron, a bowl, or a bonfire), mirror, any other objects that call to you

Suggested objects for your altar: Bright flowers; symbols of your unique joy, happiness, and creativity; gold, orange, red, or yellow candles; carnelian, sunstone, citrine, honey calcite, gold, pyrite, amber

Set up your altar. This can be a very simple altar consisting of a candle, a crystal, and a flower.

Cast your circle and get grounded. Take deep breaths up and down your spine, and into your heart.

Write down what you are burning and leaving behind. This can be outmoded thoughts, words you will no longer be using to describe yourself, patterns and behaviors you are no longer continuing, or relationships you are letting go of. You could write each thing on a piece of paper, or write a longer letter. If writing a letter, write it in the past tense. Example: "I used to gossip a lot, but I no longer find it appealing."

You may also wish to invoke the relief that the change of behavior brings. For example:

"I used to be overly dependent on my family's opinions of me, but I no longer care. I've let go of the need for approval of others who do not wish the best for me. It feels liberating and exciting. I have a lot more time and space for loving and replenishing activities now that I've set my boundaries."

When you are finished writing, burn the pieces of paper. When they are burnt up, throw some salt on top of them.

Drink half your glass of lemon water. Light your candle. Gaze at the flame and feel it lighting you up with new energy.

Meditation: See yourself doing everything you want to be doing. Envision where you will be, what you will be wearing, what is happening. Imagine your days—what will your mornings look like? What will your evenings look like? Imagine yourself calling a dear friend and excitedly telling them your news and having them come over and celebrating. If it is easier for you to write this all down, then write it all in the present or past tense. Feel the joy, excitement, and the thrill of it all fill your body. Notice any colors that are showing up for you. Notice any sounds, smells, places or symbols. Get clear on where your consciousness needs to be. Get clear on what affirmations or activities you will need to keep your consciousness clear. Before you close the meditation, promise your future self that you will begin carrying out these shifts regularly in the next few days. Know that you have the fire within you, and the bravery that comes with the self-love you give yourself.

Drink the last of the water. Blow or snuff out your candle.

Now, go do something fun. Take a walk. See a friend. Sing karaoke in the mirror. Go to a silly movie or a sweaty dance party. Promise yourself to do something fun every day for the next three days or more. Know that this pleasure-seeking is something you deserve to have, and something that is activating your desires. Allow yourself to light up a room with your smile, create music with your laughter. Drink plenty of lemon water. Allow your energy body all that it needs—whether it be rest, relaxation, quiet, or excitement.

Notes on ritual:

AUGUST 18TH: FIRST QUARTER MOON in SCORPIO, 12:49 AM PST, 1:53 PM PST MOONRISE, 12:02 AM PST MOONSET

Blood is Every Body
by Liz Migliorelli of Sister Spinster

Welcome to the Waxing Moon time. A time of growth, intensification, and structuring. Mercury goes out of retrograde on August 18th— today! This Moon is Waxing in the sign of Scorpio, a favorable time to work with blood magic as the sign of Scorpio is so attuned to exploring our deepest passions, which are often represented by blood. During a Waxing cycle, I always like to support my body with blood-building and body-tonifying herbs, to mirror the way in which the Moon is also in a building phase. Herbs that are blood-building are often called "alterative" herbs, and they nourish the blood and body with all kinds of minerals and vitamins. Tonic herbs are herbs that are solid supports for the body's natural processes, and can be taken over long periods of time. Many tonic herbs are alteratives and many alterative plants are tonics. These are herbs that are simple and gentle; we want to build the body up with ease and tenderness. Some examples of blood- and body-builders are burdock, raspberry leaf, oat straw, red clover, alfalfa and nettle. I will often make an infusion of one or two of these herbs and while enjoying this tea will focus on growing my energy with the Earth energy that I am absorbing from these plants. I offer you a recipe at the end of this piece to embody this magic of blood-building.

For a long time, my mxnstrual* cycle was the only way in which I was in relationship with my blood. I wouldn't really think about blood until I was actually bleeding. And when that was happening, the thought process was pretty limited to "Dang, that's a lot of blood" or "Whoa, why does my blood look so brown this month?" or "When will this bleeding end?" And there would be long times where I never thought about my blood at all, because I went through long periods of absence from bleeding. Today I have more awareness and gratitude for my ritual shedding each month, but my relationship to my blood goes beyond my mxnstrual cycle. And while my Moon blood is a very powerful and magical fluid, it is limiting to believe that one must mxnstruate in order to work with blood magic. We have blood in our bodies; it is something that connects us all. Blood magic is the magic of connection. When we work with blood magic, we connect to ourselves in a deeper way and we are able to enhance our work in the world with stronger commitment.

One of the first memories I have of working with the power of blood was making a pact with a friend of mine in second grade. We were meeting to commit ourselves to protecting a tree as we had seen a group of kids the day before kicking the tree for sport. We both were outraged, and decided to make a pact to hold each other accountable to speaking up to these tree bullies. We met in secret behind the school during recess, both pricking our fingers with a thumbtack we had smuggled out of the classroom. Small pools of blood formed on our respective thumbs. As we pressed our fingers together, our passions merged for the same cause and we became dedicated to our work. This blood promise remains; I still feel it in my body and am still connected to this work. Now that I am older and wiser to transmission of blood diseases, I do not recommend making blood pacts with others, but I do think having relationship to your vital force is important!

Connecting our blood to what we love is sympathetic magic; blood has always been a symbol for passion, for what excites us, for what moves our hearts. This is why blood magic is taboo. Even the idea of expressing what we truly desire is uncomfortable for many people. Sometimes what we desire isn't easy, straightforward, or considered "normal." Blood magic is messy. If we are able to work with what we are devoted to, even if we feel scared, our power grows. I often give my Moon blood to my plants, because they are what I am devoted to (and it is great fertilizer), but with this exchange I am also recognizing and honoring the plants I tend to. I give them a part of myself, and they give me parts of themselves. We are connected. Even if I don't have menstrual blood to give, I do sometimes leave blood offerings to plants that I harvest; pricking my palm open with my harvest knife. I know that this might not be for everybody, but it is a part of my magic where I have worked out what feels right to me. This is my life blood and I choose to give it to what feeds me and gives me life. At other times, I will use my mxnstrual blood to enhance the magic of a project I am really focused on, offering a deep part of myself to the work. I have also used mxnstrual blood as an offering in group ritual, as an intimate sharing of my personhood to the collective. It makes sense to also use this blood in ancestral magic, as a way to connect with those of your lineage if you desire.

It is traditional to use blood in love spells. Sure, this is something you can do, but I always err on the side of caution with love spells because they are about obtaining power over someone. True blood magic connects us with our power from within. What about casting a spell for joy with your blood? Joy moves and balances the heart. Try setting a joyful intention or working some self-love magic when your blood is really moving in your body, like during exercise, working in your garden, biking to work, having sex, masturbating, etc. Imagine that the power you feel running through your veins is also nourishing you with joy, vitality, vibrancy. Let it buzz within you. Feel it radiate and resonate around you.

Our blood tells the story of our bodies, connects us to our ancestors, and can divine our futures. Checking a pulse is attuning to the story of the body. As an herbalist, I use pulse reading as a tool with my clients—feeling their pulse as a way to feel into their vitality, to tune into how their organs are communicating with one another, exploring the quality of nourishment in their body, and listening for whispers of ancestral patterning. Feel your pulse at your neck or your wrist. Try doing this before you've had your caffeine for the day. How quickly does your pulse arrive? Listen for a minute and count it. What is the quality of the way in which it moves? Is it jumpy or does it glide under your finger? Does it feel tight or does it rebound? Take note, and see how this changes daily, or even at different times of the day. This is one way to build a relationship with your blood. Try to divine what you are hearing from your pulse. Maybe a more sluggish pulse could mean that you need more warming, vitalizing herbs. Or a rapid, hot pulse could suggest that you might want to use some releasing herbs to disperse that energy.

When we nourish our blood, we nourish the body. Every tissue and organ depends on a healthy supply of blood to perform its many functions and heal itself. Our blood distributes nutrients, oxygen, and hormones throughout the body. It carries metabolic waste out of the body. It regulates our temperature, pH levels, and immune cells that defend against pathogens. If circulation to any tissue is deficient, or the quality of the blood is insufficient, our immune system will release inflammatory substances (cytokines) to restore circulation that the tissue needs to sustain itself. While acutely helpful, this process can be harmful in the long-term, as it can lead to autoimmune tissue damage. There is a lot more to say about all of this and how blood functions in the body, but the essence is thus: nourish your blood! I have noticed that when I am taking herbs that encourage circulation and build blood before my mxnstrual cycle, my cycle is shorter and less painful. Taking blood-building herbs on a regular basis has helped me get more spring in my step, improved my memory, and has eased some anxiety/nervousness (remember that blood also nourishes your nervous system tissue!).

A simple way to nourish the blood includes eating anything that is chlorophyll-rich. Chlorophyll is a building block for healthy red blood cells, so eat your greens any way you can get them! Nettles, dandelion leaves, spinach, collards, kale, spirulina, chlorella. Don't forget to splash your sautéed greens with some apple cider vinegar to make the amazing minerals in these greens more bioavailable.

Lifeblood Syrup

An iron-rich tonic for those looking to feel grounded and embodied.

Fresh or dried herbs can be used.
1/2 cup yellow dock root
1/2 cup burdock root
1/4 cup rose hips
1/4 cup hawthorn berry
1/4 cup elderberry
1/4 cup dried cherries (or raisins, dates, jujubes, prunes, etc.)
1/2 cup nettle leaf
1/2 cup alfalfa leaf
1 tbsp fennel seed
1 tbsp cinnamon chips
3 cardamom pods
1 cup molasses
1 cup organic unbleached cane sugar
1 cup honey (optional)
1 cup vinegar (optional)

Bring 3 quarts of water to a simmer in a pot on the stove. Add all ingredients (including molasses and sugar) to the water, except the vinegar. Simmer mixture for a few hours until a lot of the liquid has boiled off and you have about 4 cups of liquid remaining. Remove from heat. If you wish, you can put all of this in a blender to really get the good stuff out before straining, or you can just strain it without blending. Try to squeeze out as much liquid as you can into a clean container. At this point in the process, I like to infuse my potion with some of my intentions for nourishing my passions, whatever it is that gets my blood moving...You can add a cup of apple cider vinegar to this mixture if you'd like more of a mineral boost. You are welcome to preserve this mix with a bit of alcohol or just refrigerate it and use it up in two to three weeks. I take a tablespoon a day, sometimes more for an extra kick—especially if I am about to bleed. The idea is to use this potion daily to build and nourish the blood. And yes, it is supposed to kind of taste like a sweet and bitter cast-iron pan.

*mxnstruate: Radical form of "menstruate" used to resist, reclaim, and re-invent dominant views surrounding the menstrual cycle. Definition by Janeen Singer of Holy Sponge!

How I am nourishing myself this week, leading up to the Full Moon:

AUGUST 26TH: FULL MOON in PISCES, 4:56 AM PST
7:54 PM PST MOONRISE, 6:26 AM PST MOONSET

The Pisces Paradox: Simultaneous Existence as Finite Human and Infinite Spirit
by Rachel Howe of Small Spells

In some ways, Pisces represents death. As the last sign of the Zodiac, Pisces contains the dying light before renewal of the self in Aries. In the darkness of the dying light, we can find insight and peace. Pisces is also the pathway into the spirit world, as of course, so is death. In Pisces is where we find our spirit self, the eternal self, the expansive self, the inter-connected self. Pisces loses the ego, and finds the soul. Ego as a construct is a tricky one; it allows us to function by providing a framework for the physical self, but it also places limitations and restrictions on the possibilities of the energetic self. Through time, the ego begins to function in response to a traumatized self rather than in response to the true inner self. It forms protections around wounds, rather than providing structural support for the potential energy of the soul.

When Pisces is in the highest manifestation of ego-less self, it can facilitate ecstatic re-connection with Source. Time falls away, wounds from the past are healed in the present and vanish, where a limitless expansion of personal energy can be felt, and where all creative and generative energy is seen, supported, and loved. When Pisces is in its lower vibration, it is a snake eating its own tail—simultaneously nourishing and killing itself, while being both the nourishment and the killer. We all carry the potential for connection to the divine within us, but we can choose to invite it or reject it, to see it or deny it. As humans, we wish to enter into the welcoming home of spiritual connection, but we have to learn the Pisces truth that this home is within each of us, not outside of us. We can become the lover and the beloved both, the creator and the created: the snake who gives birth to herself, no longer eating herself.

Pisces knows what this tastes like, what it feels like: the bliss of wriggling out of the entrapments of the physical and all its trauma and corresponding armor. Pisces thrives in ultimate freedom of the self to transcend. But when that connection is tenuous or the full connection is kept hidden or out of reach, Pisces slides into escape mode. The ecstasy of the soul flying free is hindered by the needs of the body and the mind, especially their need to continuously reinforce false patterns and beliefs about the self as a whole, about the limitations of the physical self. And so if Pisces cannot reconcile this fundamental contradiction between the material self and the immaterial self, through finding the divine in the intersections of the two, through falling in love with the paradoxes of being a spiritual human, then it will fall into a liminal space of negating the body while also not fully accepting the invitation to enter into the spirit world. It will stay suspended in this space of neither, a dream-world of partial immersion in either the human world or the spirit world, never sewing together both experiences into a holistic completion.

The symbols of esoteric knowledge illustrate the lock and the key. Pisces is traditionally shown as two fish swimming away from each other, while still next to each other. One is human, one is Spirit. One is life, one is death. The symbol shows the contradiction and the circular nature of being alive. Because I will die, I am alive. My death reinforces the fact of my living. But because I am also a microcosm of the divine, I will not die. My eternal nature belies my death, which belies the fact of my living. The paradoxical nature of being both human and finite, and spirit and infinite, while in connection with Source energy, in ceremony or in meditation, is no big deal. We understand it because it is in our nature to fundamentally feel and know the nature of Source. While sitting in connection with Source, feeling at home with Source, our minds can understand and will accept this illogical premise. But without that connection, our minds do not accept it. We look for ways out of this predicament.

In the same way, we can spend our lives trying to escape the predicament of living while knowing we will die. Even while typing these words, I feel the stigma around naming death so blatantly. I feel an urge to soften or disguise the truth that we all know. But we know it only superficially. Our minds know it, and perhaps sometimes our bodies feel it. But we don't let our emotions really feel it, and therefore we block our souls from fully integrating this truth into our lives. The struggle of Pisces is to live in the truth of death and life co-existing in all of us. The aim is about bringing light to this difficult truth, bringing it to the surface, and integrating the light and the shadow. Like a Full Moon, where the Sun and Moon oppose each other, face each other, see each other, validate each other, balance each other, love each other, allow each other, and support each other, Pisces lives between the conscious and the unconscious. To ascend into its higher form, it must acknowledge and accept both, even as they contradict each other.

Now that you've made it past the heavy stuff, it's time to play. The Sun is in Leo, connecting with the creative impulse of Pisces's connection to Source, but on a more personal level. I've channeled a Tarot spread for this Pisces/Leo Full Moon opposition. Because Leo is how we express ourselves as a human being—making art, making love, giving birth, playing games, singing and dancing—and Pisces is how we express the divine through our human energy, we might need to learn how to integrate these two so that one doesn't overshadow the other. Working with astrology is all about finding balance, and using all the multifaceted pieces of the cosmos to learn how to make adjustments. Full Moon energy is a culmination, it is like a full cup, so it's a good time to evaluate how you're working with the many streams of energy that we can tap into to create our lives with value and purpose.

Suggested Affirmation: "My human self and my spiritual self are in balance. My unique human gifts are amazing tools that I can use to create a support system for myself, one that allows me to connect with the divine, and allows Source to express itself through me. Humanity and divinity walk hand in hand in every moment of my life."

Full Moon Tarot Spread

Shuffle the cards three times. From the top of the deck, pull 6 cards and lay them in a half-circle or an arc. Pull 3 more cards and place them in an arc above, lining them up in the spaces between the first 6 cards. You are creating 3 individual groups of cards, each in a triangle formation.

Each of the top cards is a positive energy that you are working towards, or energy that is currently active. Each of the 2 bottom cards, under 1 top card, are the support system for that top card. These are energies that you need to focus on more, blocks you need to clear, actions you need to take, in order to fully support the intention of the top cards.

Meditate on each group of 3—one may be talking more about your personal life, one for business, or maybe they are all talking about the same things using varying symbols. Let yourself hear the guidance in how you can better support your path, your destiny, your calling, your soul's desire. The top cards are your Pisces wishes, the plans that are born from your higher self, from your connection to Source. Taking the road towards these wishes is fulfilling your soul's calling, which in itself is a devotion to Source and the divine. These paths take us down a road where each step is a blissful expression of the divine. The bottom cards are your Leo actions. We can choose to play out our human actions in an ego-focused way, where each breath, word, and movement nourishes and enlightens only ourselves. Or we can choose to make each breath, word, and movement nourishing and enlightening for the complete cosmos, for ourselves as a smaller piece of a greater whole—not separate, but interconnected with everything.

Full Moon Tarot Diagram

Notes on Tarot Spread:

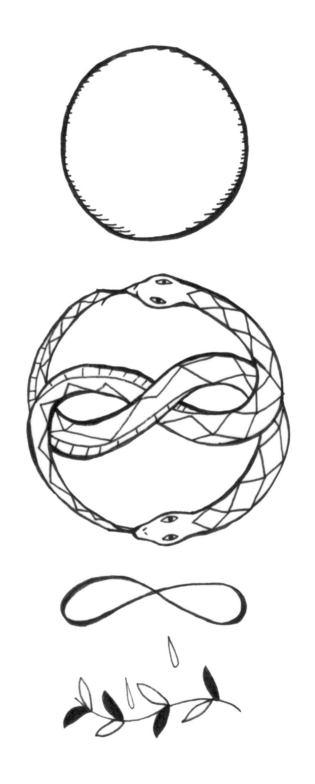

Notes on this month:

Intentions for the next:

SEPTEMBER 2018
SEPTEMBER 2ND: LAST QUARTER
SEPTEMBER 6-8TH: DARK MOON
SEPTEMBER 9TH: NEW MOON
SEPTEMBER 16TH: FIRST QUARTER
SEPTEMBER 22ND: FALL EQUINOX
SEPTEMBER 24TH: FULL MOON

September is a month that accentuates change. The seasons begin their shift with colder mornings and longer evenings. The Fall Equinox this year sits close to our Full Harvest Moon: consider what you will be calling in and expanding on during this transitional time. This month asks us to bend into any changes taking place, whether they seem daunting or are a relief. This month asks us to examine where we are ready to change, what we are growing, and what exactly we must sacrifice to make way for this growth.

The phases of the Moon dance around the Gregorian calendar, rarely lining up. Yet ancient religions' calendars were lunar, and we see remnants of this during this month. The Jewish New Year begins on the New Moon, reminding us that we can always begin again. The Ethiopian New Year starts on the 11th, while the New Moon explodes into a crescent smile.

When we are in seeming chaos, in seachange moments of collective transition, we can get caught up in "shoulds," or in toxic expectations of ourselves and others. We get trapped in self-righteous defense or indignation. It can be hard to see the forest for the trees of our pain. If you find yourself rubbing against some external blocks this month while you are shedding, if there is some stasis to your forward movement, pause. Try to take some deep breaths and zoom out. Change is difficult, but it is necessary. Realize your process might not be happening in linear time. Your process this month might be finding your way out of the forest. Your process this month might be trying to find your place *in* the forest—seeking out more fertile spaces of holding change, rooting into transitions, altering your viewpoint around transitions to be more positive, and grounding into new levels of self-discovery and collective service.

And last, but certainly not least, Lunar Lovers, is our monthly lunar temperature: let's take it. September is the month after an eclipse season summer. Some of us may be still processing any changes in our internal and external lives. Those around us may be rattled or needing extra support. As we reconcile our own changes, allow others to change as well. It's important not to forget that others are in their own processes, their own reconciliations.

This month, throughout the change, as the shake-ups settle, check in with yourself. Grounding and regrounding is essential this month. Turn inward and create your own navigational tools, forged out of commitment and communication. Our successes aren't really successes if they do not emanate from within. You'll know when to stick to the path. You'll know when to veer off of it to climb higher and to seek a better view. Again and again, be one with what you are growing. If you've been steadily leaning into the wind and letting it move you, you'll find yourself happily surprised at the Harvest Moon near this month's end.

September 9th: New Moon in Virgo / Neptune in Pisces opposing Sun and Moon / Mars in Capricorn conjunct Lilith in Aquarius / Lilith and Mars square Venus in Libra/ Chiron conjunct Moon / Saturn square Sun and Moon

September 24th: Full Moon in Aries / Sun Conjunct Mercury in Libra / Square Saturn in Capricorn / Lilith Conjunct Mars in Aquarius

High fantasy. What this means is really up to you. Early in the month the New Moon in Virgo is peering across the cosmos at Neptune in it's home sign, Pisces. Whenever something makes an aspect to Neptune there is almost always an element of fantasy, escapism, and projection. Neptune is exalted in Pisces which means it is at home—soaking in it's own undulating currents, getting hella juiced. This dream team has incredible potential to make our high ideals a little bit more real.

What do you like to dream about? Are you a stress addict and want to dream about the end of the world? Virgo moon says, do it all the way then and design an escape pod, make a bugout bag, get to know your neighbors and dream up an emergency protocol that relies on your greatest strengths. Do you want to dream about falling in love? Take some cooking classes, painting, ceramics, and violin classes—load up on romantic shit. Learn about interesting things, go to interesting places, find beauty in quiet moments early in the morning and take photos and then look at it privately and say: *damn, what a beautiful thing.* Seduce your world back into your heart and love soon follows. Harness the power of dreamy Neptune and the action planner Virgo to build out your dreams.

And, I think I want us to underachieve right now. I want us to get lost in the meticulous response to each fantastic stimuli, to order our dream sequences from a to z, and then actually, totally, *let it all go.*

Write them on balloons and release them on a hill, put them in a bottle and throw them into the ocean, find some way to give them up and see which parts come back. In waiting, you may worry. You may think, *it was all a waste.* I assure you it is not. Dreams, Neptunian dreams, are like ocean waves. They work slowly. They emerge slowly. Granular, like making sand from boulders. Neptune wants us to find not just kinship, but sincere oneness—a merger and attunement with the cosmic world. This can only be hindered if we try to escape the actual practical steps we make towards that oneness. We can try and shortcut all we want but deep down inside, this fulfilment, this connection to Truth, is only attainable through letting go of our resistance and walking the walk. If you struggle, find an act of service that is in line with what you need to create in your own life. Watch how it unfolds externally. Remember: many great accomplishments need a plan, and no plan is good without a solid dream.

Neptune in Pisces is king of paradox. All things are true. She loves you and she loves you not. On one side of things, Neptune entering Pisces in 2012 ushered in a new level of spiritual connection, psychic development, and yearning for teachers in alchemical arts. On the other end it created an escape from the political and mundane realities of life. Calling addiction medicine, calling co-dependence soulmates, and calling escapism enlightenment. The fruitful lesson in these dualities is balance. There can be a message in substances that needs to be heard by some, there can be ways to elevate the soul through deep intimate commitment, and we sometimes need to be outside of the problems to truly understand them.

Mars is all fury, intensity, and impulsivity. Transiting through timebound, patient, Capricorn, Mars has nowhere to run. it is like a race car with its pedal on the gas burning rubber waiting for the green light. Lilith in Aquarius is bringing out the higher levels of righteous rage, a higher understanding of effective communication and a greater curiosity to the collective stage. The shadow of Lilith in Aquarius is a hyper attachment to all ideas, truth, and knowledge. This combo of Lilith and Mars is in conversation with Venus in Libra which is pleading desperately, "c'mon you guys, can't we all just get along?". And the answer is: probably not. Let me tell you why this is a good thing. Libra is a sign of ambivalence and ambivalence is a word that gets a bad rep. "Ambivalent", which is usually used to describe apathy not uncaring, comes from Latin *ambi*: "both, on both sides," and *valentia* : "strength," which means the exact opposite of apathy. Libra weighs the options, and does so unceasingly because both sides can be so strongly valid. This may echo the Pisces principle so strongly that I want to make sure you are understanding the difference. Venus in Libra is about attracting and requesting attention for this very quality: deep, deep discernment.

This transit at the same time as the Full Moon is showing us our boundaries in relationship to our reputation through our need for appreciation and expression. In your wildest dreams, how do you know what you know? What may you never know? In your private fantasies, how are you given affection? How do you receive it now? In what ways to you act that are not in service to your long term goals? There are real reasons for why we do what we do, but sometimes those reasons don't exist anymore and need a refresh, require a reboot.

So, before we start anything we must stop. Slow down. Unclench your jaw, open your hands. Drop that pain. Rest, as if rest was an action. Rest is the move. That can look so differently for everyone, but actually, really, rest, rest, rest.

At the Full Moon, the Sun is scorching our planet of talk. There is something that is ready to to be expressed, and it's hard to hear, but it's written all over our faces. The Full Moon in Aries on the 24th is showing where it's difficult to speak. It's showing us a place that we are gifted at healing in others but can't heal in ourselves and it is requiring us to take a deep look inward and find our secret strengths.

Saturn in Capricorn—time and reputation— is forming a direct and challenging aspect to the Sun and Moon at this Full Moon time. We see a discipline and a strictness involved. The work we do under this Moon is enduring. How we choose to use this challenging conversation between planets will decide if we prosper or suffer in the opportunity to heal under this Moon. If we experience discipline as oppressive, expect to be oppressed. If we understand discipline builds our sense of self-worth and reputation, we might just get through this alive.

Sometimes the superficial—doing things for your reputation—is much deeper than it seems. Your reputation is like a vibration, except one that other people carry for you. It's a part of how opportunity and relationship find you. You want it tuned to the most accurate frequency possible, and though you can't control it, you sure do influence it. What are we not saying in fear of our reputation? This is in relation to a wound, or is holding space for other's secrets in fear or hiding. Speak where you must and see that as a healing action.

This September Full Moon, ask yourself:
Why is it important to be vulnerable?
What is the difference between being vulnerable and being naive for you?
How do you know who you can trust with your truth?
What are you free from? To what are you bound?

SEPTEMBER 2ND: LAST QUARTER MOON in GEMINI, 9:37 PM PST, 12:02 AM PST MOONRISE, 1:16 PM PST MOONSET

Beginning Again: Letting Go with Love

"It's hard to let go. Even when what you're holding onto is full of thorns, it's hard to let go. Maybe especially then." — Stephen King

This Sunday, September 2nd, at almost the start of this new month, the Moon shifts into Last Quarter in Gemini. As the Moon is at a 90 degree angle from our vantage point in the northern hemisphere, we only see half of her lit up. The Quarter Moons mark a time of balance in our perceptions of light and dark. The illuminating effects of our Full Moon have granted us clearer windowpanes of vision and insight. There's been some distance from the discomfort. Stairways up have appeared from the ether, built of the same mud the lotus bursts forth from. The Moon mirror gazing has its benefits. If we close our eyes and look long enough, the radiant gleams of reflection become answers. Sonnets of solutions disguised as Moon glow.

The forces of the tides at this time are lower and less dramatic. We may be feeling less. emotional. We may feel less inclined to start something new. Efforts may be best spent on wrapping things up. Ask yourself: What did this most recent Full Moon bring up? What do I need to release to get closer to my desired state? Ask yourself: If my desires were to come in the next six months, what would I need to have ready to go for them to take hold in a way I could feel? Ask yourself: This coming week, what are one or two items that I've been putting off, that I must undertake? Ask yourself: Is there a part of my thought process that needs decluttering? Ask yourself: Is there a part of my working process that needs decluttering? Ask yourself: Are there parts of my relationships that need decluttering? Ask yourself: What is stopping me from making new beginnings in service to my higher self? Ask yourself: What hard decision have I been avoiding that I know I must make in order to set something else free?

A Tarot card that speaks to changes and choices in the Major Arcana is The Lovers card. The Lovers card correlates to the sign of Gemini. The Queerest card in the first line of the Major Arcana, the Lovers is about all kinds of love: poly love, agape love, altruistic love, sexy love, creative love, and challenging love. Love as a spectrum, a healing, a getting free, a holograph, a rainbow infused action. Love of the other, love of self, love of creation, love of cosmic unions and cosmic wonders, love of authenticity and honesty. When this archetype arises, L-O-V-E is on the brain, the horizon, and it is most certainly amplified in the querent's life. The choices we make in the name of love. The places where our love has gotten stagnant and stale are up for revision. How is your action lined up with the kind of love you want to receive right now?

Another not-as-discussed topic thread that comes up around The Lovers card is about choice. Choosing. In fact, in earlier versions of the card, Key 6 was called "The Choice" (Rachel Pollack, *Seventy-Eight Degrees of Wisdom*). This archetype can be about decisions and sacrifice. When this card shows up, there is a choice to make. Keeping your self loved and charged, choices, relationships, all of the questions new creative projects bring up—all of these topics and more are on the table. We must make a decision and stay the course. The course itself, over time, will change. Even if that decision is letting go of a preconceived notion that is blocking us from experiencing this resonant, reverberant love in all of its complex glory; even if that decision is letting go of a bouquet of dead roses, so sharp they turn our skin to blood; even if that something is the holding on to a different way things could have gone, another way we could have been—we must give up something so that we can move more freely.

We don't get something for nothing.

There are some decisions that are deeply transformational. These can be some of the most difficult ones. Distancing certain family members. Moving forward with trust. Choosing to believe that the universe is a friend, not a foe. At this Waning Moon time, you may be feeling as though it is time for one of those hard choices. We get tripped up, we get scared, we get stuck, and we forget about the power of choice. Choosing is expansion. Choosing is abundant. Every breath we breathe is a choice to move on. Do things differently. With every exhale, we release the past. With every inhale, we embrace the unknown future.

Some people are resistant to choice and change as they require a sacrifice. Sacrifice can get a bad reputation in our society. It implies vulnerability, giving up things, resignation, and commitment. However, all witches know that sacrifice is not a bad word; in fact, it is integral to a successful spell. We have to give up a limiting belief of scarcity if we are to experience abundance. We have to give up a subconscious belief that we will always be lonely if we want to conjure community.

Some sacrifices are deeply transformational. Some sacrifices are painful to do. It is painful to let go of old patterns and habits. Some sacrifices are hard to do in the moment but serve our ideals, and the collective, down the line. We love the planet, so we are careful about sourcing where our food comes from. We don't want to add more waste, so we bring to-go cups to the coffee shop, or Tupperware for our leftovers when we go out to dinner. We love fellow humans, so we donate 13% of our pay to causes that protect social justice and the rights of those who cannot fight for their life all on their own. If we are white , we speak up and act to support Black people, Indigenous people, and people of color, even though that risks relationships or work. Some sacrifices ultimately are for us—for we are everyone else. Sacrifices are ultimately an act of transformation when they are born out of love.

The Lovers card can also be about reconciling parts of the self. Aspects of the inner and outer path, the mind and the body, are up for cooperation and reorganization. (A huge thank you to the work of Mary K. Greer for pushing my understanding of The Lovers into this realm of thought.) When we reconcile different opposing viewpoints or beliefs inside ourselves, sometimes that just means leaning into acceptance. Like gender, this is fluid. We accept that we can be many, many different things at once. We can revel in them. (Geminis are talented at that.) At other times we come up to the themes of release and letting go. Detachment leads to more balance. Balance leads to more freedom. At this time, it might not be release or letting go you are needing; it might be reconciliation. What relationships, to yourself and others, need reorganizing? What relationships need forgiveness? Where is it time to engage differently?

If you are feeling shaky about the risk of release, of saying goodbye, this is understandable. Remember yourself and your life and all that has passed and all of the times you let go, or all of the times something was taken from you. You took a risk. Released the doubt. Moved past the fear. Cut the confusion and moved bravely onto a different path. Think of examples of this from your own life. Every time you let something go, something else better eventually appeared. Usually, it wasn't immediate. It took time, but it showed up. Generally, the incoming item had an improved quality, provided you were conscious of what you needed.

It can be difficult to release pain and suffering when it has gone on for so long. For some of us, it runs so deep it feels almost etched into the insides of our very bones. Sometimes when we are suffering and dealing with loss, with pain, with sorrow, we become identified with it to the point that we can see nothing else. We can not fathom feeling anything else but the ache. We have to imagine what we are giving up when we give up the part of our self that has become conditioned to embody sadness, isolation, or despondency.

Do not become so attached to your pain that your pain is all you become.

Remaining static is not natural. Everything in nature changes and we are nature. Nature is the birds migrating above our heads. Nature is the egg cracking open and the cocoon opening up. What is unnatural is believing that change can't happen, must be painful, or that if your world is changing around you then it is your fault. What is unnatural is clinging to the past, especially if it was harmful.

The minute we decide to do a spell, we are letting go of the outcome. This may seem like an untrue statement at first read. In fact, letting go of specific outcomes in spell work is precisely how spells can work so well. The universe wishes to co-create with you from a point of flow, and at a level of trust and acceptance. The universe isn't usually too keen on a forced hand, or a clenched fist. When we hand over our desires and dreams to the universe, all while pledging to do our part, spell work is at its most potent. This is because we are operating from a standpoint of perfect love and perfect trust. If we have perfect love and perfect trust, we cannot also hold tight to control, unreasonable expectations, or impatient demands. Spell work is a lot like love.

Releasing and letting go are inherently an allowance for a new beginning. Magic loves a void, and so we create one when we let go of attachment to a relationship that no longer works, or behaviors that aren't supporting our creativity. It is terrifying at first, to not do the same things you've been doing for years. You knew what results you were getting! You had moved into that state of being, like the mustiest, most stained, overstuffed recliner that had molded to your body but took you nowhere. All of us have these armchairs, invisible or visible. During this Waning Moon time, please take one of these constrictive yet comfortable cloaks you have been using as a disappearing device to the curb. Let yourself make a transformative decision. Allow yourself to hold a transformative belief. Let yourself create an abundant sacrifice. Let yourself let go with love.

We can always begin again. We are always beginning again.
Endings are beginnings are endings are beginnings.
Goodbyes are hellos are goodbyes are hellos.

Some ways to practice letting go:
Give something you like or love away to someone else. Know you will never see it again. Give something you've labored over creatively (a song, a book, a poem, a painting, an email) to the world. Expect nothing in return. Feel good when people say nice things or feel bad when people say bad things but always remember that none of that has anything to do with you. Really. Repeat.

Some ways to practice beginning again:
Do the next loving thing you need to do.
How you do one thing is how you do all of the things. Therefore, imbue your one thing with as much love, presence, and attention as you can muster. If it is a hard or unpleasant thing, treat yourself as gently as you can as you come up against the sandpaper.
Ask yourself for help and then give yourself that help.
Make becoming your best friend your new practice, your new next exciting project.

If you are in the process of letting go, remember to take care of yourself. You could go back to the piece from July about soul retrievals. Ground. Connect with the Earth; let her take your pain. Nourish your body with lemon water and soup. Do you need more fire? If so, light a candle in the morning for inspiration. Do you need more fluidity? If so, take a bath if you can. Go near water if you can. Let the water hold you.

Following is a spell for protection and release. Remember that if you are letting go of things during this Waning Moon, then during the New and Waxing Moon period time, you are to focus on inviting in all of the behaviors and bounty that the clutter or confusion has been keeping you from beginning. Be clear on what you are releasing and what you are sacrificing.

A Spell to Aid One's Protection While One Is Clearing Stagnation

You will need:
2 garlic cloves
A spoonful of dried hyssop (for tea). A spoonful of dried comfrey (for tea), A spoonful of dried nettle (for tea)
Oil (any kind, such as vegetable oil or olive oil, or any other oil you use to anoint candles)
A small glass cup or jar
1 small white candle, 1 small black candle
A nail, pin, or something else to carve into the candle
1 small piece of clear quartz, 1 small piece of smoky quartz, 1 small piece of shungite
1 small glass bowl of salt water

The night before the spell, peel your garlic cloves, put them in a small glass cup or jar, and cover them with oil. The night before the spell, go around your house/room/space and clean. Especially clean your corners and under your furniture and bed. You want all dust bunnies and stagnant energy cleared away. As you clean, think about what exactly you are going to be releasing. Envision whatever it is you are releasing as all of the dust that has accumulated in your space.

Brew a protection tea. Make a tea out of nettle, comfrey, and hyssop before your spell.

Cast your circle and ground. On your altar, put your crystals and your candles. Underneath your altar, or to the side of it, place your bowl of salt water. On your black candle, carve your name, and what it is you are releasing. For example: *Ursula Johnson* is no longer procrastinating, etc.,

Anoint both of your candles with your garlic oil. Anoint yourself with the garlic oil by drawing a pentagram with it on your forehead. If you are a witch who likes to practice spells naked, as a lot of us do, draw the pentagram anywhere else on your body that feels right.

Light the black candle. As it burns, feel this behavior or relationship melt away. Feel wherever it has resided leave your body. Know that the salt water can take any sadness, sorrow, or grief. Once you feel lighter, or a shift in energy, light your white candle.

As both of the candles burn, hold your crystals in your hand. Charge them with the protective energy you are seeking. The clear quartz will keep you clear and focused. The smoky quartz will continue to release what you would like to release. The shungite will keep you psychically and physically protected.

After the candles have burnt all the way down, put the wax in the salt water bowl.

Close your circle. Dispose of the water and wax somewhere away from your home.
For the next week, carry your small crystals as a reminder of your release. Drink your tea whenever you need more support and reminders of all the loving work you are doing.

new moon in virgo
by adrienne maree brown

the new moon is a reminder that while life moves towards light—bending like trees, arcing up like new leaves—it all begins in the dark. everything new—seed bursting, brain forming, star being born—begins in darkness so total that there doesn't appear to be room to breath. there doesn't appear to be a need for air. and once it begins, life is change, change, change...changes we want, changes we don't want.

this year has brought so many changes we don't want, interwoven with changes we want.

recently a friend of mine, a black mama and organizer, was wrongfully convicted and sentenced to two years in prison. she is pregnant. the rules say this sentence is mandatory. the rules say her mother and her husband can't be present at the birth. she didn't choose these changes. there doesn't appear to be any air.

a couple i respect just had a son, a child they prayed for and manifested and wanted with every fiber in their being.

another list came out the other day showing all the environmental protections that are being stripped away under the vicious ego of this U.S. administration. some of the tears that come on my moon cycles now feel like they come up through the dirt into me. the planet is so small when you share it with short-term thinkers. we don't want these changes; the planet becomes less and less habitable with these changes. there doesn't appear to be room to breathe.

seven women i love hearing from have released or are releasing books this year, books that came out of incredible experiences, books that were written with blood, tears, octopus ink, dying breath, and sea salt.

i got a text from a friend, so full of heartbreak. my friend had offered their heart to another— genuine, wide, and wild heart love. their beloved said yes! and then, for no clear reason, said no. i went to my friend and they grasped at their chest like they wanted to pull out their heart. they didn't want this change. they aren't sure they can survive this change. no breath, no air.

someone who is precious to me has been depressed for most of the year. and they wrote me to say that today, today, they looked at themselves in the mirror and felt love. felt that they had fallen in love, finally, with themselves.

at a small scale, at a large scale, internal and external, change is constant.

the moon is its own proof, always full, always dancing with earth's shadow. and so many changes come to us, and we get to choose how to respond, who wte will be, what we will conjure and center in our lives. will we be blown around like leaves that have let go of the source of life, let ourselves become compost for some future season of growth? will we root down, will we manifest what we need down in the dark?

i write to you as a virgo, claiming the highest potential of this new moon. i like to change things because i believe they can be better, can be more perfect. it takes work for me to be with what is.

it takes work for me to trust what can only happen in the dark, in the places i can't see.

virgo in shadow can be nagging, nitpicky. but under that, in the deeper dark within, is our visionary calling. the gift of virgo: we can see something whole, beautiful, possible. Octavia Butler taught us: we get to shape change. all of us.

we get to shape ourselves for the world we are generating—we are the front lines of all the change we wish to bring into the world. each of us is a microcosm of all the possible justice, liberation, pleasure, and honesty in the universe. act accordingly.

in the face of disappointment and betrayal, we have the opportunity to become more honest about what we want, who we are, how we love. we can teach this way of being open and honest to the next generation. this will not keep us from heartbreak, but it will give us, give our species, more skill at loving.

in the face of environmental catastrophe, we can return to nature. we can respond to her cycles, we can stop consuming the earth and start living with her. we can become warriors for the planet. we can disrupt business as usual in a fight for our relative, our planet, our home.

in the face of our punitive justice system, we have so many chances to change our relation-ships to everyone in our lives. changes to become transformative with each other. when harm happens— conflict, difference, misunderstanding—we can hold hands and jump into the dark, down into the mysterious realm of roots. we can get curious about what gives us all this difference. we can wonder if it is biodiversity or if it a dangerous toxicity. together we can find the medicine, the ways to grow and change with each other.

and then the cycle continues. in two weeks, you will be able to harvest under the clarity of an aries full moon. below, i offer a ritual that allows you to plant things you are ready to harvest soon.

suggested new moon affirmation:

"all that you touch
 you change
 all that you change
 changes you
 the only lasting truth
 is change
 god
 is change"
—octavia butler

new moon tarot spread

find the moon card in your deck and lay it face down at the heart of your spread.

shuffle your deck, letting your longings come to mind.

pull three cards and place them face down in an arc over the moon card:

card 1: clarity on what brought you to this moment

card 2: clarity on what you need to be/surrender to/open to in order to truly move towards your longing

card 3: clarity about what your longing is bringing to you

with a journal and a free blank piece of paper at hand, turn each card in the arc over. in the journal, reflect on what you see, read the card's descriptions, and find the wisdom there for you. then, read the moon card and feel gratitude for what can only be seen clearly in the dark. finally, on the blank sheet of paper, write your seeds. based on this reading and wisdom, what are you ready to plant, invite, change, grow? once you have planted the seeds on this page, fold it up and put it under your bed. let it grow in your dreams for at least two weeks. keep your attention alert for the harvest.

Notes on Tarot Pull:

card 1:

card 2:

card 3:

What seeds are being planted in my life:

SEPTEMBER 16TH: FIRST QUARTER MOON in SAGITTARIUS
6:15 PM PST, 1:35 PM PST MOONRISE

Simple Recipes for Change: Experiments in Different Aims and Alignments

"You must know two things: what you are free from and what keeps you bound."
—Sri Nisargadatta Mahara

Happy Tuesday! Happy First Quarter Moon! Our New Moon was a week ago and our Full Harvest Moon is eight days away. Our energy might be picking up steam: Tuesday is ruled by Mars, and our Moon is in Sagittarius. These energetic entities spark up the wild expanse above our heads that is called the sky. We ourselves may feel ripe and for the picking at this harvesting time. We ourselves may feel absolutely ready Freddy! Totally, positively willing to take a plunge. It is time to take a risk or two, in small or grandiose doses. What juicy new treats can we pluck from our surroundings to fill our mouths up with tart tingly flavors? What divergent perspectives must we cultivate to usher in a more fulfilling paradigm?

In the self-development world, something is always wrong with someone, somewhere. People can always be smarter or faster or more something. One can always be more productive, richer, more something or another that we aren't at the moment. Something that isn't you. Comparison fever, photoshop, and the internet have left a lot of us feeling constant lack, jealousy, and an itchy, nagging feeling that something isn't alright with us. That we have to be something else entirely in order to feel ok. But what if you are perfectly fine? What if you are actually incredibly amazing and inspiring, just as you are, nothing more and nothing less? What if really, truly, the you that is here right now looking in the mirror is the you that is the one?

You aren't broken. You are whole. You were never broken. Someone or many someones tried to break you many times and yet here you are. Still here, still beautiful. Still sensitive and thoughtful, with all your talents intact, and at least two matching pairs of socks. Still here, with so, so many dreams. Many of them are on their way to you in this year or the next. You are someone else's dream. So become your own. Act accordingly. There are no excuses now for you not to be your own favorite date. There are no excuses now for who you are, what you want, and what you are going after. Brick by brick. Bit by bit. Breath by breath.

You aren't broken. Maybe there are some habits that need to be addressed. Maybe there are some behaviors that are no longer helpful. Maybe there are some interests inside of you that need coaxing out and placing onto a stage to be admired. There could be decay that needs scraping off and composting. Perhaps there are ways to look at parts of your life differently, other angles to consider, wavy ones, not so prickly. These are all puzzle pieces inside the rainbow that is you, billions and billions of pulsating colors that comprise the unique blueprint of a soul that is uniquely you.

Everything you could ever want, everything you could ever be, everything you could ever have, is already inside of you. Proceed accordingly with that knowledge.

We are halfway through the month of September. Six months ago, in March, the topic of the workbook was around boundaries. If you examined your boundaries and your needs, there most likely have been changes. Can you congratulate yourself for all the fantastic decisions you've made since March? Pluck them proudly from the ether like congratulatory bouquets of forget-me-nots. It was a Blue Moon month that was packed with magic and change. We can look back and check in on all the magic that has taken place since then.

Pause now, gentle reader. What has changed for you since March? What would you still like to see change in your world, or in the world?

Close your eyes and take as many deep breaths as you would like or need. Soften your belly and feel yourself vibrating. Imagine all the cells in your body, all 37.2 trillion of them, in motion.* Allow them to sync up in accordance with one wish you have for this week, this Harvesting Moon time. Tell them to send out the energy of what you would like. As you feel the electricity in your body circulate, remind yourself that you can imbue these vibrating cells with anything you wish, and that this energy in turn ripples out from the center of your cells to gain momentum. Pleasure. Calm. Ease. Grace. Excitement. Magnetism. Intelligence. Excitement.

Think backwards again, to March. What would you characterize the quality of your energy as? What were some of the qualities of your intentions? What are some descriptors around the feeling state of your vibration? Can you make any correlations between your energy, your vibration from six months ago, and certain events that have transpired, that are unfolding this week, right before your eyes?

This month, we are in a Harvest Moon month. Time to collect our favors from the universe. Time to ask for help as we need to. Time to call on our own sovereignty, our own strength, as proof that we are enough to receive all the bounty coming our way. What will you be harvesting this month? What harvest lies in plain sight, already around you, already in your vision, if you would name it, if you would see it?

One way we block ourselves from success when it comes to making changes in our life is to be too drastic: to make goals that are really far away from where we are. Trying to fly to the Moon when we haven't learned how to drive a car. As everything we wish to see happen comes from our sphere of influence, we have to act accordingly. Our sphere of influence is what is already in our life: current friends, community, family, our current job/career, talents, and skill sets. We must always start with where we are. Build on that. With consistent effort, our energy builds momentum and desired change occurs.

When we are working magic, when we wish to make change, we have to come to accept we are building bit by bit. Physically, it doesn't make sense to run a marathon if we are not used to walking one mile. Mentally, it doesn't make sense to try to become the most cheerily, optimistic optimist if generally you are a skeptical, sarcastic Sally. Many, many people fail to change their behavior because they are aiming much further outside their comfort zone than their brain can comprehend. The ego immediately contracts and shuts down. Our belief in our ability to conjure our desires plummets.

Magically, it is the same principle. We start just outside our comfort zone with what we want and wish for, just outside what we think is possible. If we were to quantify it, maybe it is in the 5%-10% range outside of what we aleady have and what we already are doing.

Remember, if our deep subconscious resolutely believes that something cannot happen, the chances of this happening are very slim. If that is the level you must start at, then that is where you must start: convincing wyourself, letting your deep subconscious mind believe that this beautiful thing is safe, allowed, and is real.

We start where we are: just where we need to be. While we are in the growing stages, it can be difficult to pinpoint if anything is happening. (That is why I suggest a journal, workbook, or planner to keep track of occurrences and shifts, great and small!) It is only in the looking back that we can see the change. Of course, that is what the Moon is most excellent at helping us with.

So, we start where we are: just where we need to be. Small things become everything with repetition. There are, however, caveats to this rule. If you have been dragging on a goal, dream, or wish than it is time to get going! Really, only you or a very dear loved one will know the answer to this question. You could ask yourself: could this project be finished in a month, not a year? Has this been something I've wanted to do for months or years?.

Remember that time constricts or expands as you let it. PJ Harvey wrote *Rid of Me* in a year, and recorded it in less than two weeks. Ray Bradbury wrote the first draft of *Fahrenheit 451* in nine days. I frequently see Tarot clients who think that a dream is years away when in reality it is much, much closer. If this resonates, ask yourself at this Waxing Moon time, what is my deadline? Six weeks? Six months? What would I need to focus on in order to make this a reality?

If you feel inspired by this, take action right this second. Go on, close this book and get a piece of paper out. In three months' time, what do you wish to accomplish? What needs to happen, and how will you achieve that?

Schedule it in your calendar. Make the appointments needed. Tell yourself how excellent you will feel when the task is completed. Tell yourself how committed you are to seeing it through.

Utilizing Conscious Thought

All action begins with our mind—whether we are conscious of it or not. The brain is a wonderfully elastic, retrainable, and rewireable organ. With practice, we can train our brain pathways to run along different tracks and shift overall mindset. When we practice conscious thinking, we set our thought patterns up for expansiveness. Our What if's? become believable. They move from the dreamy, ethereal zone of the New Moon and move into the tangible, building stage of the Waxing Moon.

Consistently practicing positive thinking in our lives aids us momentously with our magical workings. Our subconscious allows the sea foam possibilities to wash over the beaches of our belief systems. Our thoughts affect our behavior, which in turn affects our outcomes. If our cells are introduced to more intrigue, more playfulness, more fierce flames, they vibrate on that frequency. Overall, we just feel better. It is a win-win, all around.

If you struggle with depression, I urge you to seek help with therapy and/or medication, however you define medicine. Brain chemistry is not your fault and does not mean anything other than, yes, you have a brain chemistry makeup that is predisposed to depression, or negativity. Also: the world is totally fucked right now, evil forces are running our government, very serious situations are happening. If you are aware, this could be affecting your mental health. How could it not? This is not a call to ignore everything happening. This is a prompt to try to make your brain—your mind's home, the seat of your consciousness and subconscious—as kind, as soft, and as sweet to and for yourself as it can be. A non-allergic featherbed, not a furnace. If your mind is loving, then you can help more people. If your mind is loving, your magic is much more potent. Your sphere of influence grows. Your positivity and your love grow. Your strength grows, and your patriarchy-smashing powers grow, too!

One way that has helped me greatly with positive thinking is to practice it in calm and beautiful environments. Set yourself up for success. Go to a garden and practice consciously thinking about how beautiful the flowers are, how lovely the air feels. Really enjoy the sky and the paths of the birds' flights, tracing out codes in the patterns of the clouds. Take a walk down your favorite street and smile as you name all the best parts about it out loud in your head. If the favorite part of your day is taking a bath or a shower, decide to practice positive thinking for most of it. Decide to enjoy the hot water, give thanks for it, name how vibrant your soap smells, how silky or thrillingly stubbly your skin feels. Try to do this every day, twice a day, for at least two to five minutes. Major bonus points if you can get up to 15-20 minutes of positive thinking/narrative in your head.

Another way to access positive thinking and feelings is making gratitude and appreciation lists, for people, places, things, experiences. If you are low, and sit down and write out a gratitude list for a page or two, you will feel at least a tiny bit better. Practicing consistent gratitude, such as during set times, like meals, or when you come home from work, or when you wake up, or when you go to bed, is a powerful way to access loving feelings. When you feel gratitude and appreciation, there is no space for fear and lack.

Of course, the most tried and true way to redirect your brain power into a more constructive zone is through consistent meditation. There are books written on this, apps for this, Youtube channels for this. I won't go into it. If it is time to have a consistent three-minute-a-day meditation practice, then the Waxing Moon phase is an optimal time to start.

Experimental Thinking

Another gift that has worked wonders for me has been using experimental thinking. "When you change the way you look at things, the things you look at change," the Nobel Prize-winning physicist Max Planck famously reminds us. When we are asking, "What if? Is this true? Can I solve this problem in another way? What am I not seeing? Who can I talk to for feedback?" our thought patterns shift out of the panic zone, or fight or flight.

Curiosity changes the tone. **

You can't be mean, punishing, or hateful to yourself when you are genuinely being curious with your process. In fact, the word "curious" comes from old Latin: "eager to know, careful."

Curiosity reframes our experiences profoundly.

If change is hard for you, it is useful to practice trying—and failing—in low-stakes environments. Again, we want to set ourselves up for success! If we actively practice different ways of thinking and behaving in environments that are not stressful to our nervous system it is easier to see results and see change happen. When practiced for months, this inquisitive way of thinking can seep into the times when life is very stressful. It can get easier to try new things once we do so consistently and realize that the sky did not fall, lightning did not strike us down, the world did not end just because we tried something and we weren't amazing at it.

For me, an example of this sort of environment is yoga. Because yoga is a practice I do several times a week, and one that I am not trying to get better at, or become even really "good" at, I have absolutely no attachment to my performance. When I am trying new poses, or attempting something different, I enact a mindset of curiosity. Where does my body feel funny? At what point do I tip over and fall? How do I feel doing a new pose? Where is my edge?

Curiosity acts as a bridge from a rigid point of view. Curiosity moves us from a symphony of stickiness into an expansive terrain of possibility.

We can apply this questioning to other aspects of our life. Why am I feeling irritable today? Why did this person annoy me? What is underneath my resentment? What must I do for myself before attending to matters for other people?

Embodying New Behaviors

After all of this mental work comes the behavioral work. This is the doing part, the "pedal to the metal" aspect of the Waxing Moon time. The court card that correlates to Sagittarius, the phase that this Waxing Moon is in is the Knight of Wands. Knights are curious. Shame is a word the Knight does not understand. They do what they want when they want. They are in search of excitement, adventure, and new opportunities. When a Knight comes up, these cards are harbingers and messengers of change. Depending on your particular scenario, they can be the canary in the coal mine, or Falkor in The Neverending Story. Either way, they are an indicator that change is on the horizon, and that it is time to invoke new behaviors around certain important matters at hand.

Sometimes, we just have to do things. Sometimes it isn't about overthinking. If at this time, your homework is getting out of your own way and going for it, then that's all there is to do, sugar pie honey cup. The Knight of Wands pops up to remind us that it doesn't have to be so hard. If it is exciting and fun and interesting to us, isn't that all the reward that is needed? If there is an easier way to get results, i.e., aligning our thought patterns with our highest self, our highest dreams and desires, this Knight wants us to invest in that first. If it is time to step into the spotlight more, to share more, be generous, go ahead. If it is time to have fun, get sexy, and enjoy our minutes more, the Knight of Wands is too busy having their own thrills to actually take the time to walk you through your own process, but if they did have that time, they'd say hellllllllll yes honey! The Knight of Wands wants us to dance up that metaphorical mountain, show off our talents, and take a massive bite out of the yummiest enchilada we can find, reveling in the sauce dripping down our necks.

The Knight of Wands pops up to remind us that we are protected as we move forward. Our armor is our grit and our gumption. If we fall off somehow, we are only to get back up again. If we make a mistake, we are only to learn from it. The only way we are failing is if we beat ourselves up about it and quit an important dream. Dreams require work. The road to a dream is winding and usually does not look the way we think it will. It is okay to get lost. It is okay to take a rest. It is not okay to give up if this means giving up on yourself.

If you want things to be different, act differently.
If change is what you are seeking, change. The changes can be small: smiling at yourself in the mirror every day, waking up earlier to meditate. Or they can be large: not apologizing for existing, starting an important project,
Change is always possible. Choice is always available.

Suggested exercise for this week:
Put the Knight of Wands, or its equivalent, on your altar for a week. Every day in the morning, sit at your altar. Ask yourself: Who do I need to embody today to spark my own excitement? Do at least one thing a day that answers that question. See if you feel differently after 6 days of this.

Crystals for clarity and messages: Fluorite, clear quartz, spirit quartz, celestite, Herkimer diamond, topaz
Crystals for action: Bloodstone, carnelian, orange calcite
Crystals for transitions: Ruby in fuchsite, jaspers, agate
Herbs for a clear mind: Rhodiola

Journaling questions:
Where am I craving change?
Where am I afraid of change?
What are some very small habits or behaviors I can change in my everyday life?
What are some very small habits or behaviors I can change in my everyday thinking?
What is a situation in my life that needs a different perspective?
How can I be curious about this? What questions can I ask?
What is one big action I can take this week that will yield results in my life in the future?

*Eva Bianconi, Allison Piovesan, Federica Facchin, Alina Beraudi, Raffaella Casadei, Flavia Frabetti, Lorenza Vitale, Maria Chiara Pelleri, Simone Tassani, Francesco Piva, Soledad Perez-Amodio, Pierluigi Strippoli & Silvia Canaider (2013) "An estimation of the number of cells in the human body," Annals of Human Biology, 40:6, 463-471, DOI: 10.3109/03014460.2013.807878

** I was reconnected to this idea from a workshop on non-violent communication I took from Cecilia Sibony. Thank you, Cecilia, for all of your work on this topic.

What I am working on building and growing for the next week:

Openness + vulnerability - Work towards Cultivating these things over the next couple weeks while I am in Maine - try harder to build Community + make connections with other students in my Cohort.

How I will do this every day:

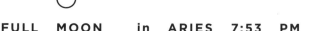

The Rewards of Risk: Celebrating Abundance under a Harvest Moon

"You can't sit around and wait for somebody to say who you are. You need to write it and paint it and do it." —Faith Ringgold

The Full Moon of September rises up strong and slowly from her horizon's nest in the obsidian sky. This Moon is called a Harvest Moon, as it is the Full Moon closest to the equinox. Harvest Moons appear very large and very close to the Earth. This was the Moon that allowed humans to stay up late and collect crops, her nighttime moonbeams falling across the fields and illuminating growth for the gatherers. This Moon is also called the Barley Moon, the Corn Moon, the Autumn Moon, and the Drying Grass Moon, among other names. This September Harvest Moon brings a feeling of completion and appreciation. Take stock of what is time to end so that there is space to begin. This Moon offers abundance and is a harbinger of the changing seasons: the loss of Summer welcomes Autumn.

Looking back is important. We have to look back to see how far we've come. Remember a time when you wanted what you now have. Give thanks to yourself and to the universe for helping you help yourself. Think back to the New Moon last April. What was beginning at that point in your life? What has grown and changed since springtime?

Two days ago, we celebrated Mabon. This Pagan holiday, which is also the Autumnal equinox, is a time of thanksgiving for the harvest as well as a recognition of the darkness knocking on our doors. Name all the lessons that you were lucky enough to be alert to this season. Give thanks by enjoying the chill in the morning air and by recognizing all of the gifts around you: light and shadows both bring openings. Cook for others, count your blessings one by one like the geese that fly overhead, soaring arrows splashed against the slate sky. Clean your home, clear out your closets, organize your cupboards. Reacquaint yourself with the myth of Persephone. Remind yourself why the descent is necessary. Give yourself time to nap or enjoy a long cup of tea. Begin to ease into the Waning Moon time that Autumn correlates with on the Wheel of the Year.

This is also a time of reflection and of easing into the change of quietude. We are now half in and out of daytime and nighttime—the darkness creeps in now, bit by bit, minute by minute. This Moon could serve as a reminder to celebrate how the dark shows us the light. How darkness and light are only perceptions that aim to serve us through their reflections, and both of them fleeting besides. How the light changes and comes around again, and how light fading, the brilliant sunsets, and the glittering grey 9:00 pm sky hold their own poignant reminders that beauty is where one finds it. The clear shift of the seasons before our eyes can grant us the permission to change as well. We can let ourselves rest more, and shed old patterns. We can relinquish preoccupations that hinder us from expressing our courage, inspirations, and our fire. We can utilize the movement of change.

Change is one of the constants that humans fear the most. Our brains are evolved to want short-term answers, and most of us equate change with uncertainty which we correspond with loss which equals failure, disappointment, or lack of resources. Yet change is inevitable. It happens around us every day. The Earth rotates every 24 hours. We lose almost a million skin cells in that time. Seeds transform into stalks which bloom and then fade away to compost into the Earth where they began. Love moves from a spark to infatuation to an unconditional promise. Let this changing season remind us of all of the wonder and excitement that can be unearthed in all different kinds of change.

The allowance of change and the ability to be flexible in the face of transformation is deep wealth. Any time we wish to progress, we will make mistakes. It is not the amount of successes or failures, lined up like marks on a wall, that determine your self-worth. A lot of value can be found in your devotion to continue tending to the soil that nourishes the seeds of your highest ideals.

At this Harvest Moon, this Corn Moon, this tenth lunation of this year, be attuned to where your energy, your efforts must go. When we are harvesting, we have to know what is ripe for plucking. Full Moons bring all the water up, up, up to the surface. That's why most farmers gather their crops at this time: the fruits, herbs, and vegetables are plump and moist, filled with the H2O that the Moon, so close to us, has coaxed up out of the earth with her pull. When we are harvesting, we take only what we need. We leave an offering to the earth. We tend to the soil. We have a plan. We enjoy the fruits of our labor. We share them.

At this Harvest Moon, during this time of change, identify where your sources of abundance come from. Define what abundance means for you and you alone. Think of some tangible ways to keep this feeling fired up through the coming months, to keep the Harvest reverberating through the cold months we have ahead.

Abundance, obviously, is not always equated with a cornucopia of cold hard cash. For some of us, abundance could about possessing a plentitude of love, time, energy, health, inspiration, and creativity. Resources could mean a surplus of ingenuity, connectivity, and emotional support. Right now, it could mean knowing where everything is on your desktop, your room, and in your apartment. It could mean knowing where you stand with your most important relationships. It could mean getting clear on your value systems, your ideals, the mission statements that drive you into wider vantage points. Abundance could mean having the privilege to live in accordance with these ideals every day. Abundance is flexible and generous. Abundance could mean realizing the endless waterfalls of love you possess at any moment. It could be cultivating confidence, finding the bits of calm in the chaos.

Our culture generally equates abundance with MORE, when for many of us abundance is defined as LESS. Less distraction, less clutter, less complication, less obligation, less stress, less unrewarding work and imbalanced relationships. Abundance for you right now could mean getting simpler. Scaling back. Doing less.

For some of us, abundance can also be defined as nothing more than a slight shift. Living life with more awareness. Doing the same things, but with less fear or anxiety. It could mean having or feeling or enjoying the same sort of life you have currently, but developing a deeper relationship with your consciousness, with your experience of that life and the people in it. A more intimate or more profound experience with creativity, spirituality, or time. A different quality of life, a different relationship with conflict, a better quality of now.

Whatever abundance looks like to you at this Harvest Full Moon, name it. Claim it. Wrap your ready hands around it and clasp it against your third eye. Get brave enough to be able to grab your bounty. Speak your truths into existence. Run after this vision through the fog. Feel it rising in your chest like so many bloodstone butterflies. Gulp it down like hot cocoa. Be clear about what risks you'll have to take to get it. Being more vulnerable. Giving yourself more space. Loving yourself enough to put yourself first. Get brave enough to sing to your desires until they can hear you through the throngs.

This Full Moon is in the astrological sign of Aries: the first sign of the zodiac. Consider the Major Arcana Tarot card that correlates to Aries: The Emperor. Let's put the patriarchy aside, let's leave the Daddy issues aspect of this card at the door for the moment. On a cosmic, archetypal level, The Emperor speaks to structures and stability. The Emperor is a card of earthly experience: the King of all of the Kings—imparting their philosophies on a grand scale. The Emperor possesses fire, bravery, wisdom, confidence, and a strong sense of self. This archetype encapsulates the integration of a hawk's eye vision and the day-to-day activities that one must undertake to get oneself to another level. This card can speak to what support one must need as they burst forth. The Emperor also reminds us that we define our empire. Our world, made up of friends, books, plants, throw pillows, tinctures, albums, movies, experiences, commutes, creation, family, food, meditations, behaviors, habits, ideals, is all defined, selected, and created by the self. You and only you decide this, ultimately: from what you eat to how you speak to what you learn to where you go to how deeply you breathe in. At this time, at this Harvest Moon, consider what world you are in and what world you are building. Reflect on what is working for who you are becoming and what is not. The fire of this Full Moon can help you move forward.

When manifesting abundance, our energy and intent must operate from a place of abundance. She's generous: abundance gives as much as she receives. Abundance knows that one person's gain is not their loss. Abundance is not in competition with anyone else. She's got her own pebbled path in the forest that she lays down one stone at a time. Abundance is patient. She knows that so long as her efforts are enjoyable, and her work is important to her, that in time the reward might only be the satisfaction of years spent in flow, hours spent in splendor, refining a craft. Pleasure is the name of abundance's game—giggles, delight, perversion, subversion, and irreverence can be found in the ample folds between abundance's legs. Abundance believes in herself. Years of trying to prove everything to anyone around her taught her this the hard way. Abundance thrives in space, and ample time: no breathlessly rushing to therapy for her! At this Full Moon time, consider the energy you are bringing into your space of manifestation. Consider the energy you bring to a space. Does it match your ideals of abundance?

When we are creatively manifesting and get caught in snags, we can utilize balancing actions to reconnect with an abundant source. If we feel lonely, we reach out to others. If we feel broke, we name all that we have, and then we give something away. If someone is cruel to us, we are kind to ourselves, then kind to others. These actions remind us that we have the ability to shape and change our world from a place of abundance. We can invoke balance in this way.

This Full Moon could also be bringing up, very clearly, what it is that must leave your life. In order to move on, we must honor completion. Something ending is a testament to the dedication that you cultivated continuously, whether the process was especially tender or heartbreakingly hard. Acknowledging a conclusion—whether it is an overripe rotting, or something simply ready to come to an organic finish like putting a favorite book back on the shelf after you've read it— describes a mature awareness. It is a gift to feel full and it is a blessing to follow the calling to begin again. Honor wherever you are in your process under this bright Moon of balance.

It's all you, darling one. You are the one. The one you have been waiting for. You are the best thing that has ever happened to you. You become this as much as you let it. May you be brave enough to let go where you must. May you be brave enough to ask for what it is that you want. May you be brave enough to move forward with grace, courage, and the flicker of a steady flame.

Say please and say thank you.

Suggested Affirmation: "I am the one I have been waiting for. It is safe for me to operate from a place of abundance. My abundance vibrates from the inside out."

A Harvest Moon Spell for Abundance

You will need:
4 candles, any size and any color you feel called to use for your particular desires
Dried cinnamon, rosemary, olive oil
Honey or sugar
4 pieces of paper
Any other items: images, drawings, deities, food, offerings, Tarot cards, crystals, or objects that symbolize abundance, bravery, and courage for you presently.

Get comfortable and cozy. Set up your altar. Cast your circle of protection. You may wish to line your candles up in a row, or create a square shape out of them, one at each corner. Four is the number of stability, endurance, strength, structure, and devotion. You may wish to put any symbols of abundance, or of courage and energy inside of the candle's square.

Charge your candles. As you anoint your candles with cinnamon, rosemary, oil, and a dash of sweetness, focus your energy on imbuing your candles with love, devotion, inspiration, and confidence (and any other attributes you'd like highlighted at this time).

The first candle symbolizes all that you have: the place of abundance you are operating from.

The second candle symbolizes all that you would like to unfold in the coming months: the most important, slightly risky things you desire.

The third candle symbolizes the belief system and mindset you would have to step into in order to receive those desires.

The fourth candle symbolizes the consistent behaviors you would have to devote yourself to in order to create those desires: how you embody those desires.

Close your eyes and center yourself. Think about all you have and where you are abundant. Allow yourself to soften into gratitude for all that you have and all that you are.

On your piece of paper, write down all that you are currently grateful for and all that you have. Stop writing when you feel really fantastic. Slide the piece of paper under the first candle and light it. Chant, sing, recite your spell, or say anything you'd like out loud.

Close your eyes and center yourself. Think about what you really, really want at this moment. Allow yourself to receive this energy inside your body. Allow yourself to fill your body up with these wonderful things.

On your piece of paper, write down what you are attracting in the present tense. Slide the piece of paper under your second candle and light it. Chant, sing, recite your spell, or say anything you'd like out loud.

Close your eyes and center yourself. Think about how you would have to set your belief systems and mindset to be someone who is comfortable with receiving all that they desire. Imagine how this mindset would be reflected in your language, how you respond to challenges, and how you speak to yourself.

On your piece of paper, write down words or sentences that illustrate this mindset or belief

system. Slide the piece of paper under your second candle and light it. Chant, sing, recite your spell, or say anything you'd like out loud.

Close your eyes and center yourself. See yourself behaving in the ways you must in order to let more abundance, more love, more goodness into your life. Let yourself see your desires playing out.

On your piece of paper, write down words or sentences that illustrate these repeated actions. Slide the piece of paper under your second candle and light it. Chant, sing, recite your spell, or say anything you'd like out loud.

Spend time in front of your candles/altar. Get all of these different aspects that contribute to the whole of your desires charged inside of your cells until you feel excited. Promise yourself you will be brave to call in your harvest in the coming weeks. Watch the dancing flames and align yourself with the fire, the abundance, the sweetness and excitement that comes with harvesting with inspired alignment, intention, and action.

Notes on Full Moon ritual:

What abundance I am working on growing:

What that looks and feels like:

Notes on this month:

Intentions for the next:

OCTOBER 2018
OCTOBER 2ND: LAST QUARTER
OCTOBER 8TH: NEW MOON
OCTOBER 16TH: FIRST QUARTER
OCTOBER 24TH: FULL MOON
OCTOBER 31ST: LAST QUARTER/
SAMHAIN/HALLOWEEN

This bridge month lies between the final harvest of the year and a time of Earth's rest. This month is the time of the witch: time of the thinning veil, and the season of the underworld. It is a time of shedding, of sloughing off the transitions of the past three months, as well as composting the lessons of the past into rich soil for future seeds. Snakes shed, lizards shed, spiders shed—all in the name of losing dead weight, all in the name of growing, all in the name of taking up more space. Take a cue from the wild: shake off the old parts that no longer have meaning. Some of the workbook prompts will help to guide you in deepening your connection to intuition, with alchemizing love and desire to movement, with considering your relationships with your ancestors, and with transforming guilt, envy, and rage for better uses.

The month starts out in the sign of Libra. This sign rules Justice, one of our cards of the year. (If you use a Marseille style deck, card 11 corresponds with Strength). The layers of the themes of the Justice card are many—psychic, karmic, and societal. We view all of these themes through the lens of truth. Not what has been told to us as the truth, but what we as humans, as beings with hearts and minds, know to be true. That every human being deserves to be safe, protected, and respected.

This card speaks to defining and refining "the truth" as it pertains to you only. Creating balance, remaining clear in your truths, and behaving in accordance with your own ideals—independent from any expectation—figures prominently. When we begin to stand in our personal truths, it is common for us to also become more in touch with our pain. The pain of feeling wronged. The pain of injustice. The pain that may have protected us at one point, but that we now feel ready to slowly release from our bodies. What do you need in this moment of shedding that no longer serves you? What do you need to feel safe as you release your pain?

Karmically, we bring balance by right thought and right action. If we want equality, we work for it on others' behalf. If we want to be loved, we love freely. If we wish to be listened to, we listen deeply. This is also a card of energetic and behavioral cord-cutting—of breaking away from harmful patterns. Some of these might be literally in your DNA, passed down from generations. It is your responsibility to bring the positive balance into your familial line, chosen family included.

Justice wants to bring the truth, and wants us to act in our truths. This month, consider your actions. Release the behavior, the words, and the thoughts that do not correspond with your highest alignment and your own sacred truths. Consider the truth that love speaks and let it guide you in navigating your Moonlit journey.

October 2018 Astrology Insights
by Diego Basdeo

October 5th: Venus Retrograde

October 8th: New Moon in Libra, Square Pluto in Capricorn / Lilith Conjunct Mars in Aquarius

October 24th: Full Moon in Taurus / Moon Conjunct Uranus at 0 degrees Taurus /
Sun conjunct Venus Retrograde in Scorpio / Squaring Pluto conjunct Mars in Aquarius / Jupiter conjunct Mercury in Scorpio

The truth is out there, but so are lies.

Call in clarity, call in completion, call in balance in all things. The New Moon in Libra is squaring Pluto in Capricorn on the 8th and it is directly confronting issues of social privilege and power. The Moon in Libra has an eye for flaws—a keen eye for what is missing or out of place. These dogwhistle tactics are exactly the kind of thing a Moon in Libra will pick up. While Libra is notoriously diplomatic, it still represents the scales of justice, and a Moon in Libra is often on the winning side. We are being asked to take an eye to our emotional environment. What is out of place? What needs revising?

Meanwhile in Aquarius, Mars (passion, fire, anger) is right next to Lilith (disruption and disobedience). Mars is hot pursuit and Lilith is the righteous rage. I see this playing out in a few ways. One is a manarchist, a macho-rugged individualist type with an agenda to create chaos regardless of who it affects, simply for the pure sense of independence. Another is the tamer of chaos, someone who knows chaos intimitely and can remain grounded and themselves in any situation. Which one are you?

Venus retrograde usually lasts about forty days and forty nights. If this rings a bell for you, you are probably familiar with the story of Jesus in the desert being tempted by the devil for forty days and forty nights. The word Lucifer means light-bringer, and refers to the morning star (Isaiah 14:12). All mythology serves to tell a history of social mores, conditions, and circumstances of existence. Our stories are psychological almanacs that help us navigate our social and emotional worlds. This month is a meditation on relationship. The relationship between mythology and reality, between love and friendship, between the past and the future. We are doing shadow work around self worth and its relationship to love, friendship, and spirit. The morning star can sometimes be precarious in the underworld, stretching our emotional, spiritual, and financial resources.

Under these phases in Scorpio we descend into the underworld with Venus, watching shadows lurch from our affections and reveal subconscious intentions. Our desire to merge and melt intensifies. Know that the brighter your light, the longer the shadow.

During Venus retrograde we could be clinging to past relationships. Write an obituary, lay some flowers, set it out to sea like a Viking funeral! Let dead things die. Let the past rest in peace. Pluto waits for no one. Let go or be dragged.

I think of the radical message of Whitney Houston in her biggest love song "I Will Always Love You," and the stark contrast it has with the highly relatable "I Have Nothing". Venus retrograde in conversation with Lilith and Mars is conflicted. She begs "don't make me close one more door," then pleads "I don't wanna hurt anymore". This is the tired and heart aching Venus. The end is hard for the Venusian. Because Venus retrograde is so uncommon—it occurs only about 7% of the time—there is a rare air, a fatedness that is often associated with love and relationship around this time. We have an opportunity to take a look at our obsessions, our powers of intuition, and see where the crux of belief and creation divine their way through us because we "can't run from myself, there's nowhere to hide".

This astrology is also connected to how pleasure or displeasure informs our day to day lives. How can pleasure be a radical action? How can pleasure not only be what we are guided towards, but what we are guided with?

I think of shame. There are those of us who are forced to live in shadow, for who we are or who we love. The New Moon is in conversation with the planet of fate, Pluto. This brings a very special highening of intuitive power and X-ray vision on yours and others' motivation. Because we may be able to see more into the darker realms of uncommunicated information, we may tend to think a little darker as well. Remember, dark can be compelling, shocking, and believable. but it isn't always the truth. This is a time for real love. Real truth.

Towards the end of the month Jupiter and Mercury will be in conjunct in Scorpio. What's important with this during the Full Moon is to move towards gaining greater perspective. Jupiter is the planet of expansion, its energy goes OUT, while Scorpio is all about introspections and the interior of things. With Jupiter working in tandem with knowledge seeking Mercury we are quickly attracted to the dark or secret truths that, most of the time, we are usually afraid to look at. The Full Moon will be conjunct Uranus right at the border of Taurus. The Sun will be lighting up the Moon right behind Venus retrograde. This could bring in energetic deep release and invitations in unforeseen opportunities concerning our relationships.

We can learn from our self-destructive tendencies right now if we're careful to balance our fear with presence. If we are always waiting for someone to take advantage of us, we eventually will be proven right. The key is to wade in knowing with your head above the water. Breathe. Don't forsake connection for paranoia.

If you are having trouble letting go, get grounded in your self worth. Maybe you are remembering yourself at your best, in love, happy, optimistic, and having good sex. Those parts of you are still you. You own that feeling. There are still new feelings yet to have. Allow release to change you.

OCTOBER 2ND : LAST QUARTER MOON in CANCER 4:45 AM PST,12:00 AM MOONRISE, 2:14 PM PST MOONSET

Dancing with the In-Between: Romancing Your Intuition

"Ninety-nine percent of you is invisible and untouchable." — R. Buckminster Fuller

The beginning of the magical month of October, like almost every other month in this High Priestess/Justice/Strength year starts off in a Waning Moon. It ends in a Waning Moon as well: two potent time periods to throw any stubborn scraggily snags in your belief system into the bonfire and watch it burn down to ash. October, a bridge month, is an opportune time to compost what is holding us back from unleashing our true power. We may feel pulls to reflect the Earth's current season and sink into quietude. We begin to settle into our own interiors with more familiarity. As we do so, our intuition rises up to take her seat on an onyx throne. Her crown is the Moon. Her shawl is made of stars. Her scepter is carved of petrified whale ear bone, labradorite, and all the spaces we are privy to when we close our eyes.

Our own unique intuition is a priceless gift. Like self-love, it can never be developed too much. Like self-care, the more we invest, the more we gain. Yet developing our intuition isn't taught in schools. Respecting and listening to our intuition does not always come naturally to all of us. Culturally, intuition links arms with feelings. Our society's viewpoint of feelings remains, unfortunately, in the deranged, disrespected feminine. The space of the Moon, the cackle, the cosmic coincidence, the wild werewoman, the oracle, and the crone. Intuition primarily exists in liminal spaces. The pause between an inhale and an exhale. A knowing so deep it resides beyond language or explanation. Precognition: a knowing before the knowing. Uncategorizable and unquantifiable. A deep and resonant well within. A gleaming orb of possibility that is only accessed by graceful digging and willful diving down, twenty thousand leagues under the self.

Intuition has been largely dismissed or ridiculed by the overculture, except for when profit is involved, of course. The military invested 20 million dollars into the Stargate Project to research "remote viewing"—otherwise known as using clairvoyance to spy on and detect enemies. Major companies in the U.K. use dowsing rods, a.k.a. divining rods, a.k.a. "witch sticks" to find water. Yet people who act on their inner guidance and trust are frequently deemed "crazy." Many of us stop daydreaming and creating and making up worlds as soon as we stop being children. Our imaginary friends fade. We still remember their names. Our daydreams collect dust. We still remember their endings.

Everyone is intuitive and everyone can access their intuition in a multitude of ways. Intuition shows up in these ways: in dreams, in clairvoyance (visions, seeing pictures or symbols), in clairaudience (hearing voices or sounds), clairsentience (clear feeling, usually with the body, such as hairs standing up), claircognizance (clear knowing), empathy (taking on the feelings of other people) and channeling/mediumship (being the vessel for spirit, guides, ancestors, and other messengers). There are other aspects on the spectrum of intuitive ability, such as taste, smell, seeing colors, seeing auras, seeing past lives, being able to communicate with animals, being able to communicate with plants, being able to communicate with beings such as angels, fairies, mermaids and more, being able to read objects (psychometry) and being able to recognize ghosts/energy in a room or space.

There are hundreds of different ways to access your intuition that include meditating, talking to your guides aloud, exercising, walking in nature, using Tarot cards and Oracle cards, breath work, paying attention to signs and signals, using a pendulum, practicing meditation, Reiki, hypnosis, Ouija boards, candle divination, channeling, throwing bones, scrying, free writing, reading tea leaves, palmistry, herbal allies, creating art, and moving your body, among many others. A lot of what these aforementioned encompass is patience and listening. Turning inward. What all these activities need is time, patience, and trust.

Perfect trust is needed to keep going with strengthening your intuition. You are trusting yourself inherently. You are trusting that the messages or sensations or energetic shifts are real. You are absolutely trusting messages, colors, feelings, sensations in any way they appear. Trust your noticing. How much are we taught to trust the intangible, especially when it comes from inside us? This may be a challenging first step when we are trying to develop our intuition.

The Ego wants to swoop in and heckle. The Ego wants to stop us from sharing and trusting. The Ego says, Don't be vulnerable. Don't experiment. The Ego says, You need Proof. How could you know that you don't know that you don't know anything? The Ego can be the 97-foot concrete wall that stands between us and free flow, free form, free reception. The Ego can shut down a lot of natural, intuitive processes.

Don't get me wrong, I love a good Ego myself. In fact, I think many of us who have lived in abuse and through attempted degradation and exploitation could deeply benefit from having a courageous, confident Ego. However, in the case of intuition-building, the Ego is really only going to get in the way. Because the Ego, Goddess bless it, is attached. And intuitive or psychic work is in the spirit of service. And the spirit of service is one of non-attachment.

When I first started giving readings, a lot of information would come in and through me. Frequently I would filter some of it. For one, it felt weird. I'm a private person. I respect other's privacy. How could I possibly say this deeply personal thing to a stranger? What if I were wrong? What if I hurt their feelings? The ways in which I receive my information shifts. One day it could be through meditation right before a client, or through cheesy '80s song lyrics that I literally didn't know I knew as I'm shuffling cards (clients who have been there for that time period, please forgive me!), or as a deceased relative who shows up as an energy field behind the client. The list of different ways my intuition comes in goes on and on.

Over time, and with practice, I began to accept my role as a messenger. My only job was to act as a conduit between my client and source. Becoming inherently unattached to the outcome of the information was essential. Any part of me that relied on my information being "true" or "false" was Ego talking. It was me, Little Miss Earthly Ego Pants. Not Source, not spirit, not service. Now, I just hand over the information. I have perfect trust it is coming in for reasons of divinity and helpfulness, so long that my own channel is clear.

When working on developing our OWN intuition for ourselves, we must also develop perfect trust. A very easy way to do this is to not rely on the internet, guidebooks, friends, or professionals for answers. Try coming up with answers for yourself. If six very large, very talkative squirrels show up for you in one short day, try to answer what this could mean for you, apart from any search or book. Literally say out loud: "These squirrels mean _____ for me right now." Make this a practice. Become your own authority.

Another way to practice trust is to trust your noticing. If patterns, words, objects, colors, or anything else is coming up for you in a short period of time, just trust it. Follow your noticing. Buy the book four people have mentioned to you. Really really LISTEN to the lyrics of the song that has come up on the radio, randomly, three times in the last two days. These noticings are portals. The Waning Moon is the perfect time to blur the lines of different realms, different worlds, different planes of realities. When something is trying to get your attention, if a symbol or image or word really resonates with you, work with it. Your noticing, your gut reaction can be enough to make it valid, enough to make it a gateway. Walk through.

How do you know your intuition is speaking to you, and that it isn't fear or anxiety? There is a very easy exercise you can do. Sitting or laying down peacefully, close your eyes and take a few deep breaths until you are as relaxed as possible. Tell yourself a fact that is irrefutable: your name, your address. Notice how you feel in your body and mind. Notice where this knowing comes from. Now, in that same relaxed state, tell yourself something that you know to be an absolute lie. Note what happens in your body. Note where in your body or mind anything shifts or changes.

Intuition thrives in calm, quiet spaces. Untouched natural settings with interesting energy increase our ability to connect with Source. Spirits and faeries love to hang in riverbanks, caves, and inside of tree hollows. What spaces does your intuition thrive in? All this means is that this is a setting where you feel calm, at peace, and where you easily receive insights and answers.

Intuition thrives in flexible mindsets. Are you so rigid you can't see other ways of doing things? Other schedules, other points of view? How many times a day or a week can you pause and ask yourself *What do I want to do now?*, and be able to answer that? Moreover, how often are you able to give yourself that time/thing you want? Every intuitive must have at least a few hours a week (or even a few hours in a day) in which they can daydream, meditate, do nothing, walk, take a bath, a hike, lay down, close their eyes, etc. Intuition needs check-ins. Check-ins need follow-through. This is also how a trusting relationship is built.

The ways in which intuition comes through are completely different from person to person. There is no better way to be psychic. Don't let the ways in which you are not able to easily access your intuition block the ways in which you are. Because I am a visual artist, for years I focused on the mindset that my psychic abilities "should" be clairvoyance. That's just not the case. Yes, anyone can become anything with practice. I have no doubt that with practice and effort I could become fluently clairvoyant. Yet I had so many other ways my abilities came through that I was ignoring— including receiving clear pictures in my mind of art work I needed to make, which is psychic in its own way. If information is coming through, let it come through without judgment. Honor it. Respect it. Trust.

Prioritize your intuition. Let it stretch out in your decision making: a mauve-colored jaguar flicking his tail towards the correct path. Don't second-guess your intuition. Allow it to guide you in your waking life. Know it can be a shield, a protection device, an answer and a question. Work with it. Learn from it.

Romance your intuition. Give it a name. Ask it what activities it desires. Make a date with your intuition. Write it a letter on lavender scented paper. Let it write you a letter back. Promise you'll feed it with plenty of water, mugwort tea, and Tarot cards. Romance your Self. Ask yourself, at least several times a week, what you desire that day. What you want to eat, where you'd like to go. Give yourself time to daydream and opportunities to fantasize. Allow yourself time every week to wander somewhere safe. To make collages, free write, gaze at the wall or into a crystal ball. Make eye contact with the Moon.

Intuition is a gift with unquantifiable gifts. Sometimes accessing those gifts and trusting them takes time to unfold. Sometimes outcomes take time to surface. We *are* dealing with non-linear time, after all. Hopefully working with the Moon's cycles has shown you the richness that rewards you when living in spiral time. Continuing to have compassion and patience as we learn to interpret our own specific intuitive language, system, and signs is a fundamental part of this process.

Suggested exercises for this week:

The Moon as a crystal ball.
The Moon is a perfect scrying device. This week, walk outside in the moonlight. Really look at her, really see what is reflecting back at you. "Intuitive" comes from the Latin intuit: to gaze at, contemplate. What are you looking at? For one person, she acts as a mirror to our most vulnerable, gleaming insides. To another, it is just a solid rock, comprised of dead volcanoes, hardened lava flows, and multiple object impacts. Another person looks up and remembers that last time she was half in shadow. What shifted when she decided to turn inside? Do this for as many nights as you'd like.

Keep an intuition journal.
This could detail symbols, signs, images, sentences, or other information that came to you in spell work, dreams, Tarot readings, meditation, your daily life, etc. It is very useful to look back and see patterns and themes over the weeks, months, and years.

Ask your higher power/intuition to provide the right messages.
Before you start your day, ask your intuition to give you all of the information or messages you need. Assure it you will be open to receiving the help and will act on the messages accordingly.

Ask your higher power/intuition to solve a problem for you.
If you are at the point where you have a strong and loving relationship with your intuition, engage with it.If there is an issue you are facing that you are having issues with, turn it over to your intuition. Before you go to bed, or in the morning, tell your intuition what you need help with clearly. Allow yourself to detach, let go from the issue, as you hand it over to your genius to take care of, or provide more answers or clarity.

Journaling questions:
What are my intuitive super powers?
When was a time that my intuition served me well?
When was a time I ignored my intuition, and what happened?
What problem or issue will I hand over to my intuition/the universe/Source/the Goddess (etc.) to help me with this week?
What exercise(s) will I commit to experimenting with that will aid my intuition?

Crystals that support psychic ability: Celestite, apophylllite, moonstone, Herkimer diamond, lapis lazuli, clear quartz
Herbs/vitamins that help support intuition: Vitamin B12, mugwort, motherwort, skullcap, valerian, blue vervain

The Love in Truth: Air Alchemy on a New Moon

"Love takes off masks that we fear we cannot live without and know we cannot live within."
— James Baldwin

On a Monday on the second week of October, our New Moon rises at dawn. A New Moon for our bridge month, our transition month, our month of apples, of Halloween, this rare month of two Last Quarter Moons. This New Moon is a natural way to start our week: in the dark, in a state of new beginnings. She'll rise with the Sun, though we can't see her. And she'll set at sunset, though her motion is invisible to us: existing more as a feeling inside of us than something we can trace with our retinas.

The Moon's reflection changes, changes, changes every single day. Really it's the angle and our perceptions that change, but it appears so very real to us all the same. And we let her change, we accept the shifts—sometimes we can make out the Sea of Rains, the Bay of Billows, the Ocean of Storms (names of the lunar seas that were named around 1651), as a face made out of shadows, other times, we know we only get to see glimmers of her (Michael Carlowicz, *The Moon*, New York: Abrams, 2007, p. 115). Some evenings, like tonight, we can't find her. She's hiding in plain sight, obstructed by sunlight. We can't see her yet we trust she is still there. We can't see her, and we name this emptiness a fresh start, a beginning of whatever we'd like.

Nature all around us changes, changes, changes every single day. The air turns colder. The animals are starting to hibernate. The trees at the edge of the forest turn red, then orange, then yellow. The ice fields are melting. All of us, every day in every way, are changing, changing, changing. Shaped by our interactions, our reflections, and hard realizations, we either stumble into or finally find—after so many hours of brushing the dirt away—an engraved marble tablet of truth. As we discover and uncover new truths, as we compost old belief systems that we once took to be the most truest truism, we have choices within. We own our own decisions to make these changes hard or easier, with our awareness and allowing of them to unfold as they need to. When the pain comes, when the choices are complicated, we let ourselves cry, we let the uncomfortableness move through us. When the tears have dried, when the journal pages have been filled, we come back around to the clear messages that reside within us.

The orbits of the planets change, the phases of the Moon change, the timing of the sunrise changes, and we all accept these changes. We too are changing. Everyone around us on this planet, whether they are interested in evolution or are simply dealing with life, are shifting, alchemizing, transforming, and changing as well. We understand this cognitively, but allowing change in our own lives can be hard. At this New Moon time, can you let yourself change in a positive and evolutionary manner? On this New Moon Monday, can you allow yourself to see others as evolving as well?

Like the Moon, we are allowed to move from one state to another. Our core soul can intrinsically stay the same while our behaviors morph or identity jumps into new territory. Under this New Moon that we can feel but not see, we open our imaginations to alchemy. We can bridge different aspects of our souls, different facets of our personalities, during this bridge month time. We can hyphenate until we can no longer count the hyphens—until they become their own constellation of dashes, an endless sea of vibrations that buoy us. We can declare "Yes AND YES AND" when we count our different states, when we explain who we are to ourselves and our loved ones. We don't have to limit our becoming. We can embody the most expansive bridge, a rainbow curving beyond the horizons of what our eyes can see.

The Earth is undergoing necessary alchemy, into a period of rest. We too must alchemize from time to time. Ancient alchemists were obsessed with changing matter: with turning base metals into precious substances, with modifying the make-up of the elements, with finding the recipes for immortality elixirs, and finding cure-alls for the human condition. They were hung up on the magical and mystical, yet their ways and findings ironically morphed into modern science. Their elemental theories still remain influential to many magical practices today.

Now we know that alchemy as the ancients thought it so is not possible: we ourselves cannot change gold into silver, coal into chrysopoeia. But we weave golden threaded webs of faith, and speak the silvery suggestions of innovative philosophies into being. We can alchemize anger into action. We can alchemize inspiration into creation, compost guilt into generosity. We must alchemize hardship into healing.

Many alchemists used "imaginatio vera," or "true imagination." Jung saw "active imagining" as a bridge between our consciousness and our subconscious. We can imagine building bridges in our own lives. We can move around the energy inside of us and alter our emotions. We can discern between what we want at this time and what we truly need. Take your imagination seriously and let it remain a lighthouse through the darkening days.

This New Moon is in Libra. Libra is an air sign, the seventh sign on the wheel of the zodiac. Libra rules the seventh house: the house of partnerships. A Moon in Libra could have us looking to others for validation or recognition. People may pop up into your life at this time to show you where you still need to learn lessons. Libra, along with Taurus, is ruled by Venus. From a spell perspective, this New Moon could be favorable for love spells, abundance spells, beauty spells, money spells, and relationship spells. You may wish to call on help and ask for cooperation from others in your life at this New Moon. This New Moon could be made up of peppermint and roses, gold plated chocolate and morning sex. Or, the disconnect between who you are and how others perceive you could be highlighted in a bitter fashion. Let the truth of how you love and what you value guide your intentions and actions at this New Moon. Align your intentions with your actions.

The Tarot card that correlates with the sign of Libra is Justice. This card, in most decks, is in the middle of the entire Major Arcana—the ultimate balance between the lessons of the evolution of the self, and the integrations of the superconsciousness of the collective. The themes of the Justice card are, well, justice oriented. How we define it and revise it, as well as truth, balance, harmony, relationships, and karma. In traditional RWCS decks, the archetype of Justice holds a sword in one hand, symbolizing truth, and getting to the heart of matters. In her other hand are the scales, that ancient symbol of balance beyond the mortal realm. It is said that Maat, the ancient Egyptian goddess of cosmic balance, creation, honor, and truth, would place your heart on one side of the scale, and a feather on the other. If your heart was lighter than or the same weight as the feather, you would go on to the afterlife.

It is here that the Justice card evokes the aspect of karma: the actions we undertake in order to evolve and move forward in service of our own particular truths. The Justice card resonates deeply with karma, or the idea that your intentions, behaviors, and actions have a very real consequence on your life. This card can be about leaving behind "an eye for an eye" expectation on someone who has done you wrong. Their behavior will have its own consequence known only to them—their punishment, in part, is living in a harmful way. Justice wants us to get clear about living in our own truths, on keeping our own actions clear and kind, not worried about the perceptions of others, nor their actions. Concern yourself with keeping your side of the street clean, not being obsessed with all the trash in someone else's backyard.

We are in a Justice year: $2 + 0 + 1 + 8 = 11$, the number that Justice in the Major Arcana correlates with. This year is also a High Priestess year ($1 + 1 = 2$), which was touched on in the July portion of this workbook. The Justice card in a Justice year means that issues of justice, of collective truths, will be in prominent placement in all our lives. We will be revising and rebuilding ideas around collective personal justice and collective personal truths. We will be cutting ties with old, toxic lineage patterns and programming that perpetuate suffering and harm. We are seeing how the law is, in this country, very frequently, designed to benefit those writing the law. How decayed our systems are. We are seeing how much rebuilding must be done, how many reparations are owed. We are seeing how much the collective depends on our participation.

Many of us on this planet right now have the opportunity to cut cords with harmful patterns that have passed down for hundreds, if not thousands, of years from generation to generation. This will in turn heal, or cause less damage for those in the present and future. What does this look like, practically? No longer staying in abusive relationships. Modeling kindness and vulnerability to others. Standing up for what we believe in, holding ourselves and others accountable, and bravely speaking our truth. Holding ourselves accountable, and redefining our truth. Living our lives as honestly as possible. No longer getting caught up in pretense, appearance, and civility. No longer associating ourselves with those that cause violence, or perpetuate violence with the silence of complicity.

Stepping into one's truth isn't always easy, but it will set you free. At the very least, living your truth will lighten your heart. Some of your heaviness will subside after you no longer accept falsities and abuse in your sphere. When we are in a process of cutting cords with a toxic lineage, we must also be clear about what we will grow that will take its place far into the future, our future. Profound manifestation is made not so much in dwelling in our missteps, or the origins of our harm, but in tilling the soil of a new path, putting the focus on a different way forward altogether. Clarity comes from acting in our loving truth. Where must you step into your truth at this New Moon?

The Justice card in a Justice year also highlights how much we are taught to obey entire belief systems as truths on both an individual level and on a global level. For thousands of years, we've watched and engaged in belief systems that are absolutely untrue, yet that have shaped laws and motivated millions towards hate, violence, and domination. These beliefs are introduced to us in fairy tales, movies, and in classic myths, to attempt to posit how these manmade manufactured beliefs stem from some correct universal order. For years, we've watched lies being disguised as truth. We see how very arbitrary the truth can be when it is in service of greed or selfishness. We are currently dismantling these systems and creating more loving definitions of what the truth is when it is here to bring loving balance to the whole. We can integrate our most sacred meaning of our truth into the collective and watch it take flight.

The element that corresponds to Libra is air. Air is life, clouds, wind, the horizon of the East, thought forms, communication, the heron touching down, the hawk soaring like an arrow in the sky, the dragonfly alighting on the water lily. Oxygen is what all life forms on the planet need to live. Air holds snow particles and moves rainstorms. Wind scatters seeds as presents to the Earth's life. Air rules whispers and opera and emails and lectures and books and karaoke. In the Tarot, air corresponds to the suit of swords: the suit that is about communication, relationships and relating, the truth, ideas, thoughts, conflict, communication, our brain chemistry, and our nervous system. In witchcraft, air is called upon when we wish to invoke imagination, intelligence, consciousness, movement, messages, innovation, inspiration, clarity, communication, and perspective. What qualities do you want to invoke during this New Moon time?

If we are alchemizing at this time, this October New Moon will bring it in through the plane of intelligence. Mental alchemy consists of combining the different processes of air. Paying attention, increasing awareness, engaging in conscious observation of one's thoughts and mental patterns, accessing more intelligence by learning, speaking our needs and desires clearly, and opening one's mind to imaginative possibilities are all ways we transform and evolve. This New Moon time is a favored time to spend with these activities. She's a blank slate, a turning page, a message waiting to be deciphered. This phase is a pause in our previously programmed cosmic movie: the moment the screen is blank, before the story begins. What new stories are you ready to see on the cosmic stage that is your destiny?

Write them down, 1-2-3. Sing them out to the sky, loud and proud. Spell them all out using the element of air. Breathe out your own fog on your cold bedroom window, and write your desires on the glass, as an invisible secret only you know about. Close your eyes and play what you wish to see happen on the screen on the other side of your third eye. Allow the different colors and sights to slide into your neuropathways and out into your energy field, seeding your aura with all you wish to attract. On this New Moon Monday, use your sentences as spells. Frequently speak using the language you wish to come back to you, rainbow boomerangs of the clarity you keep.

Like air, you live in multiple dimensions. You are the perceiver and the perceived. The observer and the actor. You integrate your internal thoughts and your external actions to align into an alchemical expression of your most pure and truthful state of being. This state, like air, moves as it must. Being many things at once is a gift: we do not have to trade one state for the other. You get to be not either/or, but yes and yes and yes and absolutely unequivocally all of the things you wish to be and all the ways you need to be them. We don't have to trade one thing for the other; we can move around our different roles like clouds, like space, like orbits in the cosmos. When we go beyond our fixed identities, when we touch base with pure intention, with our real truths, it becomes clear that we can exist exactly how we'd like, when we'd like to, simply by being, simply by knowing, simply by naming. Simply by being aware of all our integrations. Simply by allowing ourselves to the truthfulness of love.

Happy New Moon!

Journaling questions:
Who am I today? Who am I becoming?
What is my truth? How am I living my truth?
What would I like to transition into? On a personal level?
On a soul level? On a professional level? On a creative level?
How do I honor and hold all my different parts?
What are my dreams at this New Moon time?
Who or what is harming my dreams? Who or what is helping my dreams?

Suggested Affirmation: "I am true to myself. I allow and express all of the parts of myself I make my decisions from the present moment of love and truth."

*Thanks to Heather McLendon for inspiring me to focus on the subject of alchemy and transitions.

A Bridge Mirror Spread for a New Moon of Alchemy

This is a spread that asks you to be ready to alchemize between two states of being. After you do this spread, you may wish to use a card or two or three or eleven for your New Moon altar. You may wish to honor your truth and use the element of air in a way that is particular to your own brilliant imagination.

Go through your deck and pick out a card that truthfully illustrates the energy state you are in, or what you are overly identifying with at this time. Put it in the Card 1 position.

Go through your deck and pick out a card that illustrates what you really, really want, or want to change into or integrate at this time. Put it in the Card 2 position.
Pull out the Justice card, and put it in the middle. (See diagram for the rest of the card pulls/ placements.)

Card 1: The state I am in presently.
Card 2: The state I wish to be in/transition into, either in the future as a goal, or on a more consistent basis.
Now shuffle the cards:
Card 3: What next steps do I need to take for immediate embodiment?
Card 4: How do I stay in alignment with this?
Card 5: What will need to be changed, in my behavior, in my next steps?
Card 6: What is an easy way to change this?
(Justice)
Card 7: What freedom will this truthful embodiment grant me?
Card 8: What challenges come up with this truth?
Card 9: How do I get over this fear, or any upcoming challenges around this transition?
Card 10: What is the ultimate outcome of my desired transitioned state? How is this ultimately in service to my evolution, and the evolution of the collective?

You can interpret and look at this spread in a number of ways.

You can look at the cards one by one, and interpret them in this way.
You can take the cards as they reflect one another: for example cards 1 & 2, 3 & 4, and so forth. If a relationship between the cards is especially intriguing to you, maybe that's the only one you focus on at this time. You can always come back to this spread over the next 6 months.

You can see what element came up the most: Wands, Cups, Major Arcana, etc., and think about what elements can help you, and what elements you must embody. For example, if you got mostly Cups, your process may be more internal, spiritual, and intuitive, and if you got a multitude of Wands, it might be time for you to become what you want, and go after what you want. This might feel uncomfortable at first, because it is.

If you are looking at it as a whole, you can see the first half of the semi-circle (the four cards before Justice) as being what is building presently in your life, what you are transitioning towards, what to work on consciously in your life, and what hurdles or challenges you may face, internally or externally. You can view the second half of the semi-circle (the cards after Justice) as what may be hidden, what energies are to be cultivated, and cards that support your loving truths.

You can also look at it as a mirror; all of these cards are archetypes inside you that you already possess, and you may wish to focus on one or two to bring these qualities and energies up in your daily life as you move through the transitions of the season.

A Bridge Mirror Spread for a New Moon of Alchemy
Diagram

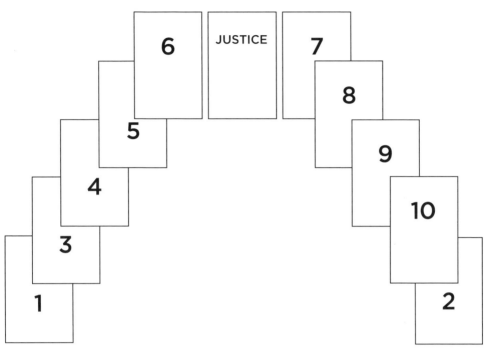

Notes on card pull:

Card 1:

Card 3:

Card 4:

Card 5:

Card 6:

Card 7:

Card 8:

Card 9:

Card 10:

Card 2:

OCTOBER 16TH: FIRST QUARTER in CAPRICORN
11:02AM PST 1:57 PM PST MOONRISE
Survival Spells: Structuring Self-Care

"If you don't like something, change it. If you can't change it, change your attitude about it."
— Maya Angelou

This Tuesday, the Moon decides to climb up into the sky, gleaming wider and wider at midday. She's a First Quarter Moon, a bowl of light holding our dreams peering back at us through the trees. So high above our heads, yet she feels so close. If we close our eyes after gazing into her milky glow, her imprint lingers easily inside our skull. She reminds us that it is wonderful to show off and ask for attention if that is what we need, so long as we don't confuse attention with love. She tells us its okay to feel shy inside, yet enact daring deeds. Our fear comes and goes. The beauty we've created remains. She whispers that some of the greatest shifts take place in a tiny, quiet moment. She wants us to hold our shaky shadows with as much compassion and space as we would for a newborn starling, cradled in our palms. This First Quarter Waxing Moon wants us to notice the messages from our inside and the outside with equal attention.

A Waxing Moon in Capricorn is good for spell work around structure, discipline, boundaries, ambitions, career, desires, health, and ownership. This is an opportune time to put your magic, attention, and focus on what you wish to build. A desire blueprint started at the New Moon really starts to take a skeleton form, bones and teeth showing, at a Waxing Moon. Focusing on long-range plans would fit nicely into an October Waxing Capricorn Moon. We can be impatient, but a Capricorn Moon wants practicality and commitment. What could you begin now that could take off in Springtime, by July? What could you give yourself now that would allow for results in the present moment? Whether it's community, trust, opportunities, pleasure, more energy, or more focus, remember to back your spell work up with action.

When working with the Moon's phases, it is optimal to take a holistic approach. If you are doing Waxing Moon spell work that is supported by building, growing, and expansion, think about how you will pair this with Waning Moon spell work and magic. What will need to be banished? What may need to be refined, revisited, reflected upon in about two weeks? What we no longer need gets released and taken away, energy reformed into something more useful. This is how we can remain energetically balanced and in spiritual alignment. Take what you need, give more than you take. Go after what you want, scale back on what is no longer serving you.

Practically, a Waxing Moon is a useful time to create one or two positive habits in your life. Using the time you spend watching television to take a night class in something interesting to you. Going outside for 20 minutes a day instead of scrolling on a phone. Simply saying "thank you," when receiving a compliment, instead of excusing it away. Being a pleasure-seeker, not a pain-chaser. We can bend time with intention and will. We can compost decaying bits that are ready to be turned over. In the beginning, changing patterns feels practically Sisyphean. Our lizard brain wants to dart this way and that over the hot rocks of stubbornness in our brains. But over time, the positivity builds up: a winged accordion of goodwill taking up space in your heart, wheezing out multi-layered affirmations of joy and gratitude. With so much focus on the fantastic, on the peaceful, on grounding actions, the time for the bad behavior and doubt fades away, a distant past self. What one or two helpful habits will you start and stick to this week?

Our New Moon prompt was around integration, loving truths, and action. About shifting identities, and mental alchemy. The air we breathe and the space we seek. Now our Moon is in an Earth sign, where she will also reside at her Fullness, in one more week. The energetics in your life might be feeling different. A more curious state might be turning into embodiment. The tone could be turning to tangibility. It is time to really take steps to put these "what if's" into action. Structuring and scheduling in our self-care is a must.

While in recent years self-care has become trendy, implementing and structuring self-care into our lives is imperative. The fact of the matter is that many of us are running on fumes. For years. Decades. The fact of the matter is that many of us have been running on fumes for hundreds, if not thousands, of years: the exhaustion of invisible labor and exploited labor and emotional labor passed down from generation to generation to generation. Many of us are so tired that we don't even know how tired we really are. There are no words to describe this type of exhaustion. Self-care can be defined as caring for oneself—with one person's care techniques and behaviors looking drastically different from another's. Self-care is what we do to take care of our emotional, mental, and physical health. For me, self-care is tied to spiritual work is tied to survival, and ultimately going past survival to arrival: taking up all of the space one needs in one's own life in order to enact our spiritual purpose.

Self-care is survival is staying alive is ultimately thriving. Because when we are taking care of ourselves, we can care for others in a more authentic way. Because when we are taking care of ourselves, we are ultimately taking care of others: those that need us literally to live (if we are caregivers and family members) and the greater collective that needs our energy, our efforts, our genius, and our brilliance that lights up rooms, inspires communities, and changes the world for the better. It all starts with knowing what we need and giving that to ourselves, consistently and resolutely. Survival spells look all different kinds of ways.

A survival spell could be blocking that caller. A survival spell could be praying for the healing of your former stalker, but distancing yourself from all of the mutual friends who still hang out with them. A survival spell could be working out a payment plan. A survival spell could be advocating at the doctors to try a new study or procedure. A survival spell could be reminders on your phone to take your meds, cancel that unnecessary obligation, make that therapy appointment, put an auto-responder on your email, call your bestie. A survival spell could be a manicure that reads "B-A-C-K O-F-F." A survival spell could be eight glasses of water and a magnesium supplement. A survival spell is speaking, screaming, repeating your story come hell or high water, for yourself, your dreams, for others like you to see and to feel less alone. A survival spell could be slipping a piece of paper in your shoe that says, "Moving forward with protection." Slipping that black tourmaline into your bra. Lighting that red candle with three dimes and a sliver of hematite inside it, *this or better, so it is.* A survival spell could be praying for your friends, praying for your community, praying for the Earth. A survival spell could be your donation, your petition, your protest. Making sure your friend gets home safe by giving them a ride. A survival spell is an ask for help, asking for a loved one to come over with soup and face masks. A survival spell could be a salt bath every day for the next few days, no guilt, no judgment, just you, your blank mind submerged in the heat and the quiet, the salt drawing out the stress.

During a Waxing Moon, a time to grow things and strengthen and build, I like to use The Magician card as a nice reminder to work with what I've got. The Magician card, patron saint of hustlers and freelancers and entrepreneurs, lets us know that everything we need we've already got. We don't need permission or that fancy equipment or that expensive candle or the backing of a celebrity to make it happen. We just need to summon up our courage and our inner strength, our own particular magic, and move forward cloaked in that magic. The Magician says, "The time is now, work with what you've got. The duct tape, the paper clips, the pencil and the piece of paper, the mental skill, all the things you are good at, bring them out at this time. Work with what you've got, because what you've got is a lot." The Magician card reminds us that sometimes, limited resources can be better, as it makes our decision-making easier and our output more immediate. We make magic with alignment and purpose, structure and inner strength.

A quick way to change your mindset is to rearrange your space. Put up new colorful pictures that remind you of what you want to see in your life. Change which way your sofa faces or add a couple of pillows to your bed. Buy a plant or two, name them, talk to them, give them enough light. Donate items you do not need, or that remind you of a less than shitty time in your life.

An easy way to change your energy levels is to rearrange your schedule. Put you first. Block off time for that 40 minutes of yoga. That 30 minutes to research therapists. That 20 minutes to experiment with new makeup. That 10 minutes to read. That 3 minutes to journal. Get used to saying "No," or "Not now," or "Can we touch base in a day or a week?" or "I'm sorry, I'm not available for that right now, but here are a few options for you to look into that I can think of in the meantime." Put the activities that fill you up— rituals, spell work, friend dates, naps, walks— in your schedule, along with your obligations, and live your life around that.

A survival spell is self-care, and self-care relies on our intuition. This month's Waning Moon prompt was around romancing our intuition. Coaxing her out of her pearl-drizzled shell. Now, the prompt is to structure intuitive practices throughout your day. Normalize the clear connection and the channel you have to yourself as you wake up, as you wait in line at the grocery store, as you sit down to work and you ask for a gentle morning, or for the solutions to come easily and joyfully. Schedule your intuition check-ins throughout the day, whether that be meditation, journaling, or speaking to your guides as you do the dishes.

Ask your intuition to show up in the form of synchronicities, signs, and symbols. Listen to the radio, open a random book, and see what the universe wishes to present to us. Trust your intuition. Trust your Self. Make decisions based upon your intuition. Trust your decisions. Just because the answers are coming from inside of you doesn't make it not real. BECAUSE it is coming from inside of you should make it even MORE real and potent! We can ask for help and pay attention when our solace shows up. We can ask for help from Spirit, our guides, our friends, and our community.

We can choose to make our process hard, or make it easier. We can choose love, or choose fear. It is up to you.

Darling reader, allow yourself to thrive, wherever you are. You've worked through and breathed through and moved through so much to get to this point. If you need to rest, use this week to rest. If you need this week to really zero in on what your body needs in terms of sleep, hydration, food, or supplements, focus on that. If you are being pulled to finish that first draft, stay up that extra hour to redesign your résumé, put you first, no matter what that is, do it. There is a driving force within you that knows who you are and what you wish to achieve. There is a strong, clear messenger inside of all of us that knows what we are capable of and how we must move forward. Listen to your intuition and give yourself what you need. Take all the space you need; save some energy for your wonderful self. Structure in your self-care and step into your arrival.

Crystals for strength-building and structure: Garnet, smoky quartz, tiger eye, gold pyrite
Strength-building herbal helpers: Nettle, motherwort, astragalus, reishi mushrooms

Some ways I am prioritizing my mental, physical, and emotional health this week:

What I need to do this week for my self-care:

OCTOBER 24TH: FULL MOON in TAURUS 9:45 PM PST, 6:37 PM PST MOONRISE. 6:37 AM MOONRISE

A Dedication of Merit
by Alexandria Bull & Pema Chödrön

This October's Full Moon falls at a time when many people are especially aware of the presence that their ancestors and lineage hold in their lives. Halloween, Samhain, Día de los Muertos, and Lhabab Düchen begin in one week, celebrations that all place awareness on those who have come before us. Today's Full Moon is also in Taurus, a sign associated with the Egyptian cow goddess Hathor. Hathor symbolized motherhood and fertility and ruled birth and death, foretelling each newborn's destiny and welcoming the dead into the next life.

Along with all of the above reasons, this time of the year brings up a lot of personal lineage-related feelings for me, as it was this time of year that my mother passed away from a drawn-out, addiction-related illness. It was also at that time that my paternal grandmother heavily intervened in my life, correctly sensing that the death of a parent was likely an ideal time for a Buddhist nun with a solid track record for working with unpleasant emotions to offer up her services. Ever since, she has been both the relative with which I have the closest relationship and my main spiritual teacher (I realize that this sounds a little cultish, but she is very cute and normal, and I promise that it isn't as creepy as it sounds). Based on the circumstances that fostered our relationship, one of the main themes that we've consistently worked with for years is healing karmic wounds on behalf of your ancestors and family members in order to release yourself from those cycles. The way we relate to and work with this has taken many forms, and the following conversation is us further exploring what this kind of practice means both for us as individuals, as well as for the collective consciousness.

Pema: We're looking at how one can heal their lineage, in big and little ways. As an example, no one in your mother's family could cook, and that's why I encourage you to learn how to cook for yourself. Even if it's one meal a month, or one meal a year—that could help you break that particular cycle. Not that there's anything so horrible about not cooking, but it is an inherited feature that doesn't serve you—a feeling of "I can't do that," or a sense of lack.

Alexandria: It's a really interesting thing to work with, inheriting the tendency to do things that do not serve you from your lineage. Especially with more serious unhealthy patterns, because it's so easy to feel anger or blame toward the people who instilled that way of being in us rather than having sympathy for them or trying to heal in the ways they couldn't.

Pema: That's right. The idea that we were talking about is prevalent in a lot of different cultures, that you can heal your ancestors by healing yourself. If they had dysfunctional patterns, you're helping them by not following that same destructive path. It's an act of love.

Alexandria: How do you work with this, in your practices and experience?

Pema: One of my Tibetan teachers said you should always learn about your ancestors, and remember them. I think about this often in terms of my distant family and the way they suffered, and how that's all in my genes, somewhere. And whether I'm being impacted by it or not, there's the sense that if I'm doing a retreat and meditating a lot and having breakthroughs, I can dedicate the merit of that to my ancestors, and even their ancestors that I don't know anything about. I want what I'm doing now to benefit them.

Alexandria: Even if they're long gone?

Pema: Well, it means not thinking about time in the same way that we usually do because it doesn't really make sense if you're thinking about time as linear. Instead, you have to think about the ways you can help them now, even if they've been gone for a long time. Whatever that actually means is kind of mysterious, but that's what Tibetans believe. You can help your ancestors by doing anything you're proud of, anything that helps other people or helps you to become more sane yourself, with the thought that you're doing this for your ancestors as far back as you know of them. Then, there's the idea that you can actually free yourself now by seeing what the patterns are that got carried down, and make the aspiration that your awareness is freeing them, too.

Alexandria: You mentioned the idea of "dedicating the merit" above. How would you explain what that practice means to someone who hasn't heard that phrase before or isn't familiar with it in the Buddhist context?

Pema: It can just mean when you're doing anything positive, for example listening to a recording that you know will be meaningful to you, you can just say to yourself, "anything I learn from this, I dedicate to my family lineage." I always start certain retreats by having everyone think about somebody or a group of people they'd like to dedicate it to, so that anything they learn or that comes out of it for the group goes to these people. And throughout the weeks of the retreat, the list may grow, since you hear about people who are in trouble, or someone dies, or a big catastrophe happens in the world. Dedicating the merit has to do with acknowledging our interconnectedness—that what one person does has a ripple effect out into the world. So if you do something that brings you closer to your wisdom, then that ripple effect goes out. And if you do self-destructive things, that ripple effect goes out, too.

Alexandria: So when we do things that are or aren't in alignment with our best nature, those actions influence our lineage and the world in general, not just us personally.

Pema: Yes. This interconnectedness is a somewhat elusive subject, and it's not only a Buddhist idea. It's a very widespread belief in a lot of traditions, and interestingly enough, in physics it comes up too...I think it's physics. I'm kind of stupid on this subject. Anyway, if you have twin photons that are seperated and something happens to one on one end of the world, the one on the other end of the world will react. Do you know what I'm talking about?

Alexandria: I think it's called quantum entanglement.

Pema: Well, there we go! In other words, this isn't just a spiritual or religious idea, it's also something that science is finding to be true—that we're part of a vast, interconnected web and what we do actually matters. So if I'm sitting in my cabin cultivating loving-kindness for others, that's why it actually has an effect. More sanity goes out into the world. But if I'm sitting there in meditation, complaining about people in my mind, just churning out negative thoughts, harboring resentments about how this or that is someone else's fault, then that's what's going out into the world.

I've been inspired by this for a long time—that how we work with our minds and our emotions really does have an effect on other people. I mean, of course it has an effect on your partner or your roommates or your boss, but it's also much more vast than that. One of the ways that I often describe this in my teaching, is that you're either adding more negativity and polarity to the world, or we're adding more loving-kindness, care for each other, empathy, and tenderness.

Do not forget to be gentle with yourself. Practicing for and working with the relationships in our family that are the most challenging can be a deeply powerful experience. However, depending on your history and where you are our on your path, it might unhealthy to work with certain people or lineage patterns at this point. Trust your gut. If there are members of your family who were abusive, caused a great deal of harm, or who you don't feel safe processing in the present—that is okay! You can aspire to do so in the future, and work up to that point at your own pace.

A Full Moon Awareness Ritual for Ancestral Healing

Suggested Affirmation: "I invoke love and empathy for myself. I dedicate my loving actions and awareness to ancestral healing for the past, present, and future."

In the morning, before beginning your day, take a moment to reflect on your lineage and ancestors, and the way their past behaviors or programming influences your life. Are there any stories, cycles, or addictions you carry that have been passed down through your lineage?

If you can identify a specific inherited tendency or way of moving through the world that does not serve you and you would like to work with healing, consider how far back you can follow that pattern through your bloodlines. How do you feel about your ancestors who also carried these traits? Sympathetic? Frustrated?

After choosing what quality you would like to focus on, commit to having a hyperaware relationship with that aspect of your experience for the rest of the day. When it comes up, contact the feelings that arise around it with as much kindness as possible. Send that quality as much love and care as possible, rather than feeling angry at it for disrupting your life. This intention goes further than just you; it also positively influences your ancestors and anyone in your lineage who may come after you and also struggle with this trait in one unbroken stream.

Since this is something you will have to keep returning to throughout your day at potentially unpredictable times, it can help to just put your hand on your heart, or cup your face in your hands as a gesture of gentleness with yourself. While working with emotions and healing tied to family, I also find it beneficial to carry bits of rose quartz, amazonite, and turquoise on my person.

If this is a practice that works for you, or you are specifically trying to work with healing inherited qualities in a more broad manner, it can also be helpful to choose a particular day of the week to continue practicing this on a weekly basis for however long it feels like it's helpful.

Notes on ritual / Full Moon times:

OCTOBER 31st: LAST QUARTER MOON in LEO 8:40 AM PST, 1:57 PM PST MOONSET

The Ghosts We Feed, the Ghosts We No Longer Need: Staying Wild under a Samhain Moon

The second Last Quarter Moon of October glides in like an obsidian bookend in our magic month. It is Wednesday. It is Samhain, the Pagan New Year. It is Halloween, a time to dress up as your wildest fantasies or silliest incarnation. Tomorrow, November 1st, is All Saints' Day. The next day, November 2nd, is the Day of the Dead. The veil between worlds is thin. There's a rustling in the atmosphere between living and dead as the final leaves fall off of the trees preparing dormancy for the proper Winter. We settle into our placement between the two worlds: between up and down, between the underworld and waking life, between what we know for certain and what the wolf howls tell us under a darkening Autumn sky. Tombstones talk to us and pomegranate seeds dissolve like sweet blood in between our teeth and our tongue. We can be our own High Priestess in the middle of the Death card. The Moon's light fades under a Scorpion sky.

Samhain marks a cross-quarter date in the Wheel of the Year. Many historians believe it began the start of the New Year in the Celtic calendar year. Long ago, Samhain was the death night of the old year; the time when cattle were slaughtered and survival was celebrated (*The Old Farmer's Almanac*). The dead were exalted, and life was honored. Turnips were carved and filled with candles—in America, they became pumpkins. Apples, symbols of love, were sought after in barrels filled with water, or attached to swinging strings.

Whether you celebrate or observe any of these holidays, there's certainly something different in the air in October. It is truly now the season of the witch. It is Hecate's time. Leave a meal for her to enjoy as she roams the forest, hiding keys for you to find in your dreams. A season of weirdness, a time to cast off inhibitions and throw them into the fire. Time to let your claws out and your hair down. Ask for what you want and follow your impulses. The iconic image of the witch riding on her broomstick is one part masturbation and one part psychedelic herbs. It is told that women would apply hallucinogenic herbs—to induce flying—via their mucus membranes. Hundreds of years ago, women would "take flight" by rubbing these herbs into their genitals and blast into a world that was much brighter, much more free than their waking life. No doubt the image of a woman on a broom flying high and happy, in more ways than one, has endured through the combination of kitchen magic, strange sexuality, and the irreverent magic and metaphors it references.

This might be the time to get in touch more deeply with your own magical practice. Get wilder: really name what you want to explore and what you want to know in the magical realms. Begin by doing research into your own background's folkloric traditions, or look right into your own lineage. This is the time of the dead; ask your family favorite stories about relatives who have passed over. If you cannot speak to your biological family, spend time with tales of your chosen family. See them as friendly guides who can inspire you with their ingenuity and innovation.

Anyone who has dealt with actual ghosts knows there are friendly ghosts and there are ghosts that haunt. Dealing with those sorts of ghosts—spirits of souls that have passed over—is another piece. There are much scarier and more stubborn ghosts inside of us we must contend with if we wish to connect to the magic that is our birthright.

The next few months could potentially be filled with real life ghouls popping up. Especially if you have done some clearing in your life. If you've started setting new intentions, refocusing on yourself and goals, begun distancing yourself from harmful patterns, behaviors, or people, they might just start knocking at your door, scratching at your window, and appearing in your phone. Stay the course. Do not engage. Or it might be you who feels like haunting others. Before calling an ex or a friend who did you wrong, just pause. Ask yourself what the best possible outcome could be. If you think a real reconciliation is useful and possible, proceed. If you are merely scratching an itch for attention or wanting to reopen old wounds, then take a bath or eat some popcorn instead. Process your feelings with anyone but the person who is harming you.

Everyone's got some ghosts that love to pull up a chair and stick around all night when you'd rather them not finish off all of your La Croix. But they do. They'll suck you and your resources dry and consume you until you feel like a zombie yourself. Chinese Buddhism calls these "hungry ghosts"—drivings of unrelenting cravings, addiction, and impulses that distract. Creepy feelings that haunt you, bring you back to past deeds and times you'd rather forget. The moments are long gone, but the stench remains. The preoccupation keeps the scary stories alive. Ghosts that are drenched in the past reek in the present.

Just because a ghost of the past pops up, that doesn't mean it is real. Sure, the ghost is real to you. It cackles annoyingly and makes your face burn and your heart race and tears your mind up into bits and pieces that get scattered here and there. We get obsessed by the ghosts of shame, comparison, rage, envy, guilt, and regret, to name a few. They keep us stuck and in loops. They can feel real to us—sometimes something very real happens in the present, with a person, place, or thing, and we get triggered. But we have to parse out if it is our reactions, preoccupations with past emotional habits, and addictions to drama, chaos, and black hole feelings that are making the starving ghosts even thirstier.

Just because a sloppy specter shows itself, that doesn't mean you have to deal with it in the same way you always have. Phantoms looked at head-on tend to shrink. One way to deal with these ghosts is viewing them as patterns you might be clinging to for a variety of reasons. Is it easier to play the victim than have accountability? Are you confusing attention with love? We all have our reasons to stay in our own personal hell.

Another reason for your haunting is that this fixation on the negative could be a distraction you've created to self-sabotage. Distractions are very effective for stopping us from focusing on really doing the really important, really meaningful projects of our life. That is a very persuasive wraith indeed. A creepy ghoul of decaying time that always wins. What are you putting off?

Yet another reason to keep a certain ghost around is that they are a bandaid for a deeper, more painful emotion underneath. One mountaintop gets climbed over and over because it is familiar. We know the particular switchbacks and slippery slopes. Yet there is another, deeper canyon we must deal with a few miles away. There are painful emotions inside this other place, but at the end of the rough trail there is solace as we finally come across the answers and meaning that we crave. How much of one emotional habit simply is a hamster wheel, a distraction keeping you from real emotional excavation?

More than two thirds of all humans have what is called a negative cognitive bias: that is, most of us look for or dwell on the negative naturally. We get 30 compliments on our painting, yet we focus on the two lukewarm reactions. It is quite literally the way our brains were developed for survival purposes, so we mustn't be mad at this occurrence. Try to develop a practice of mindfulness around your wallowing. Acknowledge it. Then as soon as you find yourself looping, change the station. Go outside, read a book, watch a television show, play a game. You can also distract yourself with goodness. Call a friend and ask them to give you compliments. Make a gratitude list. Look at pictures on the internet of baby hedgehogs swimming and baby mountain goats jumping. There are lots of ways to lose yourself in moment of positivity— or at the very least, neutrality.

All emotions are constructive, as all emotions are information. Transforming our unsavory emotions into positive outcomes is an important step to zapping any past dumpster fires that threaten to overtake the present. And, gentle reader, it is important to do that as close to IN the moment as possible. Letting icky emotions fester turns them into hauntings, which turns them into habit, which begin to run the show more than we'd like to admit. Following are some suggestions on how to work with certain overwhelming emotions.

Rage is a useful gift. It is important to connect with and love your rage and anger. At times, anger is the true voice of reason. Anger is a litmus test to our needs, our boundaries, our ethics. Once it is transformed into action, rage has the power to move mountains. It makes protest signs and changes laws. Art is created, safer spaces are made. Sometimes, underneath anger is sadness that has not been given an outlet. Made to fester inside us with no positive outcome, anger turns into a dead-end screaming match: an endless echo chamber of stress. It isolates us from others and affects our health.

Useful ways to deal with rage are to bang a drum, write a letter you will never send, scream, punch a pillow, write a song, write a book, write a poem, take boxing classes, organize a protest, transform it into art. Channel the rage productively. Become a harpy, shrieking and shrilling and never giving up in the name of justice. Become a hound of hell rattling the cages that keep people chained, fighting all the bad guys only.

Guilt is a real tricky ghost. Guilt is a sister ghoul of shame and this one tends to be both a real past life haunting as well as one that starts taking place when we are born. Guilt can be laid on especially thick in an emotionally manipulative way, getting us caught in a quicksand desert. It's appropriate to feel guilt for something wrong you've done, but when you are feeling guilty for existing, have survivor's guilt for doing well in your life after coming from a lineage of suffering, or for only getting an A and not an A+, this could be a sign that its time to let that guilt ghost go.

One ways to transform guilt is to live in the present moment. Guilt tends to begin in the past, so the more you can live in the present, the more the guilt ghosts shrink. Affirming that you are worthy of love no matter what you do is a must. It is okay to eat that ice cream. It is okay to decide not drive so and so to the airport for the third time in a month. It is imperative to have boundaries, and it is imperative to prioritize relationships with people in your life who love you unconditionally, with blame, without caveats. The most powerful way to transform guilt is to forgive yourself. Over and over again.

Envy will haunt you if you are a witch who does not fill her own cup up first. Our own well must be overflowing if we are to give another water. The ghost of envy, which leads to the goblin of comparison, which morphs into the demon of competition, is almost always rooted in insecurity. Envy and comparison is a game with the same outcome always: loss. There will always be someone with something you do not have. Someone's life will always *seem* better than yours, if you are obsessively convincing yourself.

A potent way to transform envy for the better is the practice of extreme generosity. Envy zombies suckle at the bones of scarcity. Practicing generosity makes scarcity diminish. These nitpicky ghosts vanish with the belief that there is enough for all, that one person's success is not your loss. When too much envy creeps in, it is time to put the attention back on you. Delete social media, stop scouring the internet. Focus on creating your own fantastic world, not on the projections of others' fortune. These are distractions dragging you away from your goals.

The important thing with all of these ghosts is to not keep them hanging around. They keep us living in the past, repeating our actions again and again like we are an actor in *Groundhog Day*. We must break the cycle by dealing with these cumbersome energetic drains in the present.

The ghosts that control you are sneaky, but they get easier to see with time and practice. These ghosts are not useful and the more they are fed, the larger they get. Open the door and shoo those ghosts out. The ghosts we feed, the ghosts we no longer need. Bury them in the graveyard along with our useless friends: coulda shoulda woulda. Rest In Pieces, forever and ever!

At this Waning Moon time, it is time to let go of what is standing in your way. It is time to stop feeding the starving past-life ghosts that knock up and down the hallways of your psyche. Send them on their way with some Florida water, salt, and sage. Send them on their way fast and soon.

Witch, you are wild, and it's time to revel in that wildness, free from guilt and self-flagellation. You are allowed to let the guilt, shame, envy, self-judgment go. You are allowed to enjoy life and create different, sweeter memories. You are allowed to be unapologetic. Know that in doing so, you inspire all the other witches around you to be their own brave, fun-loving, wild selves too. This is just what we all need more of: a witch alight with her own power, shooting spells like broomsticks off to the Moon and back.

Practical tips for this Waning Moon:
Go through your phone and delete all exes and all people who have harmed you that you no longer keep in your life. Do this for all your social media. Delete people you haven't spoken to in years, or people you "follow" because you feel guilty or uncomfortable. Or, delete social media for a week and only use the internet when you have to for work purposes.

Do a cord-cutting ceremony. Write down all of the ghosts you can name on little scraps of paper. Declare yourself free of all of their energy. Burn them. Bury the ashes. Declare all cords that you may have to any places, people, reactions, ideas, or things released. Take a ritual salt bath or shower. If you need to take action in real life with certain habits or relationships, follow up.

Do something fun that is a little bit scary to do: sing a song you don't know at karaoke. Pitch yourself to a magazine you admire. Apply for a job you feel unqualified for (but probably are not— we tend to underestimate ourselves!). Take sexy photos and share them. Speak up for yourself. Tell a lover exactly what you want in bed tonight. Make up an alter ego if you need to; Beyoncé has Sasha Fierce, witches have witch names. Maybe you need to rename this aspect of yourself! Pretend to be the bravest version of yourself over and over until you are the bravest version of yourself.

Stop doing things you don't like for people who don't treat you well.
Throw out any items in your space or room that no longer please you.
Throw out any excuses you have been coming up with for not shining.

What I am composting during this Waning Moon time:

Where I would like to get wilder:

Notes on this month:

Intentions for the next:

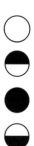

NOVEMBER 2018
NOVEMBER 4-6TH: DARK MOON
NOVEMBER 7TH: NEW MOON
NOVEMBER 15TH: FIRST QUARTER
NOVEMBER 22ND: FULL MOON
NOVEMBER 29TH: LAST QUARTER

Transformation isn't always tangible. It consists of many invisible parts, one of the most powerful being the pause. The pause isn't usually sexy or shiny, it isn't something you hang on a wall. The pause—the descent, the void, the internal turning we are asked to consider this month in this workbook—reflects the season we are in. Animals are hibernating in the earth, or preparing their nests for the winter. Preparing to slow down. Trees go dormant; they barely grow. They are still, quiet, conserving their energy. They are transforming.

In nature, darkness is fertile. It is where life incubates; it is where we plant seeds. Some of us feel solace in slow periods. Most of us are not so lucky. Who can blame us? We are taught to go, go, go. Rarely does this society extol the virtues of slowing down, going deeper, and dealing with the unknown. While we are in it, the Underground and the void can be mystifying and disorienting. Taking off the masks and redefining our thoughts can be painful when we rub against the unknown. Being asked to go beyond how we've been trained, however, creates openings, dialogues, and intriguing connections. Unpacking is messy and necessary.

This month's prompts asks you to take on a variety of topics having to do with the unknown, magic, and paradoxes. There are pieces on death, crystal grid magic, and summoning the mystery. Nothing and everything under a Full Moon. Delving into the myth of Lilith and considering how we can work with this archtype in our own lives, in our own astrological charts. Using mystery as openings into different dimensions of oneself. Empowering ourselves with our ability to question, our willingness to go deep, and have that depth eventually guide us up, into even more connection and understanding. Our magic needs mystery.

Mystery gives us myths. The word "myth" comes from the Greek "mythos," meaning "word," "tale," and "true narrative." (Wikipedia.org). Myths give our lives meaning. Myths explore our subconscious and the wildest projections of our collective high highs and our low lows. Myths act, at times, as a metaphoric guidebook on how to live our lives. Myths also serve as a mirror to certain cultures, certain philosophies, and many problematic ways of thinking. There are many myths that need revising or actual deletion. What new myths do you need to start writing about yourself this month? What mysteries about yourself do you need to explore?

The Moon themself has many myths. Moon as mother. Moon as daughter. Moon as crone. Moon as mirror. Moon as giver, Moon as controller. Moon as magic-maker. Moon as subconscious, as secrets, as cauldron to all of our desires and dreams alike. Moon as Sun's consort. Moon as the cosmic mother of everything or nothing at all. Moon as portal-maker, witch-activator. Moon as home for hares, buffalo, and extraterrestrials. The Moon is all of this, and so much more. And so are you. Let yourself be the version of yourself that resonates most—try on a different myth of yourself every day, and see what happens.

This month, let your relationship with mystery deepen. Conjure, summon, slither, glitter. Go within. Your inner Moon will meet you there, deep in the depths of your sacred pause.

November Astrology Insights
By Diego Basdeo

November 7th : New Moon in Scorpio / Squaring Lilith in Capricorn / Neptune in Pisces squaring Mercury in Sagittarius / Uranus in Aries opposing Venus Retrograde in Libra

November 8th : Jupiter enters Sagittarius

November 16th : Venus Direct

November 17th : Mercury Retrograde

November 22nd : Full Moon in Gemini / Squaring Mars conjunct Uranus in Pisces / Uranus in Aries opposing Venus in Libra

November is filled with revelations and juxtapositions. Corporeal, intangible. Fresh starts at Full Moons. Paradoxes and push-pull astrological circumstances.

Okay. New Moon in Scorpio is already a pretty deep thing. Like, to the grave and back deep. Like, Daddy's pockets deep. Like, plunging into the most secret fantasies that only your subconscious tells you in your dreams, deep. Add Lilith to the mix and we've got a powerful situation. Because of the triangular myth of Lilith herself, I'm brought to believe that the nature of this New Moon will bring us tension between the Sun (ego), the Moon (the feels), and Lilith (righteous rage). Which one is the other woman? Who is being left out in the rain? Which is the illicit relationship and how can we come clean with ourselves?

We are left in wonderment about "the others." We wonder about their desire, their anger, their curious ways. We wonder where they come from and where they're going. We watch, slowly laying scene upon scene, communicating in body languages, and I do mean body. Neptune is squaring Mercury and verbal and direct communications dissolve like sugar in water. We have to find other ways of talking. Neptune in Pisces suggests a telepathic, psychic, watery style while Mercury in Sagittarius may be too oblivious for that. So, I might suggest the body. Dance, gesture, stance. All of these movements (or lack thereof) communicate something to the viewer.

Addiction comes up fairly intensely with Lilith/Moon aspects, especially with hard aspects like the square we are seeing with the New Moon. This speaks to both addicts and people who habitually fall for addicts. There is a strong pull towards forbidden fruit and the Neptune/Mercury square can make our morals and communication boundaries very foggy. Be careful! Protect your energy.

Sex is another thing that might be closely related to addiction this month. Lilith is a thing of extremes and sex can go from embodying the sacred whore to a nun and back again in one night. It's a great time to check in with power dynamics in sex, to explore them, enjoy them, or correct them.

With our Full Moon, we have a restart. The zero degree is called an ingress. It is a threshold between one sign and another. The zero degree lies between the last and the first degree of neighboring signs. It is the first observation of an alien planet. It is a step into new territory. Zero degrees Gemini: it is an experiential degree. It is the purest expression of the sign that it is in.

At this proto-start, keep an open mind. The Moon moving into Gemini is a change from Taurus, a settled steady energy, towards an open and interpersonal energy. Taurus is the inhale, Gemini is the exhale.

A Full Moon is the opposition of the Sun and the Moon, so while the Moon is at zero degrees Gemini, the Sun is standing across the cosmos at zero degrees Sagittarius. The Sun, too, is new. Sagittarius, the archer, is high-minded philosophy. A Full Moon is, in part, the completion of a cosmic integration of polar principles of a whole. How are we integrating information right now? What conclusions are we coming to with everything we've gathered? Can we make sense of it? Does it resonate? Can we feel it? And finally, how do we share this info?

At the same time as the Full Moon, Uranus in Aries (screaming freedom and individuality) is opposing Venus in Libra (relationship and diplomacy): quick changes in relationships concerning peace, harmony, and diplomacy vs. individual expression. It's a rule-breaker, a hot and cold vibe of deep lust and fear when we get what we want. This is a reminder to detach. When we detach, we are free to feel more real love, and to feel more of ourselves.

Mars and Neptune are unfocused will. It is important to use imagination right now. There's an important usefulness to uselessness right now. This is squaring the Full Moon. It is a good time for selfless activity. Your ego energies are more subdued than normal, so charity work or otherwise could be beneficial. Your physical energy will be lower than usual, so be aware of this and try not to exhaust yourself or you may become ill. Take extra care of yourself during this time.

Overall, November is a close encounter with the unreal, the space beyond our senses, and how to speak to the ways we experience speechless moments. How can we tell our story when words won't suffice?

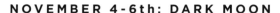

Death Under a Dark Moon

"Day to day, life's a hard job, you get tired, you lose the pattern. You need distance...The way to see how beautiful the earth is, is to see it as the moon. The way to see how beautiful life is, is from the vantage point of death." —Ursula K. Le Guin

November starts out with a Waning Moon that fades into a Dark Moon during its first week. This time would be opportune for clearing, purging, reorganizing, and FaceTiming with your inner demons to let them know you are ready to release them into the stars. November itself is a Dark Moon month, filled with mysteries and intangibilities. We might be feeling laid bare. If we are, that's appropriate. This is the time to be laid bare, to reckon with ourselves, to conjure up the skeletons of our regroupings from the smoke that is left of this year.

This Dark Moon is a time for quiet, a time for solitude, a time for casting off the extraneous concerns of the mundane, a time for no longer allowing your days to be distracted. Scrawl on large blank pages, allowing your words to wander. Talk to your ancestors, your guides. For three days, make lighting a black candle a daily practice. Really sit still and listen to the flickering flames. Remind yourself that everything you currently have, you have rightfully gained. Everything that is leaving is leaving for a reason. Name all of the treasures that are currently on their way.

A Dark Moon reminds us of what is truly important because this is a time of death. Before our charged New Moon of resurrection, be clear on what you are throwing onto the fire that you no longer need. Get ragged and raw with what you need to let go of. Do not judge any feelings that come up. If you need to snap, gnash your teeth, then release your jaw. Do not carry the clenching beyond a second or two. If your eyes are narrowed, allow them to close so you can see more clearly. You are allowed to feel safe as you navigate the uncomfortable sandpaper terrain that is letting go with love. You are allowed to be safe to experience and process suffering, rage, anger, and pain. You can use this Dark Moon as a void of transformation. You can become the Dark Moon and disappear into yourself. Dissolution requires detachment and trust. The sharp side of death's blade heightens our focus. On the other side of a death process is a deeper understanding of what is most important in life.

Death—the tiny leaf falling silently onto the surface of a lake—floats away, disappearing downstream. Death: the calm period of relief that accompanies the ending of a certain pain. The swan that glides away with no ripple. The longest blade stuck between our ribs. The greatest shock, the most ghastly sorrow, the most profound teacher. That which we all are taught to fear, to avoid, to ignore, to not speak of or about, yet we all experience. Death—the revelator, the great relator, the unblinking leveler, the ending of all endings. The beginning of all beginnings. Death: the ultimate paradox. No one gets out of alive, yet we all are, one way or another, immortal.

There are levels and layers to death. There is the death as is most commonly thought of: the end of life, the permanent cessation of an organism's being. Bodies leave the 3-D realm, animals go extinct, plants get diseased, rot, or get chopped down. It is my belief, based on visitations by clients' loved ones and my own, that the consciousness of a human goes on after their body ceases to function. Consciousness and personalities live on in different realms, in different forms, after the last breath is taken. Our bodies return to the earth, from where we began, back to the source. Dead plant and animal matter are composted, transformed into fresh soil to nurture more seeds.

Even if you are a total atheist, and do not believe in an afterworld, reincarnation, or of all of our souls returning to Source and remaining immortal, we can all agree that death is not the end of the person's legacy. It is not the end so long as we have people who remember us and who are touched by us. If you are grieving, you are lucky because that means you have been touched by someone's love, and you are present enough with this pain to honor them by remembering them. We create legacies that live long after we have passed on, whether it be by teaching and nurturing younger generations, by creating healing and helping for others, and creating ways to inspire and support humanity, the planet, and her offspring. All the more reason to be careful and exacting with the your intentions, your personal mission statements, and the energy you bring to a space. Energy cannot be destroyed. Energy can only be transformed.

There are subtle deaths: when a phase of inquiry or interest ends. There are deaths that leave you numb: processing the wound will take time. There are deaths that are exuberant: orgasms, bonfires filled with pages and pages of "no mores" and "see you never's", shaving all the hair off your head triumphantly. There are deaths that are a long time coming: changing your gender, your pronouns, or your name, ending toxic relationships, releasing parts of an identity that no longer fit, jumping on the ship just as it sails away, away, away from a harmful pattern or a stagnant job.

We all experience many, many, deaths, before we die for the final time. And even that death, the ending of the beating of our heart, is not really death, as our legacy does not end. We lose cells, skin, hair, teeth, and nails. There are break-ups, losses large and small, loved ones and others around us dying. There are brush-ups against death by way of serious illnesses or chronic disease or violence, parts of our identities dying, death of priorities, death of values, death of certain dreams or desires, the poignant death of a promise. The finality of one cycle, even if that cycle was a state of grief, or a state of anxiety, is also a death because it is an end. Every evening, as we go to sleep, another day dies. Deaths fly in and out of our lives every day.

Death is all around us, whether we realize it or not. The Earth dies every Autumn. The brittle leaves fall; the birds leave the sky wide and lonely at this time. The day fades away against the ticking clock. The Moon shows us death in every one of her cycles. We can work with the lessons death brings to give us a more potent appreciation of life. Acknowledging and accepting any and all deaths we are going through holds up a mirror to the choices we make that speak to conscious existence.

Death scares our ego down to its core. Our egos quiver, deny, ignore, and become extremely resistant when even the faintest whiff of death is in the air. We usually protest death, have trouble with endings, want to hold on tightly even when it hurts. This is because death brings real uncertainty, and humans fear the unknown. And yet, death so often brings peace in some ways. Death so often brings quiet, space, and rest. Death so often brings clarity and advancement of our own's life purpose when our ego breaks down enough to let what needs to go.

Death terrifies the ego, most likely because it lies beyond its logical comprehension. It is the true mystery of the unknown. Absolutely anything and nothing can lie on the other side of any ending. When our ego tries to step outside itself and begins to contemplate that which it cannot viscerally comprehend, it sometimes fries, short-circuits, resists, hits a wall, and casts itself in unhelpful denial. Or, it expands. We can only practice expansion this through pain, through disruption, through conflicts, through loss, and through change. We can breathe deep through it.

All of the ways in which an ego is tested—embarrassment, disruption, humiliation, vulnerability—threaten to take off the masks we all wear. The walls we have so painstakingly built to keep us separate, keep us isolated, keep us preserved, come tumbling down when we face a death of any kind. When this happens, we are reminded that safety is not a given. We are reminded that we are more alike than we are different. We all have the capacity to engage, and with that engagement dissolve inwards and outwards. With the loss of the ego comes the promise of becoming something far greater, far more enduring, far more meaningful than if our defenses had stayed erected, if our walls had remained intact. The essence of who we are, our very consciousness, gets released, begins to function. With our authentic self laid bare, we get real. When we get as real as we can, we name and focus on what is most important for our self. In some ways, physical death is the ultimate ego death because it is through the doors of corporeal detachment that we begin to live forever. Outside of our body, outside of materiality, outside of the mundane attachments, the ceaseless distractions, and the petty reactions, who are we, really? Why have we done what we have done? Who have we helped? Where are our life's lesson's buried? What must we unearth? What is our legacy?

These are some of the greatest wonders of all existence. We never truly know what happens, what the experience of this time after known time is. How strange that so many see this utterly magical, natural, mystery with such a lens of repulsion. How bizarre that our culture does not have conversations or engage with death on a larger collective level. We can expand our views around death as we embrace our inevitability. Developing a flexibility and a trust around endings can help us flow with life's cycles. Death is the ultimate reminder that we are in a cycle that is never ending, much like the tides, the seasons, the Moon, and the stars.

We are all going to pass. All of our lives will come to an end. Are we living our best life? Why not?

In her monumental book, *Women Who Run With the Wolves*, the scholar Clarissa Pinkola Estés introduces us to the concept of Life/Death/Life. This is the idea that time continues on: nothing living ever really dies. Matter is transformed. States of being are transmuted, replaced with other states of being. This is the idea that we must be in cycles of decay, death, and dissolution. We aren't meant to be incredibly productive, incredibly on, incredibly young, incredibly healthy, incredibly far away from death at all times. We all have periods of dormancy, of death, on various levels and at various times. In fact, we must have these moments of quietude, of loss, of lows, of silence. It is natural, and we are of nature. The Earth is dormant. Nothing is planted in the hard ground. We hibernate, alone in the caverns of our most internal musings. We rest in the underground, still catching our breath from the exertion of the descent. Our sky fades from metal grey to bottomless black—the Dark Moon is there, yet she doesn't shine. She needs a rest. She needs a respite from our hungry eyes. She reminds us to rest ourselves, to take quiet time for our clocks to reset. To attend to our changing interiors, to pluck out the bits we no longer need and toss them to the wind. To get really clear about what must die in our lives. These deaths are painfully necessary. If there is no death, there can be no new life.

Life/Death/Life also reminds us that straight lines are another tool of the patriarchy. Our lines are not linear. Our lines of life wobble, fly upwards, coast, find a dark grotto to rest in on their endless journey onward. Our cycles and circles go up and down, around and around. We weave in and out, out and in, sometimes with others, never alone. Even in death, we are never alone. Our actions, and the remembrance of those actions keeps us alive and immortal with the loving memories from those we have woven with, and woven alongside. As long as there is love, no one ever really dies.

Tell your loved ones you love them, whether they are dead or alive.
Be clear about which elders have taught you, and which lessons you have learned from them.
Give out praises frequently whether they are going to the dead or to the living.

A death meditation is taking conscious time to ponder the fact that we and everyone single person we know will die, yet their souls will live. The gas station attendant, our favorite singers, our therapist, our senators, our dearest loved ones will die. Their actions, their messages, their creative life, their contributions to the evolution of humanity will carry on. Their warmth, their love, their example continues on so long as we remember them and so long as we speak their names, read their stories, listen to their songs, praise their efforts. And so we accept we will die as well. And so we figure out ways to live so that our ideas, our love, our truth ring out to help humanity and the Earth for long after our body's demise.

A living meditation is identifying with your alive-ness. We can connect with the alive-ness of others: we can hold someone's hand and feel their pulse, press someone's heart up against ours in a frontal hug, we can press our face against our pet's face and lean into their body's furry electrical warmth. We can relish in the aliveness of the vegetables we eat, we can sit near the plants in our home and connect with their green growing leaves. We realize that death is a part of life, and so we choose to live more deeply, with more attention and presence given to our present moment.

If you are grappling with the pain of death, in whatever form it may take, be mindful of putting your physical and emotional needs first. There is no wrong way to process death— we will address grief during next month's Waxing Moon. There is no surefire way to get over a death. Staying mindful, conscious, and kind to yourself is always recommended. Admitting the scariness of not knowing what comes next is what a body and a mind needs. Acknowledging your suffering, dialoging with it, and not blaming yourself is a necessary component of what you must give to yourself through any process of decay and death.

A death time is a High Priestess time. The velvety veils of the dreamworlds are pulled back, reality thins out and dissolves. The somber bell rings out, reminding us that everyone gets their day of reckoning. The knowledge the dead prepare for us is collected in marble urns that we pull out like strings of black pearls to drape over our clavicles. The realm of the dead can be a space of no-time: no pain, no money, no prisons, no ladders to climb. Nothing to do but float in and out of the dark mist, and wait for the whispers to assemble into an education we can take with us back to the land of the living. The Underworld is where death takes up residence, and the Underworld is the zone of transformation, evolution, the rock bottom that aids us in our liberation. Persephone visits there, Hecate lives there, and Inanna descends there. The Underworld is a realm of redemption and resurrection. There is a portal that opens after we've bitten into the pomegranate. Do not be afraid to face your own black mirror.

During this time, allow yourself to rest, as still and silent and hidden as the Moon above. Bless the parts of you that are dying, that are dead, that are changing into something else, incompre-hensible as this shift may be. Be aware that others are in states of dying as well. Others are in their own processes and that is about them, not you. Allow others to set you free as confining relationships must come to an end. Let go of what needs to die so that different life will begin to reintegrate as it needs to, in the coming weeks and months. Remember that death is not the final destination. Allow death to reaffirm your dedication to life.

Suggested exercises for this time:
Write down all of the parts of your identity, all of the parts of who you are. Look at the list. Are there any that you want to let go, that you wish to leave in the past? Are there any you want to add, that you want to transform into?

Pretend you are attending your own funeral. What do you want it to be like? What would you want people to say about you? What are the most important parts of your life? What are the most important gifts of yours? Write down everything you want to leave behind to the earth and to the collective. Allow this framing to follow you into your life.

Get comfy and sit down with your Tarot deck. Pull out the Death card.
Shuffle the cards and ask:
What is ready to die in my life?
How can I support this release?
What is the lesson or reward that will come out of this death?

Put the cards on your altar and sit with them. Meditate near them for the next one or two days.

Journaling questions:
How do I currently feel about death?
What is ready to die in my life?
What is dying in my life?
How do I need to midwife this death?
How must I honor this death?
What will this death clear space for in my life?
How could I surrender to this death?

Hello New Moon in Scorpio
By Mark Phillips and Martin Anguiano of Spellbound Sky

So it's that time again that we are forever obsessed with—that fresh start, those new beginnings, and the endless possibilities that get us so motivated to fully embrace the blank slate that is the New Moon.

This New Moon falls in the astrological sign of Scorpio, connecting us to our personal magic on the deepest levels. Halloween and Samhain were just a warm-up to get us all in touch with our witchy ways and the unlimited power of the mystical realm. Use this energy to go within and unlock your true potential, becoming the magician of your own destiny.

Scorpio also represents transformation and we are all about that out-with-the-old-and-in-with-the-new state of mind. The death of one way of life and the rebirth of another is essential for growth and taking your New Moon manifesting game to the next level. The act of letting go is a key part of achieving the fresh start needed to create the New You. This is a time to really get the clarity needed to disconnect from whatever or whoever is holding you back. Bye. Next. Onwards and upwards!

When Scorpio passion joins forces with the New Moon, anything and everything is possible—trust and believe. That Scorpio intensity can be the driving force to take the world by storm and really start making it happen on a whole new level. On the other hand, watch out for that Scorpio sting...it's legendary. When the internal demons become external, what boils to the surface is not cute. Scorpio energy can really turn up the volume on the drama and leave you spinning your wheels for no reason without getting anything accomplished. Be mindful of this chaotic energy, but don't engage in it. Stay in your own lane and do not allow yourself to spin out of control. Remember, you call the shots in your reality and this is not the time to let energy vampires suck the life out of you. Oookaaayyy.

Instead, on this New Moon we choose to make gratitude the star of the show. Gratitude is the ultimate foundation for building all the prosperity and abundance we want to attract. There is power and pleasure in being grateful for everything in your life. If you take time to notice and be thankful for all the magical things that you are experiencing all day and every day, you will find even more of these moments will show up for you. When you are locked into the power of gratitude, even the worst setbacks and shitty days become a valuable lesson that needed to be learned. When you can identify these challenges as growth and have nothing but gratefulness for them, you will become an unstoppable force and the sky is the limit of what you can achieve. #FACTS.

This is why your connection to Source Energy through magic, meditation, and mindfulness is so important. We like to start the day with an affirmation of the energy that we want to embody. Usually it's staying in a high vibration of love and light, uplifting and inspiring others along the way. It is also important to come up with an affirmation of what energies you are not going to engage in throughout the day. Fear, doubt, lack, stress, bitterness, and bitchiness are definitely not any part of what is going to move you forward. Hold yourself accountable to your affirmations throughout the day. If you find yourself in alignment with your positive intentions, give gratitude for this. If you find yourself falling into the negative thought patterns that can sabotage you, check yourself, correct yourself, and get back on track. Now let's start manifesting up a storm with all this New Moon energy!

The New Moon and Crystals

Our love and passion for crystals has grown over the years—from making crystal jewelry in the '90s to opening Spellbound Sky in 2011, the metaphysical crystal destination of our dreams!

We have always felt that in addition to their beauty, these wonders of Mother Nature are powerful tools that can get you from point A to point B. The New Moon is our favorite time to use crystals to get us inspired and empowered. The spell work we do on the New Moon incorporates our favorite manifesting stones and we like to use these crystals to solidify the energies we want to attract. The world of crystal grids has been elevated to a whole new level lately and we always encourage everybody to explore all the possibilities of working with these mystical stones.

For this ritual, we decided to go old school and get back to the basics, sharing our original pre-internet method for setting up our stones. We like to call this simplified version an "Organic Grid."

Working with crystals should be an all-inclusive act of magic and we believe that you do not have to have the physical stone to benefit from their energies. Crystals are the tools and you are the vibrational conduit to manifest their capabilities. If you do not have the crystals we suggest, perhaps you can print out an image of the stone, or even incorporate drawing and coloring the crystals you love into your ritual. We also feel that if you want to substitute a crystal for another element, like a leaf or a stone/feather/shell found in nature, go ahead! For this ritual and all others, it is our belief that your spell works best when you personalize it and make it work for you.

New Moon Organic Manifesting Grid

Always start out with a quartz crystal generator or a selenite tower placed in the middle of your grid. These Universal high-frequency crystals are used to amplify the intentions of all your other stones, facilitating a spiritual vessel of light to co-create your purpose.

Next, we like to make a circle of stones around the quartz/selenite generator that gets us in the manifesting mode. Here's a list of our top 10 faves. Feel free to pick as many or as few that call to you:

- ▼ **Citrine** : the ultimate stone of prosperity and abundance on all levels.
- ✦ **Pyrite** : gives that warrior energy needed in order to go for it!
- ▼ **Carnelian** : allows for a motivated mindset, utilizing the power of confidence and courage.
- ✦ **Peridot** : connects you to positive energy and an optimistic outlook.
- ▼ **Lodestone** : creates that magnetic effect that draws your desires into your real life.
- ✦ **Jade** : inspires good luck, good fortune, and overall good vibes.
- ▼ **Tiger eye** : action stone used for balance, strength, and mental clarity.
- ✦ **Orange calcite** : connects you to creativity and inspiration with a free-spirited essence.
- ▼ **Garnet** : the stone of passion used to make your dreams happen in the physical realm.

Since this is a Scorpio New Moon, we want to add in a few more stones to the circle that can boost and nurture the Scorpio energy. Here are a few options—feel free to add as many other crystals to the mix that represent your story for this particular New Moon:

- ◆ **Labradorite** : activates your personal magic and elevates higher awareness.
- ▼ **Jet** : used for deep connection to the mystical realms and the inner void of creation.
- ◆ **Serpentine** : the stone of transformation, using snake energy to shed your skin in order to reveal the new you.
- ▼ **Rhodonite** : allowing love and compassion to offset the effects of that Scorpio sting.
- ◆ **Pink calcite** : supporting the heart in a state of well-being, gratitude and appreciation.
- ▼ **Black tourmaline** : the ultimate psychic protector, used for the purification of internal and external negative energies.

If it's possible for you, we prefer to create this grid outdoors, allowing the crystals to soak up the energy of the New Moon. Throughout the Waxing Moon cycle, you can select a stone from the grid circle that calls to you, to carry with you each day as a talisman on your manifesting journey for support and encouragement.

Now let's get started! Take all the elements of the grid and begin by placing your quartz or selenite in the center.

Next, mindfully place each stone or element around this generator in a circular pattern, one at a time, focusing on the energies of each one and how they are going to assist in your future vision.

Once you have the circle laid out, connect to the highest universal energies and call on your spirit guides, higher self, or other preferred cosmic helpers to provide you with the wisdom and clarity needed to fully bring power and life into this altar.

In your mind's eye, visualize all of the abundance you want to create. Feel in your heart of hearts that this is already a reality. Inhale gratitude, and exhale relief in knowing that your dreams are on the horizon!

Creating the grid is just part of this New Moon ritual. We encourage you to personalize it by adding candles, affirmations, journaling, vision boards, and any other spell work that inspires you. It can be as simple or as multi-layered as you want. With all ritual work, what you put into it is what you get out of it. Keep it fresh by constantly switching it up, and always challenge yourself to take your spiritual journey to the next level. Most of all...have fun. Laugh. Dance. Get as much enjoyment out of this New Moon ritual as possible. Now is the time to say goodbye to that wacka-doodle world of faux drama fuckery, and say hello to the magical world of your unlimited potential.

Suggested affirmation: "I am an unstoppable force of magic and power. I am worthy of receiving all the prosperity and abundance of my dreams."

Notes on New Moon feelings:

Notes on ritual:

NOVEMBER 15th: FIRST QUARTER MOON in AQUARIUS
6:54 AM PST, 12:52 PM MOONRISE, 11:52 PM MOONSET

Some Ways to Connect with Mystery, or,
Building a Healthy Relationship with the Unknown, or
Diving in without a Map, or
16 or so Ways to Get Unstuck

1. Try this affirmation on:

I learn by doing *I learn by doing* I learn by doing. I. Learn. By. Doing. I'm doing it!

2. Try this affirmation on:

Time is a spiral, not a line. I honor my current cycle of——— . I am a mystery and I love it.

3a. If you do not know what you want, free-write on a piece of paper. Start with:

"What I want, right now: ——— ."

or

"What I need, right now: ——— ."

Start writing around these prompts for 5 minutes.
Then, reread what you wrote. What are 3-6 words that pop out to you?
Is there an answer in there?

3b.(You might want to free-write, or might want to make a list. This list is the "List of Things I Do Not Want to Do but I Must So I Will Do Them, All the While Trying to Make Them Fun, or Get Them Over Quickly, or At Least Attempt to Detach Emotionally or Fear-Brained Away from Them, so as to Make Them Slightly Less Annoying or Painful. Some of These Things Are My Dreams, and I've Assigned Pain and Fear to Them. I Will Gently Work on Infusing My Dreams with Joy and Contentment. Some of These Things are Painful because They Are Unknown or I Will Be Vulnerable in Some Way. However, I Love and Honor the Unknown in the Universe and in Magic, and so I Will Honor and Love the Unknown in My Own Life. And I Appreciate Vulnerability in Others, Therefore I Appreciate and Nurture My Own Vulnerabilities.")

4. Create something, then immediately destroy it. Extra credit points if you love the thing.

5. Do some things that are invisible to everyone but you every day for weeks. Orgasms, meditation, picking up trash, sending out kind energy as you move in the world or stay on your couch. Visualizing your dreams, scenarios flowing into your life precisely at the right time, answers bubbling up from within your dreams. Those sorts of invisible things. Notice if there are any shifts in any ways as a result of these actions.

6. A black hole is the death of large star. It is a region of spacetime with such strong gravitational effects that nothing can escape from it. It is invisible and it is nothing but it is also a very big something. In fact, it continues growing as it absorbs particles from its surroundings. A nothingness that can grow. In fact, some of the brightest light in the universe occurs when orbiting gas brushes up against the black hole. A quasar is formed. The brightest light comes out of the largest darkness.

8a. Never underestimate the power of small, deliberate actions repeated countless times.

8b. Take care to toggle between working just outside your comfort zone, with efforts made from inside your comfort zone. Too much comfort can lead to stagnancy. Too much uncomfortableness can lead to overwhelm.

8c. Define your anchors. Lean on them through change. Allow new anchors to make their way into your life.

8d. P.S. Keep going, slowly and steadily. Keeping going is almost always the key.

9. Remember that every single invention, every single song you hear on the radio, every single tree that rises up to meet the sky and stretches down to root in the earth, every single sentence you read in bed, on your commute, once was nothing. Except it was also always something. It was a muse, riding on the wind, it was a message someone noticed, it was a process someone paid attention to, it was a gathering, a focus, and an action. It was water, and air, and fire, and earth, and center. It started with a tiny and weighted promise to follow through.

10. Begin at the beginning. The beginning is wherever you decide to begin. If you need to draw a start line with tape on the hallway in your apartment and cross it, do that. If you need to set an alarm to start, do that. Draw a red circle on a calendar date that feels right to you. If you need assurance that beginnings are sometimes wobbly and first drafts can be shitty and that no matter what, you are doing it well even if it is not what you envisioned, this very workbook is your assurance.

11. Be in conversation with exciting, mysterious things. Honor the experience above all else. Allow the experience of the mystery to be your teacher.

12.a. If you keep getting the same results, is it because you are doing it in the same way? Do you need to address a process, or a situation, with a completely different behavior or mindset? What if you just tried it again, in a consciously different way?

12.b. What if the difference made all the difference? What if that difference was enough, all on its own?

13. Reframe the use of the unknown in your life. Looking back on your life, remember a time when things were very unknown. What came out of that unknown state? How can the unknown be useful, thrilling, or exciting now? What is mysterious about yourself, to yourself?

14. Ask yourself: If I knew everything I needed and wanted was coming to me, what would I need to do in the meantime? Delete all the texts from an ex? Clean out the closet? Learn that language? Record the sonata? Book the flight? Apologize for snapping at that person? Make that acupuncture appointment? Say: *I love you,* a little more? Then do those things.

15. Erase the words "good" and "bad" from your vocabulary.

16. Sing a song to the Moon.

A Moon of Nothing and Everything

"Nothing is important, so everything is important." — Keith Haring

November's only Full Moon fills up fast above the horizon on a Friday. This Moon is sometimes called the Beaver Moon, when traps would be set out to capture furs. Traditionally, if the Beaver Moon is the last Full Moon before a Winter Solstice, it is also called the Mourning Moon. In North America, Native Americans have called this Moon the Freezing Moon (Anishinaabe), the Trading Moon (Cherokee), Moon When All is Gathered in (Pueblo), and the Moon When Winter Begins (Lakota). For us in the Northern Hemisphere, this is a Moon that brings us Winter on an icy platter. This weekend, many Americans will be gathering for Thanksgiving, another deceptive holiday that covers up the horrific history of our nation. You may wish to spend some time this weekend learning more about this land and the original inhabitors of Turtle Island, who have gazed up into the crystal halo of the Moon for over 12 thousand years.

This Full November Moon is the second since our Equinox Harvest Moon in September. In the Northern Hemisphere, we are squarely in the Waning part of the year—a time of rest, reflection, subconscious calibration, and shadow work. At this time, a Full Moon, so much about light, source, and energy, does not sync up with the pulse of cold, dormant earth. This death, this decay, whether metaphoric or actual, during this midnight time of the year, may turn a Full Moon somber. She could bring up the stark contrasts in your life with her gravity. Her rising could breeze past your heart roughly, showing it what it still yearns for, and leave it aching. A Full Moon in the dark days of the Wheel of the Year might amplify the shadows. Her illumination may bring up what must be revisited or released. The most fruitful work during this time of year may be around interior work, intuitive work, and what possibilities dwell in the underworlds and the liminal. Magical workings, cathartic Tarot readings, deep hypnosis, and longer meditations could be favored at this Lunation.

This Mourning Moon might bring up what in your life needs to be buried and laid to rest. Do not chase after what is running out of the door of your life, especially if what is running away has continuously sucked you dry. Let yourself grieve the emotions that demand your attention. Know that this grieving can also be a detox. Let this Full Moon allow you to remoisturize the skin of your soul. Replenish yourself with comfort and tea, eye masks and early bedtimes.

Raise your head to stare at the Moon in the night sky and you perceive a glowing circle hanging over the horizon. A circle is an endless line, a protected space. It mimics the spiral of time and spiralic orbits of the universe. We cast circles in witchcraft to begin an endless moment, a safe space that contains all timelines at once, themselves circles. It is an act that invokes our own center, and the center that is in all things, the center that sits in the middle of all the elements, the perfect blend of balance and energy. A center is a circle, the gathering together and a forming of disparate aspects of a community, a life, interests. Circles are centering.

We sit in circles to reinforce the idea that we are all equal and wise. A circle is at once an activated line and a never-ending loop. We walk in the circle of a labyrinth. Get caught up and have to circle back around. Ancient Greeks thought of the circle as being the perfect shape. The medicine wheel is a circle. There is no ending and no beginning. A circle connotes totality: a void and a portal, an entry point and a mirror. In witchcraft, as we concoct potions and prepare herbs counterclockwise and clockwise, the circle of tradition is still followed. Witches create circles of protection, summoning circles, circles of salt. We utilize the energy of our chakras: circular sources of electricity and vibrations. The circle is one of the earliest feminine signs; full bellies, cauldrons, cups, bowls, the pupil of one's eyes, and the ouroboros are the symbols we all connect to instinctually across geography, across the vast expanse of time.

We think of the Moon as a circle, but she is not. The universe does not produce perfect shapes; only pure mathematics does. The Moon is actually closer to an egg shape. The Earth is as well. The Egyptians believed in the cosmic egg; that the universe, or the great creator that birthed it, took the shape of an egg. Closer in shape to a zero.

Western culture usually thinks that zeros are undesirable. There are zeros and there are heroes. Your checking account is at zero and you panic, and there are sexually attractive savings with too many zeros to count. Starting at zero is considered daunting. This in part stems from Christianity. Medieval scholars deemed the void evil. Because their God was the creator of all, and the creator cannot make evil, then nothing (a.k.a. the void), was evil. (Charles Seife, *Zero: The Biography of a Dangerous Idea*). Jews had no such fear of the void. The teachings of the Kabbalah recognize the dual nature of God/Source/creation. The Hebrew word "win son," which means "infinite," represented the creator aspect of God. There was another name affixed to the creator: "akin," or "nothing" (Seife). Hinduism is yet another religion that collaborates with zero and the void. In Hinduism, the void is revered. It is the infinity from which the universe burst forth.

Where there is the infinite, there is joy. *There is no joy in the finite* —the Chandogya Upanishad reminds us, the early Sanskrit text from the time period of 8th to 6th century BCE. The finite can be controlled; the finite is exact and so is limited. The finite does not acknowledge the endless beyond from which our consciousness springs. The infinite is messy, the infinite is chaotic, the infinite cannot be controlled or regulated as there is literally no point in doing so. Only possibilities that swim forever, beyond laws, beyond money, beyond time. In much Eastern thought, the 0 is a strong symbol: it cannot be destroyed, it is a standalone. It is the numeral between positive and negative; it is a balanced base. Zero is the tunnel, the portal, the circle that occurs in actual nature: the Earth, the orbits, the Moon.

While the cycle of the Moon is a spiral—a circle—albeit an imperfect one, it also possesses a nature that exists beyond the binary. Inside her orbit she both dies and is reborn; she gives birth to herself, she reproduces herself all on her own. Within this process is shadow, within this process is emptiness, within this process is the void.

In the Tarot, the void is The Fool, card 0: the beginning, or actually the preexistence, or preconsciousness, or essence, or source. And of course, this means that The Fool is also the end: because a beginning is also the end of something else. These beginnings and endings are not so clear cut in our own experiences. We can have layers of voids in various aspects of our lives. Someone has left us, but the hole of time and energy they've taken with them has not yet been opened, as we cling to the idea of them to fill the void of them. We are ready for a new pattern to take hold in our lives, but are unwilling to clear the emptiness we need to flail in as we retrain ourselves and give ourselves the room to make mistakes. We like to call this "the void" when really many of us have "voids"; tiny or very gaping holes in our lives, some that are vacuums that drain, and some that are opportunities in disguise. Some that are so painful in their emptiness that we pretend they aren't there, some that would allow us to take flight if only we would crawl inside and spend time in them, running our hands over the craggy contours that line the pockets of our specific existence. Nothingness is like the nothingness of space, which is actually everything.

A void can be a deep dark well with no bottom, or a portal of endless possibilities we can step into. A Yayoi Kusama room, filled with the wonderment of no-space, no-time, or an itchy set of question marks crawling up and down our skin. In many many movies, the hero or heroine hops down a chute, or has to drag themselves through a dark tunnel in order to end up in a pivotal part of their journey. Void as birth canal, void as activation. Void as the space between the inhale and exhale. Void as pause. Pause as fruitful action.

This Full Moon, this cold Moon, this reflection Moon, this Moon that is a cipher or a vacuum or a sloshing full cup or a barren flat disc of light, is in Gemini at zero degrees. Mercury, the planet that rules Gemini, is retrograde until next month. Gemini is air, is thought, is reaction, response, communication, reflexivity, and ideas. Gemini is awareness of the self as being the other. The archetype of Gemini vibrates strongly with the famous Descartes quote: "I think, therefore I am." This Full Moon might want you to experience: "No Matter, Never Mind. No Mind, Never Matter. Either way…" (Ram Dass, *Be Here Now*). The archetype of Mercury the messenger is also strongly liminal. They are a true deity of above and below, here and there, the underworld to the above world, from a ferry to a train to a plane to a car to a cloud to the internet to love notes getting passed down a row in an eighth grade geography classroom. Mercury is everywhere and nowhere. Gemini can see this and be this. There can be great reflexiveness in this Moon, truthful messages reflecting who you are really are, and where you must embody your present self, your most spacious self, your most intriguing self. This Moon could be asking you to go beyond notions of right and wrong, shadow and light, into integration so that there is a third option: an alchemy of openings which is the combination of downloads, knowings, experiences, and experiments. Gemini is as much about thirds as it is about pairs. When ignited, contained entities come together. This results in a third, entirely distinct energy created out of the disparate, the opposite, or the kindred.

The Tarot card that corresponds to Gemini is The Lovers. Most interpretations of this card on a superficial level have to do with love and love relationships, but as always, the Tarot meanings of this key go much deeper than this first pass. Originally called "The Brothers," for Castor and Pollux, the twins that came out of the egg that Leda laid, the siblings were commemorated as stars above (Mary K. Greer, *Tarot Constellations: Patterns of Personal Destiny*). This card is about relations, choices, and the embrace of non-duality. This card speaks of the sparks that arise when we introduce disparate ideas or mindsets congenially. Some interpretations of this card speaks to integrating the balance we hold within us: masc and femme, introvert and extrovert, giver and receiver, teacher and student, seeker and knower. Within that integration lies understandings and reflections about the self that we couldn't get through a fixed gaze. We need the introduction of the other, we need to go beyond either/or, to turn our sparks into a flame.

In the RWCS deck, we see two humans in the Garden of Eden. There is safety, yet with the inclusion of the snake, the goddess of truth, we know the scene will change any moment. Presumably, the image shows lovers. When they join together, when they meet, the two become much greater than their namesake. The introduction of the third, in the form of the cosmic strawberry angel, hovers above their heads. This card does not only speak to romantic partnership; it describes what occurs when people come together with respect and dialogue about an idea, especially a complex or challenging idea, to expand solutions and understanding. In this way, this card can bring up collective consciousness and collective unconsciousness, and the spectrums of each that we are all processing and dealing with in our assorted lives. This card circles around the premise that we are our consciousness, we are beyond our consciousness, and we are run through with Source, with spirit, with any possibilities we can think of, and a lot more that we cannot quite fathom yet. At this Full Moon, you can take The Lovers card on your altar, tape it on your dashboard, put it by your bed, and meditate on choice, on different choices, on new combinations, as conscious expansion. You can ask for what messages need to come up again, for you to see them differently or engage with them more generously, more curiously. Ask yourself: what needs my attention, my mind? And what do I need to pay no mind to anymore? Ask yourself: what if I considered every interaction I had, every engagement as holy?

The Full Freezing Moon, the wide reflecting Moon, the nothing Moon, and the everything Moon of this November is in 0 degrees Gemini. The 0 point in astrology is a shift and a start, a transition, and in some cases, depending on what signs we are talking about, a jump and a leap. The Sabian symbol that correlates with this degree is:

A Glass-Bottomed Boat Reveals Undersea Wonders.

The astrologer and writer Dane Rudhyar interpreted this symbol as a "new dimension of reality perceived by the earnest inquirer" (Dane Rudhyar, *An Astrological Mandala: The Cycle of Transformation and Its 360 Symbolic Phases*). This image conjures up ideas of sight, and of seeing in different ways. The conscious mind becomes see-through. We often look up to gain insight. It is more rare to look for insights below us. There are those of us that are afraid of the deep, because the deep sea is so mysterious, it goes on without end. This Full Moon weekend could offer up moments of insight and different ways of seeing. Different ways of accessing our subconscious, our intuition, and our nothingness. What would a see-through mirror afford us? What would be a mirror that would remind us that almost everything is an illusion, brought on to our sometimes pathological attachments to something-ness? Where are the mirrors in your life right now? What mirrors are useful and which need to be shattered?

The idea of the void, of zero, of emptiness, is very important when thinking about magic. Non-attachment can stimulate growth. A seed needs a hole to grow into. Clearing away, cleaning the slate, whether that be the slate of our mind, or of our schedule, or of certain rotting patterns or relationships, is usually the first task when we perform any magical task or process. When we detach from a very specific outcome in our magical workings, we are giving the energy more opportunities to flourish. A limiting constriction of the mind into finality pushes the energy into finality. When we clear our mind of concrete expectations, even more fantastic results can occur. What wants to be in this present moment comes up to show us, unfolds to teach us, and acts as both message and messenger.

Similarly, in our relationships, whether it may be relationship to self or relationships to important humans, energies, ancestors, deities, animals, and plants in our lives, space allows in more. More love, more understanding, more time, more room to share, more information to work with. Suspending assumptions generally aids in more constructive relationships. At this Full Moon time, let your relationship to yourself—your actions, your thoughts, your responses, your affirmations—really give you that see-through glass bottomed boat of reflection. What deep visions lie on the other side when you give yourself space and time to really look?

When we speak of manifestation, the void a.k.a. scarcity, a.k.a. pain, can be used very effectively to show us what we deeply drastically DO want. Contrasts in our life: loneliness, boredom, longing, numbness, can show us where we need to show up more for ourselves. If we get really real with what we want, what we are seeking shows up in the void. Void as vulnerability. Void as answer giver. If the bright light flashlight of the only November Moon shines all of your insecurities about the unknown squarely in your face, leaving you in a sputtering state of stubbornness or sorrow, can you see them as what they are: an illusion to mask your true knowingness, a cover-up, a distraction from the potential of the present moment? An answer to the questions that you seek? Think differently. Look differently.

So, we have to build a bridge. Build a bridge from a finite place to an infinite place. Restructure our mindset so that we are in relationship with desires, not controlled by them or suffering from the lack of them in our waking life. Radically accept where we are: the pain, the chronic illness, the jealousy, the avoidance. Whatever is the block, or is interpreted as "bad," is also the information that leads us into a more generous space. Even if that self-reflexiness is a sting at first, ultimately our awareness of our selves and our connections as to why we act the way we act, why our patterns might come back around, why our wounds are so raw, so fiery, that knowledge sets us free. That knowledge grants us awareness and our awareness, over time, is what will open up different and plentiful possibilities. Knowledge is power.

With the knowledge we gain, we can practice detachment. When we practice a healthy detachment in our life, with our manifestations, our spiritual and magical life tends to grow. When we detach from outcomes, the claws of entitlement and expectation come off. Our magic is more alluring when we are meeting the universe halfway, not when we are writhing with impatience or chasing her down with a lasso. Treat your magic as you would like to be treated. Give your desires the space they need to grow into the forms they need to be in to teach you the lessons you need to learn along your path of infinity.

There is, of course, beauty in the finite. Finishing a big important project. Getting a degree. Leaving a friend who will not respect you. Certain spells that revolve around a finite result are perfectly fine: a relationship that will be supportive and loving, a different job or a different home to move into, a certain outcome by a certain date. I'm certainly not knocking spells of that nature. However, even when we cast those types of spells, we can ask for that or better. We can allow there to be some invitation for more, for a sprinkling of infinity dust on top of the cupcake of finality.

Not every Moon is one we actively honor with magical workings of a firework caliber. Some Full Moons are allowed just to exist. To be everything and nothing. No more and no less. To be a marker of eons of life that have been stirred by bright brilliant moonbeams: everyone on this Earth from Cleopatra to Mary Magdalene to Joan of Arc to Ida B. Wells to Sun Ra to Rebecca Solnit to June Jordan to you and me. And to be a cold atmosphere-less rock, chained to the Earth by a random collision and gravity, an object comprised of basic basalt, a submissive reflector of a churning sun's energy. Not even worth completely colonizing (yet), or even erecting a simple space station onto.

We don't have to actively worship every Full Moon. There doesn't have to be candles and chanting and gatherings and dance and breath work and hours of preparation. Sometimes we just witness. Sometimes we pause, we spend time interrogating the pause between our inhale and our exhale. Our exhale and our inhale. Sometimes the victory is remembering the pause is always there, and counter to what a lot of our culture says, that the pause can be a way to expand time and space. Sometimes we just get through the day, the week, however exhausting it is, and leave it at that. Bed is the celebration. The ending is the celebration. That can be enough.

Some ancient cultures looked at a Full Moon as a resting time. She is not waxing and she is not waning. She just is. If need be, follow suit. It could be a relationship Moon, a party Moon, a uniting Moon. It could be a cold Moon, a questioning Moon, a shadow work Moon. Sometimes we do the work. Sometimes we just witness (Monica Sjöö & Barbara Mor, *The Great Cosmic Mother*).

We live in an ableist culture and so our language around magic can reflect this. Some of us have no career to climb up. Some of us do not have the ability to move our bodies to build an altar or go to the witch shop for frankincense and dragons blood incense. Some of us get very sick if we are to smell that dragon's blood incense. For some of us, there is no cure. And for some of us, the Full Moon's tidal wave energy brings that up and shines a floodlight on the differences and the similarities between us. The everything-ness of our emotions and the nothing-ness, splashing around inside of us like an ironic yin yang. Please know that someone else's seeming everything-ness does not add to your nothing-ness. Please know that your everything-ness and your nothing-ness is enough, just as it is.

Every Moon is for everybody. For every Full Moon that we experience, if we cannot see her, we can feel her. If we cannot move, we can still thank her with our heart and our thoughts. Every Full Moon ritual need not be elaborate. It can be just a reminder that we are living, simply by being, simply by staying alive. The most effective form of magic is living—whether that living is messy or depressing or thrilling or tedious or all of the above and more, because that's generally what living is—it's a circle of wretchedness and beauty, chaos and devotion. The most embodied magic exists in the here and now. It is a magic that expects nothing and everything. At this Full Moon time, can you go beyond dualistic ideas in your own life? Can the not-knowing be an exciting mysterious circle of infinity?

A Full Moon is at once complete and empty at the same time. She does not generate her own light. Her dark grey surface, comprising elements such as iron, magnesium, and silicon, and covered in cold lava from billions of years ago, mottled with craters, devoid of any atmosphere, is the perfect blank surface for the Sun's reflection. She is devoid of light, yet her darkness is a conduit for the Sun's rays. When she is in her Full state in the sky, she rises at sunset, almost never in our sky at the same time as the Sun. Her presence facilitates the Sun's absence. The shadow light of the Sun, the circles we are on, the circles that surround us, the circular motions of the cosmos allow the obsidian sky to possess its own lighthouse in the form of our only Moon. Even when the Sun is not there, it is. Even when the Moon is not there, it is.

The Moon as mirror, polished or unpolished, clear or dusty, see-through or opaque, is filled up with reflected sunlight. She orbits, like all the other planets, in an circular fashion. The wheel that is the circle of time, turning around and coming back around again, seemingly without end. From the circles of the stars to the zodiac wheel that is a circle too, all the way zooming into our DNA of circles and spirals that make up the very stuff that we are. Allow the glowing orb of the Moon to allow you to center yourself. You underneath her, whole and empty and both at the same time. Limitless and another sparkling seed, another filled cup, another transparent dreamer, pausing in the in-between, floating in the nothingness and stretching out into the everything.

Crystals for this Full Moon: clear quartz, obsidian, dalmation stone, a crystal you create in your mind
Tarot cards to meditate on: The Fool, the Aces, The Lovers, The Moon, The Sun, The World, a Tarot card you make up that you need at this time

Journaling questions/questions to ask yourself as you stare up at the Moon:
Where do I feel empty? Why?
Where do I feel full? Why?
Do I need to recalibrate these states of emptiness and fullness?
How do I feel about voids? Why?
Do I need to take more space from something/someone, or give more space to someone/something?
How will I honor myself, my rest, my enough-ness and my not-enough-ness at this time?

A Ritual for Nothing

This ritual requires nothing, other than a calm, quiet, comfortable, uninterrupted space.
You may wish to have this read to you. You may wish to read this out loud while recording, then play it back. You may wish to find this recording as a free downloadable mp3 on my website (modernwomen.bigcartel.com) or on YouTube. (Google it.)

Find yourself in a comfortable position. You may be seated, lying down, propped up against a wall, or standing, depending on what is most comfortable to you.

Focus on your breathing. Focus on your inhale and your exhale. There doesn't have to be a particular rhythm, just allow for your breath to take up all of the space it needs to inside yourself, inside your lungs, cells, moving from the soles of your feet, and the top of your head. Really spend time connecting yourself to your breath, the ins and outs, and the spaces between them. Explore. Notice. (Pause.)

Now imagine a circle around you. It is a circle of energy. It is a circle that protects you. It is a circle that keeps all the you in, and all the everything else out. As your eyes are closed, can you feel how far away from your body your circle needs to be? Just notice this. (Pause.)

Make sure to fill your circle with your breath. With every exhale, expand your breath out past the skin of your body, into the circle of protection around you. With every inhale, imagine fresh energy from the sky coming into your body and filling you up.

You may imagine your breath as colors. You may imagine your body as a color. Notice any sensations or feelings with curiosity. (Pause.)

In your circle, allow all your thoughts, all your dreams, wishes, or even just mental chatter to fill up the space. Have it all there, all around you, all inside you. Take the time to see what pops up.

Then imagine a big gust of wind blowing it all away outside of your circle, outside of your body. Imagine all of the everything leaving your body, and with it, you suddenly have more space to breathe. You feel very clear. You are in the present moment completely. (Pause.)

Your body begins to sink into the earth. You fade beneath your floor, into the alive, pulsing earth. You find yourself magically in an underground tunnel, full of crags and pockets and curves. The earth is alive, and you feel grounded, concrete, and tangible.

You are safe here, and you begin to explore. Take note of where you want to go and why. Explore more, and find yourself in a small dirt room, made naturally by the cave. In a niche in the dirt wall, there is a secret object. Go over to it and see what it is. Listen to what it has to tell you. The dirt room becomes a tunnel becomes a portal to the outside. You follow the light that leads you out. (Pause.)

You break the ground, and as you leave the Earth, your body begins to get lighter. With each breath, you rise higher and higher, until you are in the sky, floatinglike a cloud, in the clouds. You allow yourself to float higher and higher like a slow balloon in the sky.

Now imagine your consciousness dissolving so that you are aware that the thoughts you are thinking are of you and are not of you. Imagine yourself connected to a source that is indescribable and imagine that source inside of you. Imagine any doubt, any fear, any stiffness or resistance to the idea that you are part of everything, fade away.

The more nothing you become, the more true that you are. As you allow yourself to become very, very still, notice any messages or new awareness you are able to receive. Keep breathing. Keep filling your lungs up with air. Feel any feelings, visualize any images, receive any messages from your vantage point high in the sky.

(Pause.)

Your consciousness slowly leaves the sky, you slowly float over the ozone, through the atmosphere, and into deep space. You see stars, and nebulae, and planets. You see the Sun, the Moon, and realize that just as you are a part of yourself, just as you are a part of the Earth, just as you are a part of the sky, you are also a part of space. You slowly allow yourself to dissolve. You slowly allow your consciousness to dissolve so that it becomes dust. You see yourself, and all your thoughts and all your actions and all your pain and suffering and love turn into the tiniest particles of matter, and float away.

A gentle sense of calm washes over you.

You tell your subconscious and you tell your consciousness that after you wake up, any downloads, any messages about your life, any realizations, or what is coming for you, will be enacted in your life following this Full Moon. We let our desires, we let our love, we let our peace, we let our belief, and we let the moment wash over us. We thank the Moon, we thank the Sun, we thank space, we thank our consciousness, we thank our guides, we thank nature, we thank animals, we thank loved ones, we thank earth, we thank water, we thank fire, we thank air, we thank the center, and we thank nothingness for showing us everything.

We take three deep breaths.

We count backwards from 12:

12
11
10
9
8
7
6
5
4
3
2
1

Open your eyes, stretch your body, and come back to yourself.

November Waning Moon: Lilith
By Diego Basdeo

Lilith:
the story.

"I am deliberate and afraid of nothing." — Audre Lorde

Lilith (or Lilitu) has over 100 names and her stories stretch from ancient Sumer to Jewish mysticism to Malaysian mythologies (*The Lilith Library*). Her archetypes, the chaotic natural world, femme sexuality, and righteous feminist rage, which appear in many worldwide religions, have been changed and recovered and colonized and covered up or completely erased. I am borrowing the name Lilith and her story because this is the name Western astrology has chosen to use for this particular energy. In our interpretation, she comes from a pre-monotheistic mythology.

One:
First woman, the left side of first man, and equal in all parts.

Adam, after observing animals in Eden, found himself deeply desiring the companionship of a creature like him and prayed to his father for a partner. God, loving his child, put Adam to sleep, and from his left side, he created Lilith. In Eden, the first home to humankind and a paradise of of both spirit (and now the flesh), Lilith was created in part to be a companion for first man, Adam, but ultimately for the joy of her creator.

As you can imagine, it was an instant sparkling romance. He saw her, she saw him, and they wasted little time getting to the business of doing what bodies do. Now y'all, the first time with a new partner can be really awkward and mistakes can be made, especially if you are the first people in history to do it, but when Adam asked Lilith to lie down and she said no, that should have been the end of the conversation. Instead he argued. Lilith suggested side by side, or her on top, but Adam was not having it. He told her, When we fuck, we look at our creator. I look at the earth because I came from dust and you look at me. End of conversation. Lilith was stunned, shook, and hurt. She was literally half of him, completely equal, made by the same creator as him. The more she thought about it, the more hurt brewed in her heart until it there wasn't any more room in her body for sadness. Hurt and pain and anger were never seen in Eden before. There was no place for them, no comforting rain or heartbreak ballads. She had no choice, and without a moment's notice, she walked straight out of paradise.

God sent three angels down to persuade her to return, but could not entice her with gifts. She left paradise, after all, so they resorted to threats. They told her if she did not return to the Garden of Eden, God would kill 100 of her children every day. And do you know what she said?

NO.

I want to pause here and look at the power of no. No is a word self-help gurus and spiritual celebrities don't like to talk about very much. No is a shutting door, a slamming door, a turn away. No is STOP.

It's good to stop. It's good to push back, to make boundaries, or send the gates crashing down.

It's good to consider, or sting, or feel rejection. It's good to say "No, and..." It's okay to say no and yes later. Lilith's NO is a point of no return. She is refusing the final threat from god, closing down all negotiation (much like Adam did before), refusing solace or repair, and rejecting his coercion to change her mind. This Lilith is about the recreation of boundaries: how, when our boundaries are violated, we can sometimes be hyper-vigilant with them moving forward and how necessary that vigilance can be to rebuild ourselves. She is a confrontation, she is saying NO, she is the explosion from a body full of microaggressions, aimless and angry.

Even under the threat of divine murder of 100 of her children every day, she refused to submit. In Lilith we find our righteous rage, our sense of justice, and a stubborn ethic.

This incarnation also raises the questions: How can we escape the binary of submission and dominance? How can we maintain a healthy exchange of power? How can we subvert dominant paradigms? When do we leave too soon? When do we stay too long?

Two:
Yes, am I that bitch.

Lilith wanders the desert, scorned, punished, and full of rage.The way her second incarnation story is told is so endemic of the patriarchal beliefs. Because the charge is around her sexuality, because she won't "put out," it is the twisted logic of misogyny that turns her into an evil ho, so what does Lilith say? If i'm gonna be a ho, I might as well be a ho! She wanders the desert, having sex with demons, making demon babies, and populating the Earth with little succubi that are blamed for nocturnal emissions, crib death, and miscarriages. She uses her sexuality as a way to transmute her feelings, she crucifies the myth of virginity, and becomes the first divine whore.

She soon learns that Adam's pursuit to bone down could not be diminished and God had the gall to create Eve from Adam's rib, ensuring that she would be OF him and therefore submissive. Lilith. Was. Pissed. She was Beyoncé Lemonade pissed, she was Kelis "I hate you so much right now" pissed. She would be damned before she let another woman be subjugated without her consent. With focused energy, Lilith turned her own ass into a snake and slithered back into Eden. When she saw Eve chillin by a tree, she slithered up the tree and broke the spell of ownership by whispering truth. Adam and Eve's world comes crashing down.

Three:
HUMBLE

Lilith retreats to her cave, satisfied at first, but soon realizes that sabotaging their lives (however righteous it was) did not ultimately change her pain. She is still in the desert, forever alone, a woman in eternal exile. She realizes that healing is the only thing she can do and, since no one was going to apologize to her, she was going to have to do it for herself. She transmutes her frustration into ownership over her body, taking agency of her voice, her life, a simple reclamation inspiring feminist rebellion for generations. This final incarnation of Lilith teaches us that, while we are not responsible for the harm done to us, we are responsible for our own healing.

According to the myth of Lilith, it wasn't Eve's knowledgeable fruit that poisoned the well; it was Adam's original sin of lust, projection, and dominance that created a lot of the evil we see in the world today. Leaders of the world are on being investigated for multiple sexual assaults, caught on camera bragging about it, and still remain in office. One in four women experience sexual assault in their lifetime. Every three days, a Trans person is murdered worldwide (*Trans Murder Monitoring Project*), and a majority of the victims are Trans women of color. Considering that Trans people make up less than one percent of the world's population,* this statistic is staggering. Lilith provides a necessary sexual dimension and explores gender non-conformity. As colonial patriarchy persisted, so too has the figure of Lilith been kept hidden. Her name is not spoken at all, and her children have been repressed and subjected to the severest controls in Western patriarchal society.

Working with the Astrological Lilith

There are several different understandings of Lilith and three different astrological points that have been identified as Lilith (asteroid, Black Moon, and Dark Moon). However, some of the leading astrologers and esoteric scientists today believe that Black Moon Lilith is the most relevant and accurate to measure astrological readings (http://montalk.net/matrix/114/food-for-the-moon).

Black Moon Lilith is the most commonly used and the easiest to access. It is not a solid object; it is a point of alignment. The Black Moon is the apogee of the Moon's orbit, the point on the Moon's orbit that is farthest from the Earth. She moves like a snake around the Moon, whispering to Eves of the world, Here, eat this knowledge, take a bite, be your own god.

Your Lilith asks you: What do you know to be true for your sovereignty, above all else? How do you embody that truth? What do you need from others, from the world, to aid you in your healing? How will you show up for your fellow sisters, not just your cis-ters?

How to interpret Lilith in your chart:

The birth chart is made up of three major components, signs, houses, and heavenly bodies (planets, asteroids, nodes, etc). What you need to know is the sign and house that your lilith is in. For this you will need your time, date, and location of birth and access to an ephemeris or have an account with astro.com. On astro.com the code for Black Moon Lilith is "h13". You can also look up "Lilith ephemeris", find the date that you were born and you will see what sign and degree Lilith is in your chart.

The sign which Lilith appears will determine how energy is expressed. For example if you have a Lilith in Gemini it may show up in a person as holding extreme dualities within their personality. The house is where it will show up. If Lilith were to show up in the fifth house we might find an avant guarde art form, using the stage to show raw sexuality and performative rejection of cultural norms. Research the archetypes of the sign your Lilith falls in.

Journaling Questions:
What is my relationship to my righteous rage?
How do I know when it's time to leave a bad situation?
When do I leave a situation that cannot be resolved?
How do I sit with ambiguous and complicated relationships? With others? With myself?
Where do I resonate with the myth of Lilith?
How can I work with this archetype?
Where do I need to explore what my Lilith means for me personally?

The magic of Lilith lies in her disobedience and her encouragement of others to be disobedient in order to be obedient to their own call. How do you will you answer the call?

*www.acpeds.org/the-college-speaks/position-statements/gender-dysphoria-in-children

Notes on this Waning Moon time:

Notes on this Moonth:

Intentions for the next:

DECEMBER 2018
DECEMBER 4TH-6TH: DARK MOON
DECEMBER 7TH: NEW MOON
DECEMBER 15TH: FIRST QUARTER
DECEMBER 22ND: FULL MOON
DECEMBER 29TH: LAST QUARTER

During the last month of this last year, we are asked to look back from a grounded present. This month can be overwhelming: so much to do, a whole year to wrap up, celebrations to attend, lights to keep on, when all we may wish to do is rest.

Allow yourself to give yourself what you need above all else.

In the cold nights of this icy month, do not let your fire go out. Process your grief, and protect your Moon magic. There are gifts on the other side of sorrow. These last workbook entries are designed to mirror the Solstice that happens this month. The prompts are meant to bring you fully into yourself by recognizing all of the parts of yourself—your flame and your grief alike—the parts of us that are sometimes called the shadow. There's also dream magic, candle magic, and a protection spell to round out the cycle and keep you buoyed in balance. Sitting with sorrow, dreaming in the dark, tending our fires, sustaining hope, visioning for the future, integrating our shadows, protecting one another—aren't these what we all need to focus on during this time?

Tender teardrop, know each one of you did not fall in vain. There is a space for the rage; there are lessons in your sorrow. Feel it all to let it out, if that is where you need to be this month. Do not forget we come home again and again, when home is our heart. Make your foundations a priority, a bottom line to remind you of what you love, where you have been, and where you are going. Tend to your roots, and continue strengthening your foundations with all types of nourishment this month.

Gentle creature, come back to yourself. Allow yourself to experience your own brilliance, your own sparkly splendor. You are like the Moon—so close to your own light that you can't quite make out your own brightness all the time. You are like the Moon—reflecting the light of others, yet with so much vision, so much gravity all on your own. When you rise up fully, you take us all with you. All of your knowledge, takes root in our soil. All of the stories you've inspired have us bending to your brilliance. Many of your lessons are wordless. There is enough of your love to gently float us all forever in your ocean.

The Moon shines her light in the dark, where it is needed most. Do not forget, when you look up in the sky, there are so many other beautiful beings also drinking in the Moon's messages. There are other seekers who are not afraid to face their truths, to step into their soft power, who wish to hold all of you, too. You may have to close your eyes to see. Do not forget to dream in the dark.

December Astro Overview
By Diego Basdeo

December 7th: New Moon In Sagttarius / Mercury goes Direct / Mars conjunct Neptune

December 22nd : Full Moon in Cancer / Jupiter conjunct Mercury

Things are shifting and we will stay grounded. We receive messages and we will stay grounded. We understand all cycles. All knowledge sharpens knowledge and we are knowing.

Uranus in Aries is here for the shifts, move it shake it turn it upside down. When Uranus entered Aries, it came in with a bang with the start of Occupy and the Fukushima disaster and has been shaking shit up ever since. Uranus is dramatic and unforeseen change. It is uprising; it is wild and unthinkable. Uranus in Aries is about pure independence to be different and during the New Moon, it is opposing Venus in Libra who is unshakably riding the middle ground. These things are literally diametrically opposed and yet we need them both in our lives.

During the first few weeks of December, we have the chance to see a new perspective on order and instinctive balance. The need to change and adjust, coupled with the Venusian willingness to work with what's on the table, can bring about some really beautiful changes. Venus needs dignity in Libra; she's willing to give the world but under the right conditions, to be kind, to be fair. Uranus needs change, needs to do something totally different, needs to undermine the status quo. Which one calls you? Which one is your growth edge? Do you know when to play nice? Do you know when to speak up? To quote a famous Libra, Oscar Wilde, "Everything in moderation, including moderation."

Under the wild December New Moon, Neptune will be side by side with Mars in telepathic Pisces. This is an opening for psychic electric connection to the cosmic world. Mars comes through in a dynamic and very disarming position. Mars, the infamous planet of war and aggression, transmutes into passive aggression sometimes. And watch out for huge energy fluctuations; look for outlets for excess. Take in wisdom of all cycles.

All things, our energy, our blood, our lust, and wonder all move in cycles. The knowledge of a New Moon in Sagittarius is a hopeful one and to maintain that hope we must understand that hope is a part of a larger waxing and waning of emotions. Sagittarius New Moon also knows a full cycle of experiences. We need variety and freedom.

Deep breath.

Are you ready? Jupiter (abundance, expansion) conjunct Mercury (communication) in Sagittarius tells me that speaking our dreams out loud gives them tremendous power. Say it out loud, shout them, whisper them, write them, and touch them to your heart. Let them be true. Let them serve the highest most good. May they be clear. May they be abundant. May they grip your tender core and pull you closer to your incredibly beautiful, outrageously brilliant, and cunningly surprising destiny.

Chiron, the wounded healer, is aspecting the Moon along with the piercing sword of Mars. We have direct access to our great wound which means we have our finger on the place of our greatest healing. Pour pour pour love love love. In pain be soft, then softer. Be patient. Be giving.

Finally, there is a Uranus/Pluto square that calls us to a very important conversation. Where is your POWER? Are you staying in that old familiar shell for fear of how powerful you would become? We have to step out, expose ourselves a little, get a little vulnerable, to claim what's ours sometimes.

We end the year with a Full Moon in Cancer. Cancer is the mother, nurturance, nourishment, and the Moon is its planet. A Cancer Full Moon is an amazing thing and I want us to take the last weeks of the year to reflect on how incredible we are. The Moon opens the doors to accessing or demanding care by putting us as close to our feelings as possible. I want you to celebrate your development through this workbook. Revisit, and be recharged by your revisiting. Let your growth and insights belong to no one but you.

Then, prepare to walk through the next door of your spiritual journey.

Bring it home to you.

DECEMBER 4th-6th: DARK MOON

Into the Dreamtime
By Liz Migliorelli of Sister Spinster

Welcome Dark Moon! We know that this is lunar time for resting, observing, releasing our energy, and shifting our power. There is so much magic that can happen in this darkness. A chance to restore and transform. We are offered the opportunity to engage with the dark in an intentional way every night, not just during Dark Moon times. We dream in the dark of night. This is a fertile ground for our minds. We can empty out, replenish, incubate, or receive new dreams. Every night, we are offered an opportunity to participate in the mysteries of the world when we dream. And there is so much that can come through! My dreamwork practice is essential to my work with plants, my work with ancestors, and the work of self-transformation (which are all connected anyway!). Since we are in Winter, this is a great time to establish a dreamwork practice if you don't have one already. We are in the time of hibernation, the time of turning inward, the time of divination, sight, self-reflection. We are in the dreamtime.

To begin a dreamwork practice, consider your bed as an altar to your dream. It's hard to honor the dreams as important when I don't shift the energy of the space or set an intention. If I am watching TV, scrolling the phone-void, or doing work late at night, I have found it to be pretty unrealistic to push my computer off my lap, roll over and expect a big, healing dream to come in. Create an exalted space for a dream to come through. This might look like moving your clothes off the bed before you fall asleep. I will use my bedside table as a place to leave an offering for the dream, which means that I clear away the three or four water cups that have lingered too long. I will usually burn some plants before bedtime, as it shifts the energy of my bedroom and changes my state of consciousness. Since so much of my dream life is held in intention with my ancestral practice, I like to burn plants that my ancestors burned, because it is familiar and healing for them, too. For me, that means cedar, rosemary, garden sage, juniper, and yarrow. I leave my screens outside of my bedroom and try not to do phone/computer stuff at least 30 minutes or an hour before going to bed.

Setting the intention to dream is often referred to as "dream incubation." Incubate means develop slowly without outward or perceptible signs. It is really as simple as saying out loud: "I ask for a dream that shows me how my ancestors worked with this plant" or "I ask for a dream that gives me a tool I need to move through these next few weeks." Speaking or writing the intention is important. It's good manners to ask for what you are looking for and not just assume the spirit world knows what you want. I will often write this incubation on a piece of paper and put it under my pillow.

In working with the lunar cycles, you have been leaning into experiencing time as cyclical: noticing the different patterns of energy that are available to us and the art of waiting for the right time to take action in alignment with the Moon. Just remember that dreams work in non-linear time; they are omni-directional. You may have already dreamed the dream you incubated last night. You might dream it three years from now. You might also dream it as a waking dream! Also it helps to remember that having a dreamwork practice isn't necessarily about getting a direct result, in the same way that lunar work isn't so cause-and-effect oriented. We are learning about the quality of time, the ways in which we are in relationship with the practice and the dream world itself.

No one knows your dream vocabulary like you do. I'm not a fan of dream dictionaries, or asking the internet oracle to tell me what my dream means. Part of this practice is asserting and trusting your personal sovereignty in deciding what rings true and what needs to be dropped.

Only you can decipher your dream of an egg carton full of bees, or whatever it might be. The best way to begin to build your dream language is by taking really good notes. Start a dream journal. I have been recording my dreams since age 16, and I have a good idea what it means at this point when I dream of spiders. That magic is specific to me and the way in which I engage with mystery. Even if you think you can't remember your dreams, just start by writing one word or a color from the dream that resonates. The practice of it opens the door for the remembrance. It's like taking herbs: if you don't take the herbs frequently, they don't work in the body. If you don't show up to writing the dreams down, you won't be able to develop a deep relationship to your dream vocabulary. Over time, you will be able to map together patterns of dream energy, symbols, and deeper meanings.

We can be more fully engaged in the dream world with the help of plants. Not only can the plants help our minds and bodies prepare for rest, but they can do the magic work of enhancing our dream states. I love asking plants for help in the dream world! There are some famous dream herbs that you have probably heard of such as mugwort, but all plants can be used as dream plants. They all have their roots in the underworld, and can tap us into the dream of Earth. What plants are calling to you in the dreamtime?

I spoke to burning plants earlier as a way to set intention for dreaming, but there are many other ways to do this work.

 Have a cup of tea. Setting time aside for a cup of tea to connect with the taste, medicine, and energy of your plant ally while setting an intention for the dream time is great! A general guideline for making a strong cup of tea is to infuse one tablespoon of herb per cup of hot water for 20-40 minutes.

 Take a spirit dose of tincture (a spirit dose means 1-5 drops of the tincture, so you are receiving an energetic dose of the plant rather than a medicinal dose). You can also put a few drops of the herb on your pillow.

 Sleep with an herbal dream pillow. You can make a dream pillow by sewing two pieces of fabric together and putting the herb of your choice plus some rice as filler to rest your head on or keep next to you as you sleep. You can also put some of the dried herb under your pillow or hold some in your hand while sleeping. I really like using fragrant herbs for this, such as lavender, mugwort, chamomile, rose, rosemary or jasmine. These scents alone will shift your dream state!

Some plant suggestions:

Rose: A favorite for relaxation, entering into the dream space with a centered heart.
Burdock: Keeps anger, sadness, and fear away from the dream state, acts as a psychic bodyguard.
Skullcap: Helps to quiet the mind, relax the body, and release tension before bed.
Mugwort: Has a very long history of dream enhancement and is ruled by the Moon. It opens the door between the worlds, helps us shapeshift into a more vivid dreamstate. Very bitter, so use with more pleasant-tasting herbs if you wish. Do not take while pregnant/nursing.
Valerian: A classic sedative, can bring deep and intense dreams. I recommend finding a tincture made with the fresh plant, as the dried plant tincture can often make people feel anxious, which is the exact opposite of what we are trying to do!
Lavender: Opens the crown to facilitate communication with spirit realm while calming the body.

Only you can decipher your dream of an egg carton full of bees, or whatever it might be. The best way to begin to build your dream language is by taking really good notes. Start a dream journal. I have been recording my dreams since age 16, and I have a good idea what it means at this point when I dream of spiders. That magic is specific to me and the way in which I engage with mystery. Even if you think you can't remember your dreams, just start by writing one word or a color from the dream that resonates. The practice of it opens the door for the remembrance. It's like taking herbs: if you don't take the herbs frequently, they don't work in the body. If you don't show up to writing the dreams down, you won't be able to develop a deep relationship to your dream vocabulary. Over time, you will be able to map together patterns of dream energy, symbols, and deeper meanings.

We can be more fully engaged in the dream world with the help of plants. Not only can the plants help our minds and bodies prepare for rest, but they can do the magic work of enhancing our dream states. I love asking plants for help in the dream world! There are some famous dream herbs that you have probably heard of such as mugwort, but all plants can be used as dream plants. They all have their roots in the underworld, and can tap us into the dream of Earth. What plants are calling to you in the dreamtime?

I spoke to burning plants earlier as a way to set intention for dreaming, but there are many other ways to do this work.

Some plant suggestions:

Rose: A favorite for relaxation, entering into the dream space with a centered heart.
Burdock: Keeps anger, sadness, and fear away from the dream state, acts as a psychic bodyguard.
Skullcap: Helps to quiet the mind, relax the body, and release tension before bed.
Mugwort: Has a very long history of dream enhancement and is ruled by the Moon. It opens the door between the worlds, helps us shapeshift into a more vivid dreamstate. Very bitter, so use with more pleasant-tasting herbs if you wish. Do not take while pregnant/nursing.
Valerian: A classic sedative, can bring deep and intense dreams. I recommend finding a tincture made with the fresh plant, as the dried plant tincture can often make people feel anxious, which is the exact opposite of what we are trying to do!
Lavender: Opens the crown to facilitate communication with spirit realm while calming the body.

Dream Tea Recipe

2 pts Chamomile
1 pt Skullcap or Passionflower
1 pt Rose
½ pt Mugwort
½ pt Lavender

This tea can be made with fresh or dried herbs. Remember that you might want to add a little more of the fresh herbs if that's what you are working with. If dried, blend the tea together and keep in an airtight jar in a cool, dark place. Use the tea brewing ratios offered above! Drink one hour to 30 minutes before bed to help you prepare for dreaming. Don't forget to imbue your cup of dream tea with your dream incubation, whisper your spell into the tea, and drink up!

May you dream deeply of good medicine.

DECEMBER 7TH : NEW MOON in SAGITTARIUS
1:20 AM PST, MOONRISE 6:58 AM, MOONSET 5:23 PM PST

New Moon Fire: A brief primer on candle magic

Happy New Moon of the last month of this year! Happy December and happy fuzzy knitted sock nights and short brisk days! Happy Mercury out of retrograde, not to appear for another three months! The early Winter sunset gives way to the blank slate of night. More time to get cozy, cook elaborate meals for ourselves and loved ones, watch our favorite movies, and spend our time on indoor projects to be presented to the world in early Spring.

This New Moon is in Sagittarius, with our Sun in the archer's constellation as well. In India, this constellation is called the Bow. In ancient Persia, it was the Centaur, and in ancient Rome, the sign of Sagittarius was associated with Diana, who ruled the horse-riding Amazons who lived by the Black Sea (Barbara Walker, *The Women's Dictionary of Symbols and Sacred Objects*). This New Moon piece is all about fire and candle magic. Working with the element of fire is fitting to do in December. Staying warm and inspired is a must to wrap up the last month of the year in an activated and optimistic fashion. We still have time left in this year: What would you like to start? What would you still like to say you did in 2018? One day might be enough to change the dial to a song you'd rather sing along with. Maybe your affirmation for the next seven days just needs to be:

Someday is today.

Working with fire can speed up our magic. Since humankind discovered fire, we've used it in all aspects of our life. Fire is the great transformer. Fire cooks food, shapes metal, heats houses. Fire helps us to see in the dark and to keep us protected, smoke cleanses us, fire aids us in ritual. We have many secular activities that involve candles. You blow out birthday candles, sing songs around a campfire, light a candle or two to romance your beloved. Fire brings everyone around it—it is a magnetizing element. The simple act of getting warm in a group feels carnal and familiar. The flames seem alive; they dance and give us messages about our existence.

Candles have been associated with magic since the dawn of time. Early on, candles have been associated with spirit and with the soul. Candles as memorials, candles as a metaphor, candles as the brightness of the spirit and a reminder of our internal flame. Many Pagan and folkloric traditions—that continued on in Christian practices—involved torches, bonfires, and candles. These ancients dedicated this fire to the gigantic fire in the sky: the Sun and its cycles. We can look to this present as a continuation of these ancient practices. Currently, it is the fifth night of Hanukkah, the festival of lights. Later this month, just before the Full Moon, many people will light candles for the Winter Solstice, or Yule, the festival of lights! One day after Christmas, people who celebrate Kwanzaa will light a kinara, and celebrate the resilience of the African Diaspora by the ritual of candle lighting. These holidays also mark the return of light to our days that will happen soon at the Solstice. For now, our days remain short and our evenings are long: the best time to dive into candle magic.

Candle magic, without a doubt, is most witches' tried and true effective form of magic-making. Candles themselves are little portable altars of life! They have a beginning, a middle, and an end. Fire is used for purification, activity, ignition, illumination, celebration, passion, and clarity. They soothe our mind, help us focus and remind us of our sparks. Within a candle we can work with all of the elements: we have the fire in the flame, the earth in the wax and/or the herbs/crystals we add to dress the candle, water as anointing oil, the air of our chants over the charged candle and the air that fans the flame, and our spirit, source, and our center—our intentions, the energy we pour into the candle, and the time we spend with it.

The Tarot suit that correlates to fire is Wands. Wands are all about action; they activate in the external. This suit has to do with inspiration, passion, sex, illumination, courage, will, creativity, as well as quality of energy. If Pentacles are the hours in the day, the actual items we build, the way we work, our magic, and what we are doing with our time, the Wands possess the quality in which we think of our work, how we think of our time, how we think of ourselves, and all of the ways in which we think of our magic. If the suit of Pentacles is the hourglass, Wands are the way we hold the hourglass, the way we speak of the hourglass, and the way we use our energy, will, excitement, and enthusiasm to create shifts and bend time. Wands, like Pentacles, are very physical—they are to be embodied and learned through life experience. Whether it be a party, a conflict, a new business, or a trip around the world, the Wands generally process by doing. They act first, and because of this, they are an intuitive suit. Wands go for it, wands act now! Wands, like fire, can move at very, very, very fast speeds, so buckle up when you see a lot of Wand cards in your reading—things are about to get spicy!

Wands, which are sometimes called Clubs/Rods/Staffs, also deal with power and force, war and conflict. We can use our will for the highest goals or in petty and egotistical ways. In the Minors, the shadow side of the Wands suit pops up to be dealt with in the Five, the Seven, the Nine, and the Ten of Wands. Egoism, selfishness, shortsightedness, competitiveness, defensiveness and a stubbornness to reflect, as well as overwhelm and burnout can take place with too much fire! We must rest, think of others, ask for help, or shift gears so our fire doesn't fade away.

We can work with the attributes of the Wands suit at this time. We can summon inspiration and charge our desire with candle magic. If there is absolutely no way you can burn a candle, or if for some reason you are averse to candle magic or afraid of fire, there is an easy enough way to access the energy of candle magic without using candles. This is creative visualization. Creative visualization is very useful and can be used in tandem with spells or on its own in meditation every day. In general, the key to creative visualization is belief and repetition. Try creatively visualizing every day for up to 20 minutes. Usually, focusing on one area at a time is best, but I suppose you could try it every day for month with different topics, and give yourself an entire energetic and mental vibratory makeover!

Candle magic is sympathetic magic: like attracts like. What this means, precisely, is that the attributes of the spell you are creating are being activated by the objects you are using in your spell work. Symbols are powerful—we see this everywhere in our culture, from hieroglyphics to Tarot cards to app icons to bus billboards. Similarly, using symbols in magic, whether blooming flowers on an altar, spicy ginger in ceremonial tea, or seeds scattered to the wind, imprint in our mind and move our energy in our desired fashion. As within, so without. As above, so below.

Sympathetic magic is amazing because we are very likely to believe in optimal results when we are literally seeing a metaphor of them on our altar. Spells that move one candle to another slowly, over a course of a few days, remind us over time what we are drawing to us. At its core, sympathetic magic operates on intent and on belief. Sometimes the results within the spell working itself are incredible and affirming. Following is a very brief overview of some of the aspects of candle magic, with the intent to inspire you to create your own New Moon Candle Magic Spell.

Choosing Your Candle

When doing any spell, you will first want to get very clear on the outcome you want. You will also want to be practical, and take into account the amount of time, effort, money, and energy you will want to put into a spell. I've only said this about one hundred times in these workbooks, so I'll say it one hundred and one times: fancy tools and expensive equipment do not make a spell effective. Intention, your energy, discipline, devotion and your personal power does.

Another aspect you will want to take into account is whether you want a votive or a tapered wax candle. Votives you "dress"; you put herbs, oils, crystals, and other magickal ingredients on the top of your candle, and try to carve your words, sigils, or symbols in the small space at the top. Votive candles burn longer, so if you want to have your attention focused on the intention at hand for up to 7 days, you might want to go that route. Tapered candles you can anoint and carve more easily, and smaller glass-free candles have an easier cleanup. With both tapered and votives, you can create your own custom label if you wish and put it on your candle. Tea lights work as well!

Last, but certainly not least, you will want to think carefully about color, and the amount of candles you want for your spell. One candle to start is enough. If you want to do a magnet spell (draw something to you), two candles are better, with one candle symbolizing you, and the other symbolizing the thing you want. You might want to use 3, 4, or 10 candles in a spell. It is truly up to your intuition and what your particular spell is. Some witches use the correspondences of the days of the week, various planetary correspondences, chakra or energy center correspondences, or deity correspondences to pick their candle's color. As always, my advice is to go with your intuition and pick a color that deeply resonates with you, not what books or the internet say. There are many magic makers who sell beautiful candles that they make and fix themselves. If you feel drawn to go that route, do it! It is nice to have an added boost of intention in your spell work.

Charging Your Candle

After you purchase your candle and right before you start your spell, you will want to charge your candle(s). Get in the comfortable, quiet altar space area that you will be working your spell in. This goes without saying, but when lighting a candle, be sure to have it in a safe space: high up, away from dogs and cats, and far away from curtains, tapestries, or other materials where it could catch fire. Place the candle in both of your hands. Close your eyes and as you breathe, invoke the energy of what you are putting forth with your spell into your body and move that energy into the candle. You can speak, sing, or chant if you feel called. Take as long as you'd like, until you feel an energetic shift or a click.

Carving Your Candle

This isn't a must, but many practitioners will carve a candle with words or symbols specific to their spell. When carving your candle, you can use a pin, scissors, a sharp pen or pencil, a nail, or a knife. A good rule of thumb is to keep this item separate from every day use. You can carve your candle with words, symbols, astrological glyphs, numbers, images, or symbols. Generally, the simpler the better. Some witches will do the same symbol 3 times, or another special number that resonates with them.

Anointing Your Candle

Anointing your candle, also known as dressing, is simply rubbing your candle with oil to leave a further imprint on it. Anointing oil seems to have come from ancient practices—Hebrew, and continued with Christian and Hoodoo religion—where oil is used to bless one in ritual. Many witches anoint themselves with oils, Florida water, water, or drawing on their body with these liquids before ritual. Anointing oil is usually blessed, charged, and only used for spell work/ ritual work. I generally use olive oil that has an infusion of herbs or crystals in it that correlate to what my spell work is around. (Garlic and rosemary for protection, rose quartz for love, etc.) Some practitioners may frown at this, but sometimes if I have leftover charged oil that I've made specifically for a spell, I'll cook with it for a few days after so that the energetics are inside of me, nourishing me, as my candle burns as well.

Some witches anoint their candle in a specific fashion: top to bottom, or from the middle outwards. Use whatever is in your tradition. Again, your focus and dedication are what is most important. You don't need any more than a drop or two. If your candle is a votive, sprinkle a drop or two on the top.

Herbs and Crystals

After carving and anointing, we add herbs or crystals that correspond with our wishes and further amplify the energy. You can roll your candle in herbs, or simply sprinkle or rub it in. Powdered herbs work really well here: cinnamon, hibiscus flower, and salt work well. You can also use dried flowers like lavender. For self-love spells, I'll use dried rose petals from roses my sweetheart has gifted me. Honey is great for attracting spells. When in doubt, use what is around you and what is in season.

Decorating Your Candle

There are many other ways to decorate your candle. You can make your own labels. If you buy a simple glass candle from the dollar store, you can draw and design your own spell label, customizing it to exactly what you want! All that extra time and intention creating a piece of artwork that is the total flavor and tone of deliciousness that you want the universe to bring you is extra time you are spending vibrating on the frequency of what it is you want! Simply glue your paper on the glass, or dip it in water and affix it to your raw wax candle and let it dry. You can save your labels as a reminder of your spell work, or burn or dispose of your label as a further offering. I tend to offer my label up to the fire, as reminder of the time and energy I will be committed to in making my intentions a reality.

Glitter, sand, and collage are all used as decoration. You can use other elements with your candle: put your candle in a bowl of water, ground it with earth, surround it with flowers or crystals, place it on a drawing you've made. You can sprinkle salt or other powdered herbs around your candle. You can use a small magnet embedded under your candle. You can tie multiple candles together in a banishing or reverse hexing spell, then cut them apart to signify liberation. You can braid thread, yarn, or grass around candles to strengthen bonds or qualities that you would like to invoke.

Lighting Your Candle

When it is time to start your spell, cut a bit of the wick off your candle. It will burn cleaner and clearer that way. When lighting your candle, you will want to stay focused on what you are doing. See the lighting of the candle as a metaphor for the igniting of your magic.

Flame as Focus

After the candle is lit, relax into the flame. Focusing on the flame is a fantastic way to focus. Imagine the flickering energy of the fire as your soul, your self, your dreams taking hold. Stare at the blue part of the flame. Imprint the flame in your mind. Bring the fire into your heart. As the energy from the charged candle gets burned down, you can imagine the energy of the intention going out into the universe. This fire can aid and help you in your daily efforts as well, a sparkly reminder that there is movement.

In general, part of the reason I love working specifically with smaller candles that burn for an hour up to three hours is because I can customize the candle much more easily. Also, I like to be present for the entire time it takes for the candle to burn down. While I wait for the candle to burn, I focus on my intention, I sing, I chant, I do breath work, meditate, journal, and draw. In my opinion, this charges the spell even more. It is also easier to observe the candles and attempt to do candle divination.

Candle Divination

Another way to work with candles in your spell work is through candle divination. It is amazing to watch the flame move in a particular way, and to see the candle behave in a particular way. There are different ways to work with candle divination.

There is pyromancy, the observing of the flame. You can use the flame as a scrying device and see what images show up for you. There is ceromancy, or signs or images seen in the wax. You can observe images or forms either in the wax, or slowly pour your burning candle into a vessel of cold water and read the wax, as you would tea leaves. There is also capnomancy, which is reading smoke, or interpreting images left on the glass after the candle has burned down (Catherine Yronwode and Mikhail Strabo, *The Art of Hoodoo Candle Magic*, Forestville, California: Missionary Independent Spiritual Church, 2014, p. 48).

Again, use your intuition for meanings and remember this isn't rocket science. If the fire jumps around wickedly, that could be a sign that there is a lot of energy around your intent. If the candle burns slow and steady, your spell might take a bit more time to take off, but the results will be positive and long lasting. If your votive cracks, the energy of your spell might be electric and you might have to go out of your comfort zone to achieve maximum results. Observe and engage with your candle for added information. Please note that there are psychics and candle workers who read candles as their speciality.

Once I did a candle magic protection service for myself and some friends. (Always get explicit permission from friends and be clear as to what the service is for, if casting spells for others.) What all my friends had in common, sadly, was dealing with repeated theft and copying of original creative work. The service was enacted to protect us all from harm in that arena. A yellow candle was used for our spirit and our unique creative spark. Pink candles were used for each one of us. I put a ring of white candles around the pink candles to protect us in clarity and neutrality. And around the white candles were black candles, as a double ring of protection, sucking up toxicity from thieves, and another ring of neutrality. An interesting part of this service was witnessing which candle was left burning after all the others had melted down. It was the yellow candle for our creativity and spirit, even though I had lit that candle first! This felt like a lovely reminder that even though our work might be stolen or copied, our true authentic creativity would remain with us always, as it was a gift from spirit.

Other Ways to Use Candles as Ritual

Light a candle in the morning when you meditate. Visualize what you'd like to see in the flames. Light a candle before beginning a creative project or an important project that will require focus and dedication. When you are missing a loved one, dead or alive, light a candle to remind you of their spirit.

Similar to the Moon, you can use a candle as a "charger" of objects or energy. You can place a

Tarot or Oracle card behind or in front of a candle, to charge it with fire. You can write out petitions (letters or poems for help from the universe or deities) and slide them under your candle. The flame of the candle can be used to burn up little pieces of paper with your wishes on them, or these bits of paper can be burned in the candle. (You can use a ceremonial bonfire in this fashion as well.)

You can carve a candle in the shape of something meaningful, and you can buy candles in the shape of things. As mentioned previously, you can do a candle service: not just for you and your friends, but to a deity, an idea, a planet, or a person.

Blowing out Your Candle

Some practitioners say to leave your candle burning until it is finished, but I will tell you now to NEVER leave a candle burning unattended. Starting a fire of destruction is not what candle magic is intended to do! I leave my candle burning as long as I or my partner is in the house with it. If I have to put my candle out, I do not blow it out. I either snuff it out by covering the candle, or I wet my fingers and extinguish the flame myself. The second option certainly feels a lot more magical! Again, one practitioner will advise you to blow it out and never snuff. It really depends on what feels right to you.

Disposing of Your Candle

Disposing of your candle should be carried out with the same thought that you have considered your spell. If you have used a votive candle, more precautions are necessary. In general, I put a few sprinkles of salt in a candle when the candle has been burned down to neutralize the energy. A candle used for banishing or protection must be disposed of in a recycling bin/trash bin not on your property, somewhere you rarely go. Environmentalists may frown on this, but sometimes I feel called to bury my votive. Other people will also frown on this, but once in a while, if I am feeling particularly superstitious after a powerful spell, I'll put my votives in a paper bag and smash them with a hammer before disposing of them.

A candle votive used for a positive spell, in general, I salt and recycle in my own recycling bin. Please keep in mind that many practitioners suggest disposing of ALL votives outside of one's property. If you are a crafty magic maker, you can use the votive again and pour your own wax in it. Or, you can use it for something else entirely: to hold your crystals or spare coins. I sometimes save particularly important candle votives, and use them as a vessel to put all my petitions and pieces of paper in. After about six months, I take them all out and review them to see what has transpired, and what hasn't. That also gives me a chance to reflect and see what parts of my actions have not been focused on my desires, and if it is time to reignite them with another candle spell!

If it is a candle without glass, only a bit of wax will be left that is very easy to dispose of. Again, if it is a banishing spell I will generally bury it or throw it away in a place that is not my home.

Candle magic is fun, easy, and part of every single witch's lineage as the flame is everywhere. This New Moon Candle Magic Spell is now entirely up to you! Maybe try something you have never done, so that your mind and intentions are expanded!

Happy New Moon!

A New Moon Candle Magic Spell

Using your intuition, create your own candle magic spell. The only "rule" is that the New Moon is an opportune time for starting new projects, tending to seeds, and creating fresh starts and fresh habits. It is a time for dreaming, moving forward, hope, and aiming high. This New Moon starts in the middle of the night on a Friday, ruled by Venus, so spells around love, sex, money, abundance, beauty, bravery, health, fertility (metaphorically and actually) would be favored today. If you decide to do your New Moon spell any time in the next three days, you could change your color, herb, and crystal correspondences accordingly. Sagittarius rules philosophy, innovation, healing, faith, expansion, positivity, travel (actual and metaphorical), and learning, so you could also think in terms of those themes, and adjust your candle ingredients accordingly.

Suggested candle magic colors for a New Moon in Sagittarius: Red, orange, yellow, pink, green, dark blue

Suggested herbs for anointing: Cinnamon, honey, cayenne pepper, basil, rowan, rosemary, lavender

Suggested crystals to surround your candle with, or to embed in your candle: Carnelian, bloodstone, orange calcite, rose quartz, serpentine, malachite, lodestone

Notes:

DECEMBER 12th : FIRST QUARTER in PISCES 3:49 AM PST | 12:28 PM PST MOONRISE | MOONSET

Sitting With Grief

"Grief has no distance." — Joan Didion

This Saturday, the Moon touches in on her First Quarter: a mere seven days to the culmination of a cycle of a set of particular energies, wishes, and intentions. We are halfway there to the last Full Moon of this year. Halfway through to a new month in a new-to-us year. Here all of us sit: fragile and alive, as distinct and different as every star up above. And here we sit: evaluating, reevaluating, considering, reconsidering, wondering, accepting, reflecting, and dreaming. The First Quarter Moon can feel like a time of balance: her surface is halfway lit up with glow and shadow. This time can feel like a ticking clock counting down inside of us, needing to be manifested in some tangible way: late night writing to channel our fervent dreams, early morning stretching as a metaphor to our own expansion, afternoon decision-making for what we need, not what we want. There are millions of different ways to reach towards the top of a wave.

Today, the First Quarter Moon lands in the sign of Pisces: sign of cosmic creativity, sign of emotional intelligence, the archetype of the connected collective. Together, we are greater. Pisces time is its own clock entirely: stones turn to sand over millennia, rushing rivers move upstream as if by magic. The cosmic egg has been laid in every last one of us, if only we could choose to crack it apart. The alarms would ring by way of holographic snowflakes alighting on our eyelids, if only we would open them to receive their colors. If only we decided to get out of our own way and meet our own markers of creative expression, allow our own definitions of transcendent success pulse between our hands, outside of fake ribbons, bows, and badges. If only we could dissolve out past the controlling limits that have been placed on us and float on into rainbow time, Moon time, spiral time, to enjoy the flow is to be in it.

As the Moon rotates farther away from us on its orbit, more of it is lit up, as the Sun's rays lick at its surface hungrily. The tides shift accordingly, as does our energy and emotions. Theoretically, we are in a Waxing Moon phase, and a Waxing Moon phase brings enhanced enchanted energy. A Waxing Moon traditionally references honeycombs, radiant orbs of the most beautifully striped brown tiger eye, and glittery bits of carnelian and citrine. This Moon phase encourages us to stretch out and grow. A Waxing Moon is an ask to take all of that glitter, all of those bubbles of inspiration inside, and translate that into the world with your actions. If you feel that buzzing calling inside, if you feel the impulse to follow up your New Moon Fire Magic with some Real World Fire Action, then do it! Write that poem, hit publish on that web page, focus on getting all your creative communications out out out of your fabulously divine body. There's still time to shine out, out, and up this year. There are still ways to fulfill some of your goals, if you are a goal-oriented person. Remember that your voice is powerful. Your authentic expression helps us all. Your artistic outputs are a gift to humanity. Your healing heals the collective. If this Waxing Moon time wishes to pull stanzas of sustenance out of you, stream them out onto the page. This is an opportune time for cosmic check marks and metaphoric victory laps.

However, we are in the Waning Moon time of the year. It is truly the darkest time of the year, as we creep towards a Full Solstice Moon. Soon the energy moving up and accumulating during a Waning time of the year might bring up sadness and sorrow. What wells up inside of us might be tears, not jubilation. In front of us, a tipped-over cup, completely cracked and empty. So, we acknowledge where we are. So, we feel. Surrendering to any and all feelings that have to come up in order to make their way out. We wait here, in the process of the parsing out of pain, in the weaving of our sadness into stronger threads of survival. We reflect on this painful year. Our losses and our regrets. To feel awash with grief is normal at this time. Do not push your feelings away from you, brave dove. Sit with grief. Watch it stretch out its hand, fold into its beckoning breath. Allow it to pull up a rickety chair at the table.

All of us sit and converse with grief at some point. We grieve for the past, stolen from us by cruelties. We grieve for our ancestors' past—what they had to go through to get us here. We grieve for violence and needless suffering. We grieve for whole peoples, known and unknown, mistreated and exploited. We wail for the theft of our freedom and our joy. We grieve for the Earth and her flora and fauna, polluted and ravaged. And we grieve for ourselves. We grieve what we never had. We grieve what no one gave us. What we were never promised. Who we were told we were and what we were capable of. We grieve for ideas about fear and scarcity that were dumped on us by society, or by our families. We grieve what we had to take back for ourselves, all alone, triumphant in the most melancholic way. No one may ever truly know what another has gone through to get to where they are. Know that one person's story is a story of many: those that they lost, and the those that came before them. Behind the curtains of a supposed success most likely lie mountains of pain, and salt pillars of grief.

Grief is loss, and profound change. Generally, but not always, it resides with a lack of control. The death of someone you love, separation from friends or community, getting sick, watching someone you love get sick, moving, loss of a job, the inability to do certain things due to disability, being forced to give up something you want to keep—these are some ways that grief weaves its way into our lives. There are certainly more.

Grief is also more existential. The experience can feel both vague, nameless, and yet deeply entrenched in bone and muscle. If you are in a group of people that have experienced persecution, there are the remnants of grief as passed through blood. If you are part of a group of people that is in a diaspora, there is grief that comes with that loss. There is sharp grief that comes with being colonized, with so much of the violence that this entails. There is an existential quality to not have ever received easy and abundant chances to experience freedom, joy, safety, encouragement, and basic respect that haunts many of us on this Earth. When so many of us have had that taken away from us, there is longing and there is grief that must be processed. There may be deep grief that resurfaces when we begin realizing, more and more, that all that has been stolen from us could never be quantified. This grief is collective.

Someone in some way, somewhere, is grieving. And so we do our part to really see and really be with them. We can witness them in their process. We can provide a support with our connection. We ask: how are you? Can I bring over soup? How are you? Can I sit next to you? Can I witness you in your grief? Can we live here, together?

Once grief comes to stay, it never really goes away. She settles in the corner of our consciousness like a shadowy cat. It lodges in our throats like so many burning, jumping frogs. Grief is an ongoing process, and we must treat it as such. Only more pain is created with the expectation that one day we will wake up and be done with the feelings that accompany such a loss. There is no rushing through this. Only when we accept that interfacing with these feelings is to be an ongoing part of our existence, will our grief change. We can we move into a deeper healing, we can exist in a deeper experience of the complex stages of this sorrow. Grief is not to be "fixed." Grief is to be worked with, listened to, and allowed to take up space. Grief is to be listened to and engaged with, another teacher in the classroom of life.

Grief is a somatic and visceral state of being. Grief is a painful, stark wave to be floating in. Yet, in order to move through it, in order to move with it, we must be in the experience holistically.

Grief requires suspension of time: there are moments when we are in numbness and denial, moments where we are sucked back into the past. There are times when the anvil of loss comes hammering down on our heart, a mournful cacophony of boulder-sized proportions, raining down unexpectedly. The only task to complete is to meet grief where and when she shows up. Tears are cleansing, so cry. Laughter is useful, so try to find humor when you can.

Grief shows up in unexpected ways. Sometimes, when we have great success, we find ourselves numb, or sad in some way. Sometimes, when something wonderful happens in our life, we grieve, because it doesn't feel the way we had expected it would. Or, something wonderful happens, and we grieve because we've lost an important person to share our joy with. Sometimes, waves of rage and anger can still bubble up over a loss you thought had been processed. This is normal. A grief timeline is not made of logic. The timelessness, of Moon time, the timelessness of magic, can be helpful to realize, witness, and work with. We can go back into a painful scenario, reimagine it, rewrite it, and leave it behind. We can still include our loved ones in our lives even if they have passed. We can speak to them, write them letters, and share our lives with them. The number one message I receive from deceased loved ones wanting to make contact with the living is that they simply wish to tell them how proud they are of my client. We can remember that our ancestors, whether blood or not, want us to carry on and create lives that are a testament to the lessons they've taught us.

Grieve what you need to and where you need to. There is no grief hierarchy and no grief handbook. (Though On Death and Dying, and On Grief and Grieving, by Elisabeth Kübler-Ross, are helpful. As is Bluets by Maggie Nelson, and The Year of Magical Thinking by Joan Didion.) Grieving is a somatic process: it must be experienced in your body. It must make its way through your nervous system. It must be experienced viscerally: through breath, clawing, and rest. It must be allowed to make its way through the veins in your knees, the hairs on the back of your neck. If grief needs to flatten you, if grief needs to send you to your bed for hours each day, or days each month, let it, with no judgment. Do not hold back from expressing emotions. Do not force yourself to go out or be there or be the same way you were before the traumatic event happened. Let the grief hold you as it needs to hold you. Let yourself be in a relationship with your grief until you are holding it. Notice the numbness. Notice the shifts of tone that come as it waxes and wanes. Notice what you need on a daily basis, on an hourly basis. Ultimately, over time, the gripping will shift into holding, the holding moves into integration, and the integration moves into more insights.

We can look to nature as a reflection of how she deals with grief. When a mother deer loses her baby, she mourns. If she is a leader in her group, another deer takes over—the mourning mother must not make decisions while she is in mourning. She visits her lost child, then slowly backs away, revisits, and backs away again, as part of her process, until it is time to separate. You may wish to take cues from the deer and refrain from major decisions, return again to your loss, then give it the space and time that goodbyes need.

Swans notoriously mate for life. It is true: widowed swans have been known to die of heartbreak. Many carry on. Many swans repartner after a mate dies before them. Swans remind us to look for love again. Float on the current; let the trust take us back into reverberations of resurrection. Our hearts need time.

We look to more reflections and can see archetypes of pain over time—symbols of grief, sadness, sorrow, and rage. We have the harpies: those wailing winged creatures of soul-snatching and stormy winds. There's the Grey Sisters, sharing one eye and a tooth, whomping and wishing for their pain to be acknowledged. Hecate glides over the expanse of the underworld and the in-between world, her black cloak gliding over headstones, her hounds gnashing their teeth in the hell that can be reality. She's comfortable being a solace to those who are in-between worlds. Indeed, Hecate was demoted by colonizers from being the ruler of all worlds, to a sub-deity forced to roam; she expresses a particular form of feminist grief. Hecate wants us to show up to her messages in the dark. These images of pain-ravaged femininity present to us the ways that pain literally mutates us; made out of claws, teeth, missing parts, and too many heads, pain and grief transform us into surreal pain bodies. These archetypes speak to how we must not ignore our suffering. We are literally physically and psychicly augmented by our grief and trauma.

Every culture has its own rituals around grief. We can find solace in our heritage of mourning rituals. We look to the stories from our own culture about grief and grieving, about sadness and sorrow. We create our own rituals based off of the ones we've been taught. In the Jewish tradition, my background, we sit shiva—we sit in grief actively—for seven days. There is a 30 day period of mourning. After that, the mourning period lasts for 11 months. On the anniversary of the beloved's death, Yahrzeit, we light a candle, create an altar, and pay our respects. Think about what is meaningful in your own ritual work. If something is missing from your own particular process, look to how your culture traditionally grieved.

We look for reflections in the Tarot of grief and we can see suggestions of it in many places. In the Minor Arcana, there are many places where loss pops up. With The Tower, there is a profound loss—a no-going-back loss. The loss that changes us irrevocably. And we need to be changed when this card comes up. The Tower illustrates a dark night of the soul. A time period when we experience the pain in order to move through how it threatens to overtake and control us profoundly. In The Tower, there is trauma, healing, dissolution of ego, and a surrending to this. We fall through the expectations of what we thought life would be, and the idea of who we are, the idea of who we have been clinging to as a wedge or a numbing device from the truth. After we go through The Tower, we realize our soul's truth: we are stronger, we are more brilliant than we could ever know. We break through the low ceiling of the doubt and fear we've been using as protection, allowed to finally fly free into the starry night of possibilities.

In the Minor Arcana, tales of grief and loss are scattered throughout the suits. In the Five of Cups, the figure is only looking at the overturned cups that I call "shoulda, woulda, coulda." They are choosing to stay in disappointment—there is a regret that must be addressed. In the Eight of Cups, we have a loss that comes with leaving, or being left. The Six of Swords, while a positive card, reminds me of Mercury taking the dead on the River Styx to their new home. Like the Eight of Cups, it is a card about moving away and moving on through pain. Both of these cards speak to making the right choice, not the easy one. The Three of Swords asks us to unbreak our own heart, to deal with our own deep traumas that we internalize. The Nine of Swords is about the anxiety and suffering of others that goes far beyond our experience. And the Ten of Swords, like The Tower, is about an ending or a rock bottom that we must go through to get clearer and lighter, and ultimately redeliver ourselves back to our ourselves in a different way. These cards remind us to be in our suffering. Learn from it. Address our pain. Sit with it and in it. Our suffering is not shameful.

You can take all of these cards out, and others that resonate with you, and meditate with them. Ask them to speak to you. Pull one or two other cards to help give you more information about how to move through loss.

So, we look to others for help and for guidance, for support and aid. Therapy and support groups might be what you need at this time. Reading others' experiences of grief, of love lost, and of trauma can be helpful. There is heartbreak in life—to expect only sunshine is harmful denial. Be around others who can show up for you in the ways you need.

We come to find that grief is a teacher. Grief teaches us patience, as there is no way out but to sit with it. It reminds us of our vulnerability and of the importance of surrender. It wishes for us to reach out, to lean, to open up, to soften our spines and to melt more into the seashell of time. Grief reminds us to treat one another very carefully, very honestly, and very, very tenderly.

We can expand the ways we view grief—as ultimately transforming our grief leads us to give so much. Research is grief. Fingering the broken shards of a cracked window and slowly repiecing them into another meaningful form, filling the cracks with gold—a wabi sabi treatment of our heart. Grieving is revisions—going back over to right the injustices, to retell the stories that must be told. Justice is grief. Transformative justice is grief. Protesting is grief. Honoring those who came before you is grief. Ancestor work is grief. Grieving is doing the work that your grandparents needed you to do but could not—their hands were tied, they had to keep the heat on, the mouths fed, the bill collectors satiated. Grieving can in some cases mean resurrection, tribute, and the pleasure of keeping a torch lit and carried forward.

This is a time where so many of us are grieving. Many of us are sharing in the nameless sorrow that is watching a world die, we are experiencing a jagged, ragged pain as we watch people around us be lost to greed and senseless violence. Remembering that—remembering that almost all of us are dealing with loss and sadness—is to nudge us towards compassion and forgiveness of one another. We may want to check on our loved ones constantly, and not just for a week or a month after a loss has occurred. Recently, I had a real friend reach out to me to ask if I wanted to do a grief ceremony around my dog that passed away six months prior. That felt like the right timing, and I was touched that she was still thinking of the fact that I would still be processing my loss. There was that understanding that the feeling of loss does not ever really go away. There was that acknowledgment that served as a bridge to my isolation. Reach out to your friends. Ask them if they want to talk. Bring over soup, tissues, or just yourself, a compassionate ear to listen. Normalize grieving as so many of us are in states of grief and processing loss. Let the grieving speak; do not shut them down or close them out when they express their pain.

Call your friends together and have a grief night. Everyone can bring snacks and mementos. Have plenty of water, tea, and tissues. Gather together and talk about who or what you are grieving. Listen very carefully. Do not interrupt one another. Do not try to make anyone feel better. Do not say anything like *It was their time. It is a relief.* Simply witness them and listen. Cry together if you need to. Tell one another you love each other. Afterwords, you may wish to clear the energy of the grief circle by jiggling your bodies, or moving or dancing around. You may wish to clear the space by opening a few windows for an hour or two, and by sprinkling salt in the room then sweeping or vacuuming it up after everyone leaves.

The souls of the dead need your grieving. Whether they are strangers or intimate, they need the love that transpires when you actively grieve them. The rainbows expelled from your heart are a love song to them, to all that they are, all that they showed you, all that they gave. The cries are testaments to the love they built out of years of steady care, unwavering fortitude, home-cooked meals, and middle of the night phone calls they picked up just for you.

Actively processing your grief helps the larger community. The collective needs your grieving to soften the sorrow that has been made into stagnant concrete by denial and delusion. In these actions are a righting, are a cosmic tipping of the scales into balance. These scales might need some oil, the imbalance has been so heavy for so long, there's rust on the gears. These scales will need more than just one of us, pushing with all our might to move the dial towards decency. To give grief her day in court, her expressive moments in the sun, her tears splashing down through, cleansing us through their salt. Active grief is a salve to the whole. Working with our sorrow is a testament to the depth of how we love.

We can think about the type of life that continues even after death. Even the Earth, so hard and so cold right now, in this December cold, is alive. Even as you grieve, you are very much alive. Your heart, cracked open, still beats, still leaks out gold. Tell stories of life, and tell stories of your process.

At this time, if you find yourself grieving, honor yourself. Deal, don't dwell. Spending energy in blame or in judging the length of the time your grief is taking, or how it wants to turn up, is not useful. Processing it is the most useful work you can do. Lean into the sensations and let them pierce you, let the waves in. Take a long shower to sob in. Pour salt in your hot bathwater and sit with tourmaline and smoky quartz in the bath. Let the water hold you. Put on *The Notebook* or *Bambi* and cry, cry, cry with no shame or judgment. Put on *Channel Orange* and sing along until you find yourself sobbing away the grief of the life lost, the love lost, the parts of yourself that you lost. Sob until the waves subside from a crash to a gentle rocking. Center quietly and take in the knowledge that grief is also love. Letting yourself be changed by love is priceless. Evolution is finding your way through the change, for yourself, for everyone, over and over again.

Pay attention to how grief is coming up for you and what it needs you to know. Let your grief inform your life. Let it change you, let it show you its specific melancholic beauty and offer you new vantage points. Let it break you open. Let it pull you through. Let your life be shaped and made meaningful by your pain, let your suffering make you softer. Let it show you what your mettle is made of: bone and crushed violet, fire and liquid gold. Grief is loss and love. Grieving is actively choosing to honor love in ways that give it the weight that something as precious as love deserves. Grief is powerful. It is unmasked vulnerability. Vulnerability is caring. Caring is one of the only uses of the heart.

Helpful herbs for grief: yarrow, gorse, oat straw, violet leaves
Helpful crystals for grief: rose quartz, Apache tears, desert rose, apophyllite
Tarot cards to meditate on: The Tower, the Three of Swords, the Five of Cups, the Six of Swords, the Eight of Cups, the Nine of Swords, the Ten of Swords

Journaling questions:
How has grief impacted my life?
What are the useful ways that grief has changed me?
What has grief taught me?
Is there anything I still need to take time to grieve?
Where, if anywhere, do I feel shame or judgment around my grief?
How can I clear that up?
How will I honor my grief?
Do I need to have a weekly, monthly, or quarterly grief practice?
How can I constructively process my sorrow?

DECEMBER 22nd: FULL MOON in CANCER 11:49 AM PST, 5:09 PM PST MOONRISE 6:43 AM PST MOONSET

You are the Moon: A Full Cold Solstice Moon

The Full Moon rises from her nest on the opposite horizon as the Sun sets. One celestial body disappears as the other gathers sparks in the cauldron above called the sky. Our last Full Moon this year arrives on Saturn's Saturday. Nine days before the end of the year, or the beginning of the next, and we might be feeling both accordingly wrung out and expectant. This Moon has been known as the Cold Moon, or the Long Night's Moon. This year, it is a Solstice Moon. The Winter Equinox, and Yule, just occurred. We may still be celebrating: final celebrations, illuminations, revelations. This Solstice Moon reminds us to keep going. Yesterday was the darkest day of the year. Today, we experience minutes more of light, on this first official day of winter. Even after the darkest night there is dawn. The cycles of light continue, and the Sun begins to come back around again.

"Yule" is a name that comes from Germanic peoples; the earliest references to it were in regards to it being the name of a month, hundreds and hundred of years ago. (Wikipedia.org). One of the Norse god Odin's names correlates to "Yule-father." As Christianity was derived from folk-loric Indigenous traditions, we can see the correlation between this Sabbat and other Christian Holidays. At the Solstice, we celebrate light and dark, our survival, and community. There is ritual, eating, and gratitude. We gather with beloved ones in front of a fire or near a heater. We set up an altar and thank the Sun for returning. We praise the light returning outside and honor the light inside that still remains. If you have the energy cook for others, or show up in an authentic way somewhere somehow. Do something for those that have less than you. We have to keep others going too. There are the times that we need the lights in the dark. There are times when we are the lights in the dark.

From a magical perspective a Full moon on Cancer on Saturday could be good for any psychic activities. Turn all the lights out and meditate. Get your pendulum out and ask all the questions you've been pondering lately. Ask for messages to come through the radio waves, via sentences in books, or in other unmistakeable ways. Cancer is psychic ability and emotional depth and Saturn is boundaries. Saturn is success derived through discipline and expansion through true, hard, work. Think: The World Card. Refine and focus on your intuitive abilities this weekend. Give your emotional body what it needs to recharge or transcend. Once you are clear, Saturn will help to build what is meant to last. The Sun in Capricorn provides a base of reality that could be jarring, but is ultimately grounding. A Cancer Full Moon wants you comfortable, connected, and understood. Understanding starts within.

This is a Full Moon for long term amplification. This Cold Solstice Moon, like the last Moon is at 0 degrees. Last month the 0 degree Full Moon was in Gemini, this month is Cancer (more on this later). This lunation might bring up a very tangible knocking at the doors of your mind, body, and heart. It is time to dig into the lengthy marathon that is called life. Plan what you want to have happen 6 months from now, at the New Moon in June or July and work backwards from then. If you possess even more patience, think even longer into the future. Where do you want to be in 2 years, 5 years, 8 years, 10 years? Emotionally? Character-wise? Self-love wise? Talent-Wise? Ability-wise? Pleasure-wise? Honey bunny, if your goals are not something you actually enjoy doing almost all of the time, why are you doing them? This might be a Full Moon of reset its and forget its. It is more than ok to actually love what you do, find stability through your relationships, have a life that is devoid of major drama, and not be so hard on yourself. Challenges are different than repeated tortures. Results are not achieved by limiting yourself by perfectionism, guilt, and comparison.

This is a Full Moon that might leave us wired and tired. Sleepless nights go up, from around 3 nights before to 3 nights after a Full Moon, usually, if we are sensitive to them. We can work with this energy productively. If you can't sleep, write. If you can't write, rest in a bath or listen to a guided meditation or calm music. During the day, try not to react if situations come up—pause is always an option before responding. Wait a few days or more. Be sure to stay hydrated, especially if your sleep is being compromised. This is just a another warning to be gentle, gentle, gentle with yourself and others. Especially if some of us are going into family situations that might be difficult on this Full Moon weekend.

From a spell perspective, this Full Moon favors a variety of magical workings. This is a good time for securing safety, accepting where you are and asking for the help you need. Spells favored at this Full Moon would be love spells, protection spells, psychic ability, fertility, growth spells, right work spells, spiritual power, discipline and devotion, spells of a long range nature, such as starting a new business, looking for a new medical or healing team, wisdom, right timing, finding a new place to live, spells for health, as well as spells for community and greater humanity.

Magical actions that would be supported at this moon are kitchen magic: make a pot of soup, and add herbal ingredients to boost your immune system like ginger, parsley and garlic. If you haven't made fire cider yet this season, this is the perfect weekend to throw together a batch. Find an excuse to invite chosen family over to your house and play records, card games, and decompress from the year together. This could be a Full Moon weekend spent nurturing the people and activities you hold dear. Spend the afternoon writing love letters to the most important influences in your life: dead or alive. Tell everyone you adore you love them. Even if they can't hear you, their souls will be able to feel it.

This is a Full Moon to think about the types of support you will be needing long-term to carve the life of your dreams out of the mottled seagreen marble of possibilities.If you know ultimately this requires more vulnerability, think about the ways in which you can do that. If you will need to ask for more help, save more money, put yourself out there more, write them all down. Consider how these unfamiliar actions will move you from the shaky colt stage to the swiftly moving deer stage. Remember that any difference can be hard at first but that any difference being made in the spirit of your highest self is a difference that matters. Little things become big moves with time and consistency. Consider your support systems and be honest about how much more you need to invest into the things that help you grow, help sustain you, and keep you dreaming in the dark.

It is time to take stock. Count your blessings. Write down your lessons. Accept where you are. Acknowledge how far you've come. The last Full Moon in Cancer was this past year in January— how much has transpired since then! You can go back to your 2018 Vol I edition of Many Moons to see what was happening in your interior and exterior world. You can see the spells that came true and the magic that has yet to unfold. You can use this Full Moon to recommit to your faith, your hope, and your belief in yourself and in the universe. Under this last Full Moon, whisper *I believe* and *I know*. Under this night sky full of glittering winking stars and for some of us, surrounded by sparkling sheets of snow, remember. Remember that you shine too. Remember that the stars and the Moon don't know they are shining but they gleam and enchant just the same. Give yourself a wink in the mirror. Let yourself smile a smile that lights up your face.

Get serious about what you need. Get clear about what you require. Get real about the boundaries, sometimes scary, that you will have to uphold with yourself and with others if you are to truly refresh and revolutionize your moments. You can love someone and let them go. You can love yourself enough to let yourself go somewhere else— safer or riskier or another different part of the sea. You can love yourself enough to throw the biodegradable trunk full of guilt, shame, blame or judgment off the side of the boat and know it will decompose and turn into benign sand for the fish to nibble on. It doesn't have to be yours to carry anymore.

Everyone knows the Moon. Everyone has a relationship with it.

I come out to the desert to write. The rocks are actually the bottom of an ancient ocean and the Moon and stars are so clear that evening viewing becomes an almost a psychedelic experience. At the dog park one morning, an older gentleman and I get to talking. He asks me what I write about. With hesitation, I tell him. "Do you really believe in this?" he asks me. I tell him that I wouldn't be spending all my time and energy writing books and books about the Moon if I did not believe in her power. I explain that we try to act separate from nature, but we are nature, and we are effected by the seasons and the weather even if some of us pretend it doesn't matter. *We are talking animals*, I add. *Evil animals*, he says. I tell him not all of us talking animals are evil. On the way out of the parking lot, he stops my car. I roll down the window, and he remarks: "The Moon out here and the stars are especially beautiful." I tell him that's why I come out here— to view the Moon and the stars on their most stunning stage. I don't tell him I stand underneath the Moon and listen to what she has to tell me. How the Moon's voice comes from inside of me, almost silent yet undeniable. I don't tell him I cast spells with her moonbeams, happily cry the tears of joy and of sorrow that she brings out of me, and feel her holding me as she reflects myself back to me, every time, without any asks of reciprocity. Instead I say: "There's a Blue Moon tonight, the second Blue Moon of this year." He tells me he noticed her filling up. "The next time we will have two Blue moons is 2037." I proclaim. "Oh, I'll be gone by then," he answers, turns away, and raps on my car hood as a friendly goodbye.

Everyone knows the Moon. Everyone has a relationship with them.

One of the men at the printing press that prints *Many Moons* asks me one day: what is this about, anyway? I tell him, and as a diagram I made about the Moon's cycles is printed on the table in front of us, I point to what phase we are in currently. We stand next to a gigantic whirring printing press, yelling over the noise of industry. I let him know that coming up this weekend there will be a New Moon. He is ecstatic. He tells me he is going on a fishing trip with his friends, and a moonless sky means they will catch more fish. He explains that when the Moon is Full, the fish can see more easily. Because of this they eat more food so are less desperate, and do not get fooled by the hooks dripping with worms or false bait in the water. A black sky means the fish are hungrier, and more likely to get caught.

Everyone knows the Moon. Everyone has a relationship with her.

I don't tell these men that the Moon is why the witches got murdered. The reason why women and intuitives and psychics and shamans and queers and tarot readers are hated: their healing powers too terrifying for men, or anyone else afraid of healing before they die in this body, to accept. I don't speak about how the resistance in our culture to healing and to wildness and vulnerable connection and to magic and to intuition and to the inexplicable is so deep that anyone or anything that provides tools of empowerment, compassion, and empathy are so reviled they are shunned, shamed, shut down. I don't tell them that the Moon made me truly love myself, and as result, made me truly love them. I don't share that living with the Moon's cycles in a holistic way, and as an extension really living with myself in a holistic manner, with all my mistakes and radiance and pain and laughter and death and rebirth and knowing and listening and channelling and wondering and generosity and scarcity and sureness and faith and patience and surrender saved my life. I don't tell them this is how I know that magic is real, and how I know that Moon magic is especially potent.

Everyone knows the Moon. Everyone has a relationship with him.

No one owns the Moon. Not technically, at least. The Moon treaty of 1979 states that no country, organization, or corporation can own any planets or cosmic objects. There is a man named Dennis Hope who has made millions of dollars selling off parts of the Moon to buyers: he thinks he found a loophole because he is an individual, not a corporation or organization. Time will tell if he can land on the Moon and erect a Walmart. Sadly, the S.P.A.C.E. act of 2015 allowed space extraction. The law made it so that anyone, any corporation, or organization can take any resources off of a planet, asteroid, or Moon. They can mine on Mars and suck up the fabled underground water from inside of our Moon. It is only a matter of time before outer space becomes another place to pillage and rob.

This world is so extractive, of course it would extend to this Moon: this globe can barely contain the emptiness disguised as greed that courses through it. Even the men who landed on the Moon left trash on her. Litter is still regularly left on the Moon. The most famous item the astronauts in 1969 left were footprints and the American Flag. All in all, there are about 413,100 pounds of debris dropped by humans on the Moon. Tossed In the Sea of Tranquility, strewn about in the various Lunar Marias are backpacks, Hasselblad cameras, 12 pairs of moon boots, a plaque signed by Richard Nixon, 96 pounds of human waste, golfballs, hammers, 5 American Flags jewelry, and much more. Because the Moon has no atmosphere, these will never decompose or get blown off (George Got, *Weird things that have been left on the moon*, futurism.media). Nowadays, of course, the new space race is funded by corporations. Nowadays, a future of lunar tourism, and a universe filled with empty candy wrappers, plastic bottles, and diapers floating past one's spaceship window is not so farfetched to imagine.

This is the extractive way we are taught to view the sacred nature and nature's mysterious ways. This is the extractive way we are taught to consider relationships. The extractive way we try to use and sell magic. This is the trash that we leave quite literally on the holy face of the cosmos. The Moon doesn't care. She was there for Alexander the Great, and there for Shakespeare. She tossed moon water down to Sappho to catch in the forms of poems we can still cry tears over. They were there when the buffalo were almost completely murdered off the plains, when the trail of tears left a whole land almost empty of its stewards. The Moon shone down steadily while the first gay lovers kissed gingerly, as peashoots peered out of the soil, as secrets were shared between strangers. The Stonewall riots happened under a Waxing Gibbous Moon and ended on a Full Moon in July. The Moon shines still as coral reefs disintegrate and we protest another injustice and we continue to figure out ways to love one another without destroying ourselves. The great Moon, Mother of the heavens, doesn't care. That doesn't mean we shouldn't care about her.

Just because the majority of people's practices are extractive, greedy, short-sighted and violent, doesn't mean ours have to be. If you are reading this now and care about the earth, care about humanity, care about equality and other non-talking animals and exploitation, if you are engaged in any kind of nourishing and challenging work: then you know. You know that we do this work for a future we can't see. For a future, quite frankly, we may never see. We know that this world, this patriarchal colonizing greedy maddening world was built up in someone else's imagination and we are living in the remnants of their ideas, formed thousands of years ago.*
We know to never underestimate the actions and intentions of one person. We know that this is a long road, but it is one that can be pleasurable, beautiful, and connection-filled. We know that we are healing the wounds of those that came before us. We know that we are one bead on the string that is all of existence. We know we are interconnected and interwoven in this silver web. We know that to love something is to want to protect it, to save it, to nourish it, and to share it. We know that love offers us a way to live on after our bodies are no longer.

*thank you to the work of adrienne marie brown for reminding me of this fact in her work and inspiring me with her perspectives.

Once upon a time, this planet lived by the Moon. Our calendars were Lunar. We planted by the Moon, made decisions by the seasons and the stars. Over time, the solar life—productive, rational, competitive—won out through war, violence, and colonization. Instead of living with intuition, the unknown, and in cycles, mysteries were deemed scary. if you couldn't explain something if did not exist. If you could not explain something, if you could not understand something, you could not tame it, you could not control it. Therefore it was not useful to you, therefore it was negative and was either demonized, exploited, extracted, locked up or killed.

Creativity, intuition, inspiration, and compassion is moontime and it is a natural state for us talking animals to exist in. Without the use of our intuition we are computerized and robotic. There is no room for chance, for change, for wonder, for adventure. Without qualities of the feminine: of inspiration, of healing, of relating to one another, empathy, recognizing that we are the whole, and that if one of us is hurting then we all hurt, we are a cold state of existence. When the value of emotions—of depth, connection, empathy and compassion—are gone, the humanity is gone.

Our ancestors lived with the Moon. They learned from the Moon, the Sun, from nature, from the sky, the seasons, from the elements, from animals, from their own rhythms and patterns. They worshipped and appreciated all the cycles of life, or at the very least, dealt with them head on. They prepared for the winter. They saw the death in life. They lived their lives in Moontime: flowing with the tides, not against.

This Full Moon is at 0 degrees Cancer. Traditionally a femme archetype, Cancer has to do with mothering, with nurturing and with caring for others, and with emotional abilities and depth of intuition. Cancer can have to do with who or what ideals you keep close to your heart. What do you love, and why? What are you protecting, and why? What is sacred to you? Why? How do you reflect this, in your behaviors, your actions, your thoughts, your work in the world? What around your heart, your home, your defenses, your life, is ready to be refreshed, reset? How will your new world be a reflection of the world you wish to see, even if you know that you may never actually get to see it?

The 0 degree is a beginning, pure potential. At this time, we can reimagine our heart as an open, gold-plated chalice of opportunities, ready to receive. The more we give from a grounded and honest place, from an aligned place, the more we receive. Making our decisions from a loving place, from an open heart, affords us true freedom to garner deep insights. In the moment your ego has nothing to gain you end up gaining everything.

The Sabian symbol for this particular Moon is resonant for this idea, and mirrors our Full Moon from November.

The Sabian symbol for 0 degrees Cancer is:

On A Ship The Sailors Lower An Old Flag And Raise A New One

This is a visual that speaks to an old paradigm being shown the door. There is a collective energy to this image. We need one another. When we dream together our dreams become more vibrant. Collective power blooms permanently. Last month our Full Moon at 0 degrees Gemini found us also on an oceanic vessel: the glass bottomed boat. We were looking down, into our subsciousness, looking into the depths to glean new information, beautiful new pictures. This Moon, we are still out at sea, we continue to float on the waves of intuition and emotions. A decision has been made to shift old symbols. Flags have traditionally been a symbol of communication. Whether it is telling others what type of vessel you are, what you are carrying on your vessel, how you need to come into the port, or where you are from, a flag is used. Now we are ready for a different form of communication. The sea of the collective unconscious is our base, and as more aligned communication and ideas are elevated, others become the wind beneath our sails, as we become theirs. At this Full Moon, there is a chance to make a decision that will impact the collective—whether it be our families, our friend groups, or other communities we are a part of. We might be making these decisions together, or it may be time to go it alone as you reorient yourselves in the flow of the flashes of inspiration that have been coming up to the surface of your water in the last few months. This is the 2nd Full moon at 0 degrees. The 2nd Full Moon at a starting point. Start at your beginning, which is all you know and all you've experienced. Start wherever you'd like on this imperfect circle of the year. Envision, create, and discover your journey as you embark on it.

We search for ourselves in a world that wants to stop us from being found. And yet, here we are, finding ourselves together. More and more by minute. More and more by each Moontime.

We are in a different stage of becoming. We can raise our new visions for our ideal futures high. We can seek out those who in reality meet our deepest needs, who will not hide from our brilliance or from our vulnerability. We can give to others from the most true and generous places within us. These offerings become a buffet of stars we can all enjoy freely.

No one owns the Moon. We don't need to own her to enjoy her. We don't need to exploit her to derive pleasure from her. We don't expect anything from her other than what she shows us. What she gives us is wild and free and magical. She needs nothing from us yet we need to give her our love, our protection, our gratitude and our tender care. Moonlight follows us and infuses us wherever we are.

Look at yourself now. Changing with the stars, merging with the sky, revolving with nature. All of the seasons that have traipsed and trudged on, around you, under you, and over you, and you've lived through them all. Look at yourself, changing for no one but you. Look at yourself, changing for everyone around you to view.

The Moon reminds us of who we are what we've done. Who we were and what we've become. We carry the Moon inside of us. She was you once. You were once her. She turns out and turns away. Cheers and cries big salty tears. She grows the seeds, waters the dreams. The Moon shows us ourselves, changing and being. Even in the dark, we glow. Even in the dark, we love ourselves.

Let's dream in the dark for one another as we weave spells for our futures. Let's remind ourselves of how we must live and what we must protect as we remember the things that can never die.

The Moon is us and we are the Moon.
The Moon is herself completely.
Nothing more, nothing less.
Call yourself the Moon.

Happy Full Moon!

Suggested crystals: garnet, ruby, onyx, moonstone, pearl, clear quartz, rose quartz, selenite, opals of all kinds
Suggested herbs: motherwort, mugwort, moonwort, jasmine, violet, rosehips, elder flower

A Spell to Protect the Moon

You will need:
A candle or tea light (s)
A bowl of filtered water
3 clear drinking glasses
Optional: moonstone, selenite, rose quartz

You may wish to do this spell in addition to any other personal spells or rituals you are planning on.

Place the bowl of filtered water outside or by a window that catches moonlight. You may wish to put any water-safe crystals in the bowl to charge in the water. Leave the water outside for at least 30 minutes, longer is better.

Set your altar up. Simplest is best. White, silver, and blue are the colors of the Moon.

Go outside if you can, or by the Moon viewing window.
Ground yourself and cast your circle.
Spend time connecting with her. Open your eyes wide and have a staring contest with the Moon. Close your eyes and see if any images come up. Listen for any messages that want to come up from inside of you. If able, plant your legs wide, and lift your arms up so that you are a pentacle. Feel the energy of the Moonlight cascading into your body, filing you up. Really feel the energy inside of you: energy that is your own, and energy that is a gift.

Take your moon water bowl and go inside to your altar. Pour the water carefully into the 3 glasses.
Put them on the altar. Light your candles.

Say:

I vow to protect you, Moon. I vow to protect myself. (Or something like it.)

Drink one glass of water.

I show frequent appreciation of the Moon. I give myself constant gratitude.
I promise to love the Moon inside of me. I promise to keep my heart open. (Or something like it.)

Drink one glass of water.

I honor the sacredness of the Moon. I honor the sacredness in all of us.
So it is. All this or better. Blessed be.

Drink one glass of water.

After you put the last glass of water down, give thanks. Thank the Moon for being your guide. Thank any other beings, deities, animals, or guides you have. Any teachers, any ancestors you will be including in your protection prayer. Thank all the other Moonbeamers. As you wield this powerful love spell of protection, know that somewhere, out there, there are other compassion and strong humans also thinking of you, a stranger, and thanking you for your work. The spells become amplified in this way.

As the candle light flickers, as the moon water enters your system, let yourself breathe. You are yourself now, you are the Moon, you are also everyone else who are themselves and who are also the Moon. Let yourself be. Sing any songs, chant any chants, say any words you need to express. Write down any wishes or dreams. Let any visions or feelings come to you that need to waft in or up.

Close your circle. You may wish to keep your candle burning. You may wish to continue your practice of staring at the Moon of every night, of being the Moon every day: unabashed, wild, completely yourself whether hiding or glowing for the heavens to behold.

Notes & Reflections on ritual or on myself at this Full Moon:

"How can I be substantial if I do not cast a shadow? I must have a dark side also if I am to be whole." — Carl Jung

Today, December 29th, the Moon goes Last Quarter in the sign of Libra. Our Full Cold Winter Moon was one week ago. Now in the Waning phase, the light fades from her face. She needs her turning away time. With the chilly nights almost as long as the grey days, we need tea, cuddles, and a promise of a New Moon New Year reset. The Waning Moon time is the perfect time to pause, reflect, revisit, and give more attention to feelings that came up before that we may not have had the language to talk about in the moment. Our breath hitting the icicle air gives our words and existence cloudy form.

It is the end of the year and many of us may feel quiet. You may wish to be still as snow before the sun rises. Let the ice cubes in the vegan nog do the talking. Let the fire in the hearth give off all of the warmth needed to warm our skin. You may feel wrung out, and ready for rest before the next year. Ready to see the past depart, ready to release the hurts and hopes alike that all the days couldn't quite promise us.

This is the time of shadows: the Waning Moon time in the Waning Moon portion of the season of the year. If you feel called to do shadow work at this time, to deep dive into your subconscious, your fears, your limiting beliefs, it makes perfect sense. Air them out, pull them out of your psyche and into the fire. Name the harsh truths one by one as they parade past, on their way to dissolve into the past where they must remain for you to see clearly in this present. What are you letting go of, on this last Waning Moon period of this intense year? What truths are still staring you down in the middle of the night? What vulnerabilities is it time for you to face?

The "shadow," as popularized as Carl Jung, is the aspects of the personality and the self that we reject. It is the part of your self that you have not fully integrated into your consciousness. Those parts you try keep at bay, the parts you avoid and ignore looking at, keep at arms length, try to hide behind facades and masks or shove into the closet. We've all got them, no matter how skilled we've gotten at hiding them. All of us were taught at some point that we needed to stifle either aspects of our personality, aspects of our desires, or aspects of our shining gifts. Sometimes it is our glow that society makes into the shadow, and we internalize this. Part of spiritual growth is acknowledging, examining, and loving all of your shadow self—viewing these rejected components as teachers and resonant reflectors, going beyond the pain into understanding of the cause. Some of these parts are your deep desires and your dreams. Some of these are basic ego traits that we all grapple with: jealousy, insecurity, control, or arrogance. Some of these aspects hold integral truths about who you are and where your soul needs to evolve into in this lifetime. It is important to recognize that shadow work is ongoing work. It is a lifelong process of discovering, uncovering, accepting, loving, and transforming.

The trick is to be aware of our shadow, but not to identify as it. The trick is to see it for what it is—a part of you that can help you step into your fullness, hug your wholeness with both arms.

Mindfulness will help you parse out whether you are being consumed by your shadow side. Procrastination, avoidance, projections, passive aggressiveness, uncontrolled anger bursts, pronounced vanity, running primarily on ego, and extreme defensiveness are all some indicators that your shadowy subconscious is running the show.

This is deeply harmful to our magic. When we aren't working our magic to the highest of our abilities, even our spells become more safety structures for our ego to hide in. When we are practicing magic without truly getting to know who we are, at the core of our soul, we are limiting our magic. We are not clearly in alignment with our true desires, and either end up selling our desires short, or fixating on the external only as a marker of success. This is very "The Secret" level magic and manifestation: needing the car, needing the accolades, needing the attention, needing anything and everything but our own permission, our own witnessing, the love and recognition that comes from within. Everything other than ourselves is looked at when we are out of balance.

It might be time to hold these aspects of your behavior up to the light.
It might be time to stop playing safe, playing small.
It could be time to connect with who you really are beyond all of the noise.
Identify where your deepest fears—and therefore, your deepest needs—come from.

Take a moment to set this workbook down and close your eyes. Are there patterns or themes in your life that have popped up this year (or longer) that you have been running from? Is it time to stop running and use these themes as a source of guidance and expression?

In popular New Age culture, many practitioners like to "love and light" everything away. Spiritual bypassing is the name of the game—ignoring structural inequities, the history of colonization, and other various oppressive systems in the form of denial, gaslighting, and deeming anyone who speaks of the human condition and oppressive systems as being "not high vibe." This impetus is always a sign of someone who has not integrated their shadow. This impulse to deny is a clear sign of someone caught in huge projections, trapped in their own delusions created by an imbalanced ego. This is the astrologer who only wants to exist in 5-D, the six-figure white money coach who never discusses their own privilege or mentions the word "capitalism," the male New Age leader who victim blames the women coming forward as part of the #Metoo movement. We can acknowledge the harm of this behavior publicly. It can be a blueprint of exactly how not to let our unchecked shadow blot out our compassion and our awareness of others' suffering.

Exposing our vulnerable parts in safe settings is a powerful tool. Our shadow holds all of our fears, all of our ego's motivations, all of our limiting beliefs—and in this way, it is a veritable Pandora's Box of insights and lessons to our own behaviors. The emotions of our shadow side give us creative fuel. Ironically, it is usually the parts of ourselves that we run from that are the parts of us that will redeem us, give our souls purpose, and give our life fuel. What are the unique gifts that only you possess, that feel scary to show the world? Why? What would happen, ultimately, if you began sharing them? Would this sharing open new worlds, different experiences? How are you ready to begin releasing your resistance to embodying joy, and sharing your gifts?

We can turn aspects of our shadow into our greatest strengths, by giving them the space to tell us what we need and how we really are. There is great power in expressing our vulnerabilities. We find we are not alone. We find that we are worthy of love and respect. We are humans, and humans are messy. Out of true honesty comes true freedom. When we lay ourselves bare, and listen to what our shadow self needs, and we give that to ourselves, we reconnect with our ultimate personal power. That is the love only we can give ourselves.

Shadows are among humanity's oldest timekeepers. Before the Gregorian calendar, it was observing the shadow of the Moon that marked time and the earliest holidays, the earliest times to celebrate, the ways in which we learned to grow food, and survive. Sundials, Stonehenge, and Mayan pyramids all marked time by using shadows. Over 2,000 years ago, Eratosthenes, a head librarian at the Great Library of Alexandria, was the first person to calculate the size of Earth by using the measurements of shadows. The ancients believed that one's shadow was a detachable part of one's soul. Shadows were held sacred, and were protected as such. Ancient Jews feared their shadows being stolen by the "noon day demon," and took extra precautions around midday, the time of day when our shadows are most likely to disappear (Barbara Walker, *The Woman's Dictionary of Symbols and Sacred Objects*, p. 353).

While our shadow can be difficult to look at, it serves as one of the most potent antidotes to our healing. Last year, when I was in Glastonbury, England, having the dreamy experience of being surrounded by acres of nettles on a hike, I got stung. My friends immediately showed me a plant that always grows next to nettles that acts as a salve when you rub it on your inflamed skin. The plant was called dock, and indeed it stopped the itching. I've heard that in the United States, the antidote to nettles is horsetail. In nature, we frequently find the antidote next to the poison. The Chechen tree and the Chaca tree. Echinacea and goldenrod. Poison ivy and jewelweed. In self-development, working with the shadow is the antidote to much of our blocks. Always next to us, we can go deeper into it and use it as a balm when we get stung. The shadows right next to us have been the antidote all along. Our true selves, right next to our shadows, are the reassurance our shadows yearn for.

There are many ways to explore shadow magic in your practice. Shadow magic is simply focusing on working with the shadow aspects of the self first and foremost. We do this by putting the majority of our focus on working with shadow; the subconscious, trance, underworld journeying, and embracing and moving through our inner demons are all aspects of shadow magic. Not to be confused with dark magic, which is the type of magic that consciously causes harm to others and attempts to control or destroy others without their consent, shadow magic is powerful. Datura and obsidian. Burying ashes, breaking glass, and cracking eggs. Black mirrors and grey moonstone. Hecate and Medusa and Inanna and Kali and Ishtar and Sedna and Pele and Isis and Morrígan and The High Priestess and Lilith and Baba Yaga and every witch who has screamed into the night, walked squarely into the void, every innocent human who has ever been vilified or misunderstood, every person who has ever protected herself or or stood up for herself or wanted to protect others. We call upon these deities and archetypes for guidance and protection.

Shadow cannot be set on fire, nor can it be made wet by water. We cannot hold it in between our hands, but we can feel it in our belly and in our throat. Shadow doesn't make noise, but we can hear its whisper. It is free to roam, distort the truth, or offer new insights from our subconscious. It can be a block, a distortion, or a Rorschach masterpiece of where we've been and how we've internalized our experiences.

Mirror magic is a wonderful tool for shadow magic. The mirror is simply the prop, our superficial reflection the mask we must see through. Light a candle, turn off the lights, and stare at yourself in the mirror. Stare until the superficial reflection dissolves. Wait until you receive messages or information. Mirror magic is so potent because as we stare into ourselves, we are able to detect that we are not who we thought we were. There is some other energy there—that energy is our true source, beyond our mundane issues and petty distractions. We see both ourselves and the mirror, but we recognize we are neither (Sri Nisargadatta Maharaj, *I Am That*, p. 315).

There is nothing wrong about living in shadow realm. That is the work that many of us are called to do. The life of being present with our pain long enough to start healing it. Knowing it is a slow process—always evolving, always moving through the cycles and spirals we are meant to unravel and regroup around. Those of us who feel called to venture into their shadows usually also end up holding space for those other brave souls to examine their pain. Speaking of taboo subjects. Inspiring others through their art, their messages, their transformation of the wounds into poem about a beautiful bruise. We watch others come out of their own bramble bushes bleeding, yet with a handful of ripe fruit. We are reminded that there is nothing bad or repulsive about our battered bits, the puzzle pieces inside of us that do not ever seem to fit.

You aren't stuck, you are just figuring it out. You aren't broken, you are just more aware. This gives us the courage to face our own forests, our own caverns. We are reminded to keep our eyes open and unblinking as we discover ourselves in the darkness.

Do not let the pervasive perfectionism that is rampant in our culture stop you from moving forward with your dreams. Sometimes we think: "Well, I need to do XYZ and learn XYZ before I can start my acting career." Or, "I still cry over my ex; I can't be a relationship coach," etc., etc., and so on and so forth. Life does not wrap up in a little perfect bow, no matter how much the media wants to tell you so. We will have our shadows until our last breath. You can have challenges and still step into a beautiful life. You can have debt, a learning disability, trauma, chronic physical pain, and still be allowed to go for whatever you want. (Hello, hi, it's me, talking about myself, your fucked-up Moon Witch who currently is living the life of her dreams featuring major abundance, deep love, and all kinds of fun and fulfillment!)

There is no light without shadow. The darkness is the light. The light is in the darkness. Both must exist with the other. They are not separate. We can hold both, experience both, sometimes at the same time. Integrating our shadows is being whole. Not perfect. Just a human, embracing all the parts. A human being, in alignment with their truest self. Integrating our shadows goes far beyond either/or.

Looking at the shadow leaves us witnessing the parts of us that are beyond definition, beyond compartmentalization. The mess, the wonder, the incredible survival, the weirdness, the aspects of ourself that have no easy language, or plopped into a commercial to be bought and sold. Those of us who are between worlds—between genders, between identities, between defini-tions—are beautiful bridges. Sadly, in our culture, bridges are walked on, not exalted. View your between-ness as a gift that helps others to see themselves. See the aspects of yourself that are beyond definition as affirmations of your unique imprint, your mystery, and your magic.

This past January, an old dear friend visited me. She brought along her heart, her two-year-old daughter named Ruby. A vibrant young spark who was a New Moon baby, Ruby was so alive, so very much *in life* in the way that so many young seedlings are. On their trip, in the blinding Los Angeles sun, outside of Griffith Observatory where we had looked at sculptures of planets and figured out how much we would all weigh on Venus, Ruby noticed and became obsessed with her shadow. She couldn't take her eyes off of it, and didn't want to move. The little two-year-old crouched down, entranced and enamored of this reflection of her. We explained to little Ruby that her shadow would always be with her. Even if she couldn't see it, even if her eyes weren't glued to the sidewalk, it would always be a part of her: another side of her escorting her through life. All three of us made hand puppets and figures, and laughed at the different shapes our shadows made together.

If only all of us engaged with our shadows in the way this child did: curious, engaged, not afraid to really look, really accept our shadows s part of us that it will not go away. Our shadows can be great helpers. In a lot of self-help, or coaching language, there tends to be goals to erase and obliterate the shadow altogether. That is problematic—we never lose our shadow side. What changes is the way we choose to engage with it. That is what shifts our energy. That is what diminishes its hold on us. We learn to listen to our shadows and collaborate with them as helpers, as markers of desire, as places that need more love, not more rejection.

Living in Moontime is the greatest helper psychically, energetically, and magically for shadow work. The Moon is light and dark, reflected and projected, the cosmic egg connected to our water inside. The Waning Moon and the Dark Moon are the perfect times to go deep within. There the shadow is most comfortable. Release is supported. Intuition is piqued. Under the Waning Moon, it is easier to see with our eyes closed.

The Moon comes around, again and again, bringing up similar emotions and energy to help us with our evolution. The Waning Moon time comes around again, reminding us how our shadow might be tripping us up, causing us to stumble. The way we interact with it can change. When similar patterns or themes arise in our life, they can change as a result of these different interactions.

Is it time to stop repeating the harmful past? Is it time to float out of one hindering spiral, and into a more fruitful one? Is it time to let your Dark Moon self, your shadow self, your intuitive self, your cord-cutting self help you?

You deserve to feel loved fully, seen fully, no matter where the light is or is not. At this time, I urge you to view your progress as a process and your feelings as friends, not potential foes. Be kind to yourself and others around you, whether they are family or the person in front of you in line. Send love to your ancestors and your enemies. Stay in the dark as long as you need to come up and resurface with new insights, with different light.

View yourself like the Moon—integrated and whole whether you align with light or with shadow. Accept that all of your experiences are valid. Both are needed. Imperfectly perfect, beaming back at ourselves.

This was the year of Justice, The High Priestess, and Strength. We saw the truth. We changed our behavior and actions from the ground level up. Cords were cut. Lines were drawn in the sand. We stepped more fully into ourselves. We listened to our intuition more and witnessed the fruits of that trust. We transformed our pain into brilliance, into being, into gifts for the future.

Look at yourself. Count all of the blessings and all the lessons. Look around at your support system and sing songs of gratitude. Expand out into the collective—acknowledge what we are building, separately and together. Weave a spell of collective protection and collective liberation.

Look at yourself. Feel your tenderness. Engage with all of your undeniable power. Go beyond the mirror. Go into the Moon.

Journaling questions:
How is my shadow currently coming up for me right now?
What does it wish to tell me?
What is the gift, the strength of this message?
How can I practically or magically integrate my shadow this week?
What are some helpful truths that I know now this year?
What are some harsh truths I am still working through?
What gifts did I receive as a result of working with my intuition?
How did my intuition come up most strongly this year?
How will I continue to connect to and trust in my intuition?
What am I releasing from this year during this Waning Moon?

This is a Tarot pull designed to spotlight some of your lessons and highlights of the year. Do this in a comfortable place where you feel calm and have time.

Pull out a card that right now, is an accurate reflection of you. Put it in the center of your table.

Pull out the High Priestess card, the Strength Card, and the Justice card and put them in a row underneath card 1, in that order.

Shuffle your cards.

Ask: What does the Moon want me to know? What did I start or continue healing by trusting my inner voice? Place the card underneath the High Priestess.

Shuffle your cards.

Ask: What is the secret superpower of my heart? What did my wildness and energy put into motion this year?Put the card underneath Strength.

Shuffle your cards.

Ask: What is the truth of this year's lessons? What can I take with me? Put this card underneath Justice.

Shuffle your cards.

Ask a question only your subconsious, your inner knowing can answer. Put this card underneath the card you pulled for Strength.

Shuffle your cards.
Ask: What does my higher power, or source, or my guides, want me to know about where to focus my energy for the beginning of next year? Place this card above the card you picked to symbolize yourself.

Notes on spread:

Reflections on this year:

JULY 2018 SIGNS: CANCER: TO JULY 22 LEO : FROM JULY 22 GEMSTONE: RUBY FLOWER: WATER LILY

SUNDAY	MONDAY	TUESDAY	WEDNESDAY	THURSDAY	FRIDAY	SATURDAY

AUGUST 2018 SIGNS: LEO : TO AUGUST 22 VIRGO : FROM AUGUST 22 GEMSTONE: PERIDOT FLOWER: POPPY

| SUNDAY | MONDAY | TUESDAY | WEDNESDAY | THURSDAY | FRIDAY | SATURDAY |

SEPTEMBER 2018 SIGNS: VIRGO TO SEPTEMBER 22 LIBRA : FROM SEPTEMBER 22 GEMSTONE: SAPPHIRE FLOWER: MORNING GLORY

SUNDAY	MONDAY	TUESDAY	WEDNESDAY	THURSDAY	FRIDAY	SATURDAY

NOVEMBER 2018 SIGNS: SCORPIO TO NOVEMBER 22 SAGITTARIUS : FROM NOVEMBER 22 GEMSTONE: CITRINE : FLOWER : CHRYSANTHEMUM

DECEMBER 2018 SIGNS: SAGITTARIUS TO DECEMBER 21 CAPRICORN : FROM DECEMBER 21 GEMSTONE: TURQUOISE

FLOWER: HOLLY

SUNDAY	MONDAY	TUESDAY	WEDNESDAY	THURSDAY	FRIDAY	SATURDAY

Contributors:

Diego Basdeo is a writer and astrologer in the Bay Area. He believes fiction, memoir, and astrology have provided a space for understanding, transformation, and healing. Astrology has a particular beauty in illustrating our unique challenges, natural talents, and reminds us that we have a place in this universe as a part of the human experience and offers tools to heal present and ancestral trauma in ourselves. You can contact him for readings and other offerings at diego.basdeo@gmail.com

adrienne maree brown is author of *Emergent Strategy: Shaping Change, Changing Worlds* and the co-editor of *Octavia's Brood: Science Fiction from Social Justice Movements*. She is a writer, social justice facilitator, pleasure activist, healer and doula living in Detroit.
Find adrienne on-line at: adriennemareebrown.net & on IG: @adriennemareebrown

Alexandria Bull is a writer and Buddhist practitioner living in Oakland, California. She has a bachelor's degree from the Jack Kerouac School of Disembodied Poetics at Naropa University and is the granddaughter of Buddhist teacher Pema Chödrön. Her passions are mindfulness based education, ancestral and karmic healing, and positive death awareness and preparation. She is currently writing a biography about her grandmother. Find her on IG @alexandriagloria

Pema Chödrön is an American Tibetan Buddhist. She is an ordained nun, acharya and disciple of Chögyam Trungpa Rinpoche. Pema has written many books and is the director of the Gampo Abbey in Nova Scotia, Canada. Find her at: pemachodronfoundation.org

Rachel Howe is an artist and healer based in Los Angeles. She runs Small Spells, providing inspiration and healing through tarot readings and reiki sessions, as well as regular astrology posts and channeled messages on her Instagram feed, @smallspells. Her work empowering others to find their way to healing also takes the form of teaching workshops on tarot and accessing intuition. Her drawings find their way onto various products like t-shirts, books, and a self-produced tarot deck. Reaching a broad audience through her illustrations that embrace mysticism while staying firmly rooted in the culture of modern design —drawing on the imagery of cartoons, tattoos, handmade illustrations and low-fi graphic design, Rachel has found a voice that is both accessible and aspirational. Find Rachel on-line here: smallspells.com & on IG: @smallspells

Liz Migliorelli: Liz Migliorelli is a western herbalist and magic maker who believes in affordable, accessible, community-based health care and the healing power of plants. She is the head witch behind Sister Spinster, a line of flower essences and other potions. She teaches ancestral remembrance, folk healing and magic classes across the country. She lives on the Mendocino coast in California and enjoys blowing kisses to the whales. You can work with her and learn more about her work at: sisterspinster.net & on IG:sister_spinster

Layla Saad is a writer and speaker, whose work focuses on centering the stories, art and magic of people of colour. As the founder of Wild Mystic Woman, Layla's work explores the intersecting themes of spirituality, social justice, creativity, feminism, business and leadership.As an East African, Arab, British, Muslim, feminist, soul seeker, living in the Middle East (Qatar), and sharing her work with the global community, Layla stands at a diverse intersection of identities, from which she is able to draw rich and intriguing perspectives. Layla's own personal journey as a black Muslim woman, her work with her clients and her writings often confront the oppressive cultures of patriarchy and white supremacy.

Find Layla on-line here: wildmysticwoman.com & on IG @wildmysticwoman

Spellbound Sky is a metaphysical crystal destination in Los Angeles, founded by Mark Phillips and Martin Anguiano. The couple spent their first 20+ vibrant years together as fashion designers, always sharing a passion for an unconventional point of view with a mystical twist. Metaphysical interest played a big role in their lives, and eventually crystals evolved into a mutual obsession that inspired them to take a leap of faith toward creating a world that reflected their true spiritual passion. Spellbound Sky opened in 2011 with a goal to share their love of crystals and the magical realms, keeping the integrity of their personal modern and free-spirited vision intact. Year after year, Spellbound Sky continues to inspire and empower, connecting the community with the wisdom and tools needed to unlock their unlimited potential and turn dreams into a reality.

Find Spellbound on-line at: spellboundsky.com & on IG: @spellboundsky

Credits:

Sarah Lyn Rogers was the copyeditor of this book. You can hire her at: sarahlynwrites@gmail.com.

LinYee Yuan was the line editor and provided additional editing and guidance for this book. Check out LinYee's magazine at: thisismold.com

Rhiannon Dexter Flowers provided additional consulting and encouragement through-out this process. This book—and of course, my life— would not be the same without her. Thank you Rhiannon for your support over the last decade plus of magical living!

Marlee Grace provided insight and feedback for the outline for this workbook. She also provided vast emotional support as a friend during the course of writing this book. I love you Marlee!

Jenstar Hacker deepened my practice with the Moon in 2011 and with her example. I bow to you, wonderful human!

Classic Litho is the fabulous printer for this book. Thank you Masoud Nikravan and your incredible team for all of your help, incredible service, and amazing printing.

This is a self-published book. If you find typos, bless them! Thank you for supporting independent publishing and independent artists!

Thank you:

Thank you to my incredible partner Oliver who provides me with all the love, care, support and laughter I need in order to do my work. You are the most brilliant, sweetest, funniest, best person I know and I thank the universe every day for your presence and love in my life.

Deep thanks to my family for making me what I am today. I am grateful to be from you and with you.

Thank you to all the places that have hosted workshops and sold this publication. Thank you to all my beautiful and amazing clients who have taught me, and continue to teach me, so much.

Thank you so my wonderful contributors. A huge special thanks goes out to Diego Basdeo, for writing for these publications for 5 editions, and Liz Migliorelli, for writing for the last 3. Endless gratitude to Sarah Lyn Rogers, the copyeditor of the book, LinYee Yuan, the line editor of this publication, and Rhiannon Flowers for her compassionate consultation.

Thank you for reading this. Sending you nothing but love and the best or better for your highest self's desires and wishes. Thank you to the Queer community and to all the other witches and creatives who have taught me, inspired me, helped me, and supported me. I have too many thank yous, far much gratitude for far too many specific people to fit into one small page—and for that I know I am deeply, deeply blessed. Thank you to my guides, and thank you to source.

This workbook is dedicated to the memory of my fiercely beloved familiar Phaedra, who passed on unexpectedly one day after the October 2017 Full Moon. Thank you for being my loyal and loving companion throughout the last eleven years, including the last five editions of this workbook. I will carry your spirit with me as long as I love and live.

About the creator, writer, and editor: Sarah Faith Gottesdiener is an artist, designer, Tarot reader and writer. Her feminist gear company is called Modern Women. She has a bachelors from Smith College and a Masters in Design from CalArts. Sarah has taught workshops metaphysical subjects all over the USA and Canada, and has taught visual literacy and design at institutions like CalArts, Otis, and Scripps. Her design clients include Nike, Sephora, Uniqlo, and many, many small businesses and wonderful individuals.

See her design work at : sarahgottesdiener.com, Her spiritual writings and images at visualmagic. info, & her store at modernwomen.bigcartel.com.
She thinks you are probably doing a great job. She wants you to keep going.

This publication is intended as a guidebook for the curious human's use. It is not intended to take the place of a professional therapist or professional medical attention. For speaking or lecture engagements, to hire me for consulting, Tarot sessions, or to book me for design work, please feel free to contact me at
modernwomenprojects@gmail.com
Love & Health, Peace & Joy and
Blessed Be.